STEPHEN S. WISE:

SERVANT OF THE PEOPLE

Stephen S. Wise:

SERVANT OF THE PEOPLE

SELECTED LETTERS EDITED

By Carl Hermann Voss

FOREWORD

By Justine Wise Polier
and
James Waterman Wise

THE JEWISH PUBLICATION SOCIETY OF AMERICA

PHILADELPHIA   5729/1969

TO THE GRANDCHILDREN

AND GREAT-GRANDCHILDREN

OF STEPHEN S. WISE

*(Excerpt from a
letter written in
Philadelphia, Pennsylvania,
Autumn, 1919)*

TO LOUISE WATERMAN WISE

. . . A moment ago I was touched by something that I prize more than a French decoration—a poor Jewish newsboy came to me saying, "I know who you are and what you have done for the Jews. God keep you alive for the sake of our people." More than I deserved but exactly what I most coveted. Well, dearest, we have some form of immortality before us—for you the blessings of the babies [Child Adoption Committee of the Free Synagogue], though they know it not, and as for myself a day's remembrance by my people. . . .

FOREWORD

From many thousands of letters written by Stephen Wise over more than half a century, Carl Hermann Voss has chosen those that best portrayed to him the man, his growth and his work.

The letters recapture so much of the spirit of our father, his strength, his power, his compassion and his love, that it would be folly to attempt any objective judgment concerning them. They recall too many shared experiences. Despite busy days and nights our father never seemed pressed for time so far as we were concerned. He would travel all night by coach to wake and walk with us to school. It was on these walks that we learned of his passion for freedom of the pulpit, of his trips to Christian churches to speak as a Jew, long before the idea of ecumenism was known. We heard of the early efforts to protect Jews in foreign lands against persecution and to establish a state where they could be citizens as of right, rather than by tolerance, a word he loathed. The fights against civic corruption, the battles for humane conditions for workers and their right to organize, plans for social legislation to protect the old, women and children, the struggle to achieve freedom from discrimination for all Americans were shared. While scenes and individuals shifted, his involvement, as we later understood, was an inevitable expression of his commitment toward the building of a just society.

In the earlier letters, Carl Voss has chosen some that throw light on an era in which our father and the Jewish community were coming of age. One finds glimpses of the early gropings to discover the meaning of being a Jew and a minister in America at the turn of the century. At that time the many newcomers who had fled pogroms in Czarist Russia were poor and deeply Jewish, while the comparatively small Jewish population, which had arrived earlier, saw assimilation, the "melting pot," as the road to full Americanization. The concept and ideal of a pluralistic society had not yet been expressed. Instinctively he responded to the newcomers, to their needs and to spiritual values which he saw as essential to a vital Jewish community.

The later letters include the tragic and lonely struggle to make the Christian and the Jewish worlds understand the meaning of Hitlerism. They tell of the days and nights of agony in the face of apathy and indifference to its victims. And they reflect the increasing labors to seeks ways to save all he could reach.

This volume contains letters of import to American and Jewish history. Besides such letters there are those that show the undramatic and unending day-to-day work that preceded public action. The pages reveal some of the issues and the men with whom our father battled. Swift anger and great generosity toward opponents, as well as friends, are here. Always, behind and beyond public action, one senses the compassionate understanding and tender concern for every person whose life he touched that made his ministry what it was. Happily, the letters include flashes of the robust humor our father could turn against himself, of his sense of fun, and of his zest for life that make understandable how he could carry so many burdens and yet smile and laugh as a child.

The letters compiled by Dr. Voss with great understanding provide a challenge to those of us who assume that the problems faced in earlier times were less complex and more easily answered. They suggest that while battles may be dated, the way in which a man encounters life is far less ephemeral.

JUSTINE WISE POLIER
JAMES WATERMAN WISE

August 19, 1968
Lake Placid

INTRODUCTION

I recall telling our family, during the 1924 National Democratic Convention, about the wonderful prayer I heard on the radio by a rabbi named Wise. My parents then told me who Stephen Wise was. I shall never forget his prayer at that session; its beauty and the extraordinary power of his voice remain in my memory.

In the mid- and late-1920s, I often read about this courageous, controversial man. His utterances, in the pulpit and on the lecture platform, to workers on the picket line or in newspaper reports, kept him in the public mind.

During the early 1930s, I saw Stephen Wise at closer range in New York City. When I was a student at Union Theological Seminary, I went to hear him whenever I could at public gatherings, or at the Free Synagogue services in Carnegie Hall where his dignity and reverence were unforgettable. I soon realized that the American people could not escape the impact of Stephen Wise's personality as he denounced chicanery and corruption, joined with John Haynes Holmes in the work of the City Affairs Committee to speed James J. Walker's deposition as mayor of New York City, thundered against the menace of Adolf Hitler and, when the Nazis swept into power, warned of their threat to the peace of the world and to Israel as a people and a faith.

Preaching occasionally as his guest in the pulpit of the Free Synagogue, I also worked with him in a number of causes and came to know him well in the 1940s. It was easy to understand

why tens of thousands of Jews and non-Jews were grateful for his
leadership and felt their hearts warmed by his friendship, why
so many people queued up for blocks in patient silence and then
moved solemnly past his bier in the Free Synagogue in April,
1949.

Three years after his death and the posthumous publication of
his autobiography, *Challenging Years,* his successor at the re-
named "Stephen Wise Free Synagogue," Edward E. Klein, suggested to me a dual biography of Wise and his cherished friend,
John Haynes Holmes, minister of the Community Church of
New York from 1907 to 1949. In working on that book, *Rabbi
and Minister,* I read hundreds of Wise's remarkable letters and
was able to render assistance to his daughter and son, Justine
Wise Polier and James Waterman Wise, as they edited *The Personal Letters of Stephen S. Wise.* To the Wise family, as to myself, all his letters mirrored the man as he really was: they not
only reflected a loving interest in people but bespoke his passionate convictions about freedom, justice and equality. The belief that such letters would show even more of a rich, warm-
hearted personality eventually brought *Stephen S. Wise: Servant
of the People* into being, for as I pored over the material in the
Archives at Brandeis University, I anticipated an anthology of
which letters would be only a part; but as the work progressed, it
soon became apparent that his letters merited a separate book.

I made my selection on the basis of Wise's leadership on a half
dozen fronts: the political outreach of the Zionist movement, the
development of Palestine, his involvement in Liberal Judaism,
the advancement of Jewish learning, Democratic party affairs,
social reform, and interfaith cooperation in America. These letters, marshalled for convenience chronologically, highlight Stephen Wise's activities as a rabbi and as a public figure and reflect
his absorbing interests and activities, his varied concerns and
causes; they give information of historic significance as well as in-
sights into his character. If asked about ranking the many aspects
of his career in order of importance, Stephen Wise would have
responded that, first of all, he was a Jew and a Zionist; then an
American; after that, a rabbi; finally, as he himself phrased it,
"an educator of men for the Jewish ministry." To his vast public
he was all these, but also an orator, an organizer, an impresario,

a prophetic figure, an implacable foe of tyranny and injustice, a civic figure, a world citizen.

His creative will and ability to translate vision into reality were part of every aspect of his unique career. Thus his deep religious commitment led him to become founder-rabbi of the Free Synagogue in 1907 and founder-president of a new rabbinical seminary, the Jewish Institute of Religion, in 1922. He sought to make religion more than "relevant"; he wanted to make it real, vital, and enduring in people's lives. His was a liberal religion, a progressive, yet traditionally oriented Judaism, combined with a sensitive and informed social conscience. He was always, but especially in his letters, a thoughtful, deeply committed rabbi, a patient teacher, a wise counselor.

Wise's growth as a Zionist was a major thread in the varied, colorful tapestry of his public life, for Zion reborn was to him, as to his friend and mentor, Theodor Herzl, the vision to become a reality. He saw early the gleam of Zionist hopes and a possibility of their achievement. His meeting Herzl, author of *The Jewish State,* at the Second Zionist Congress at Basle in 1898 was for him a milestone. Wise had just helped bring into being the Federation of American Zionists and had played an important part in developing it. Later he occupied a key place in the formulation and announcement of the Balfour Declaration of November 1917, which pledged Great Britain to "view with favour the establishment in Palestine of a national home for the Jewish people." Whether in the Zionist movement prior to World War I or in the frenetic 1920s, whether in the grim '30s or the catastrophic '40s, Stephen Wise was a major figure in the drama of this epoch. *Stephen S. Wise: Servant of the People* covers many aspects of Wise's long and active career on a score of fronts and can therefore only touch on this fervent Zionism which ranges from correspondence with Theodor Herzl in the 1890s to his deep happiness as Israel proclaimed her independence and, a year later, prepared to join the United Nations. At Boston's Ford Hall Forum in the last month of his life, as his audience celebrated with him his seventy-fifth birthday, he said: "I have lived to see the Jewish state. I am too small for the greatness of the mercy which God has shown us."

Just as Wise was for years one of the few Zionist leaders in

SERVANT OF THE PEOPLE

the Reform rabbinate, he was always in the forefront in his work
on behalf of inter-religious comity and mutual respect long in
advance of the now fashionable "Brotherhood movement" and
the widely hailed "ecumenical spirit" of Pope John XXIII and
Vatican Council II. Wise's never-ceasing work to achieve
equity and freedom may now seem easy to emulate, but in his
day these causes were not popular and few dared embrace them.

As an orator he was without an equal, ranking in eloquence
and influence with such masters as Henry Ward Beecher and
Robert Ingersoll, both of whom he had heard when he was a
boy. By the time he was seventeen, he had started on the road
to fame as a public speaker of skill and power. Several weeks
before his eighteenth birthday in 1892, a speaker's flyer was dis-
tributed by Congregation Beth-El in Greenpoint:

> *Dear Sir:*
> *You are cordially invited to attend a Lecture by* MR. STEPHEN S.
> WISE, *The Great Orator of Columbia College, and aspirant for the
> Ministry, on* FRIDAY THE 5TH INST. *at the Temple, 110 Noble St.
> Services to commence at 7:30, Lecture at 8 P.M. sharp.*
> *— Subject —*
> **"WHY AM I A JEW?"**
> *It is expected that this lecture will be a very interesting one, and
> to make it a success, you are requested to attend with your friends.*
> *By order of the President, etc.*

As these letters show, Wise gave strength to a sorely harassed
Jewish people everywhere. But what is less known is that he also
brought courage and tenacity to those Christians who stood for
rudimentary justice and basic human rights, and sought to safe-
guard freedom of the pulpit. In this book we honor the extraordinary legacy of his thought and action, and keep Stephen
Wise alive in grateful memory.

CARL HERMANN VOSS

Saratoga Springs, N.Y.
April, 1969

ACKNOWLEDGMENTS

In the preparation of this book I am indebted to many:

I am grateful to Abram L. Sachar, first president, now chancellor, of Brandeis University, for a research associate's grant from a larger special grant of the Charles Merrill Trust to the University which enabled me to work among the papers of Stephen Wise gathered, with the cooperation and consent of the Wise family, in the Archives of the Goldfarb Library on the Waltham, Massachusetts, campus; to his colleagues, Nahum N. Glatzer, Louis Kronenberger, Harry Tarlin, and Ronald V. Glens, for their guidance and assistance; and to Ned Rosenbaum for his contribution as a research assistant.

I express thanks for the many kinds of help given by Jacob Rader Marcus and Stanley F. Chyet, both of the American Jewish Archives at the Hebrew Union College–Jewish Institute of Religion in Cincinnati, Ohio, and Edward Kiev, their colleague in the Library of the H.U.C.—J.I.R. in New York City, and the staff of that institution in both cities; Sylvia Landress, Zionist Archives, New York City; Alex Bein and Michael Heymann, Central Zionist Archives, Jerusalem, Israel; and to the following libraries: the Jewish and National Library, the Institute of Contemporary Jewry, and the Jewish Historical Society of the Hebrew University, Jerusalem; American Jewish Historical Society, Brandeis University campus, Waltham, Mass.; the Lucy Scribner Library, Skidmore College, Saratoga Springs, N.Y.; the Beinecke Rare Book and Manuscript Library, Yale University, New Haven, Conn.; Meadville Theological School, Chicago, Ill.; the Manuscripts Division, Library of Congress,

Washington, D.C.; and the Houghton Library, Harvard University, Cambridge, Mass.

I want to thank Hyman J. Fliegel for permission to quote letters from Stephen Wise to Gertrude Wolf in the collection he has made available to the American Jewish Historical Society in Waltham, Massachusetts.

Harry Starr of New York City, Nahum Goldmann of Jerusalem, and Charles Rosenbloom of Pittsburgh, Pa., gave practical assistance. To the Lucius N. Littauer Foundation and the Memorial Foundation for Jewish Culture I am grateful for grants-in-aid for my research and writing.

For counsel and editorial assistance I owe much to Justine Wise Polier and James Waterman Wise who have written and edited several books about their father and mother and have therefore shed light on my own writing. Their love and devotion to Stephen Wise did not cloud judgments or blunt critical faculties. To them I am obligated for formal permission to quote these letters, the contents of which are by copyright law their property. In gratitude for our friendship of more than twenty-five years I have dedicated this book to their children and grandchildren.

To my wife, Phyllis Gierlotka Voss, I owe a great debt, not only for encouragement and assistance but also for patience and understanding, as I delved into dusty cartons, scanned crumbling manuscripts, and shed flakes of paper, large and small, all over our home. Fortunately she believed in this book as much as I did.

Editing these letters has been an exciting, often thrilling experience, especially because I saw anew how loved and respected Stephen Wise was during his life, despite opponents and enemies who detested and excoriated him. Such love and respect live on decades after his death, for he sowed better than he knew. His enormous affection and genuine concern for human beings, his fidelity as a rabbi and his passion for justice on every level of life have borne rich fruit. To these qualities and achievements I must attest as I thank those people mentioned here, and many more, too numerous to list.

C. H. V.

CONTENTS

xv]

CHRONOLOGY OF
STEPHEN SAMUEL WISE
(1874–1949)

1874   Born March 17 in Budapest, Hungary, son of Aaron Wise and Sabine de Fischer [Farkashazy] Wise.

1875   Brought to the United States where his father had become rabbi of Congregation Rodeph Shalom in New York City.

1889   Enters College of the City of New York at age 15.

1890   Instructed in rabbinical subjects by Alexander Kohut and Gustav Gottheil.

1891   Transfers to Columbia University.

1892   Graduates with honors from Columbia University; studies with Thomas Davidson in his Summer School, Glenmore-on-Hudson, N.Y.

1893   Pursues postgraduate and rabbinical studies in Vienna and at Oxford University; ordained to rabbinate by Adolph Jellinek, Chief Rabbi of Vienna; installed as assistant rabbi to Henry F. Jacobs, Congregation B'nai Jeshurun, New York City, in the spring and, on his death, elected minister in September.

1894   Continues doctoral studies at Columbia University under guidance of Richard Gottheil.

1895   Carries on graduate studies at Oxford University while on several months' leave from rabbinical duties; studies under Adolph Neubauer.

1896   Death of his father, Aaron Wise.

1897   Joins with Richard Gottheil, Harry Friedenwald, Bernard Ehrenreich and others in founding Federation of American Zionists; chosen honorary secretary.

1898   Attends Second Zionist Congress in Basle; meets Dr. Theodor Herzl, who appoints him American Secretary of World Zionist movement.

1899   Journeys to West Coast on speaking trip on behalf of Zionism; invited to become rabbi of Temple Beth Israel, Portland, Oregon; becomes engaged to marry Louise Waterman.

1900   Installed in autumn as rabbi of Portland congregation; married on November 14.

1901   Birth of son, James Waterman Wise; completes translation of Book of Judges for *Holy Scriptures,* published in 1917 by Jewish Publication Society of America.

1902   Awarded degree of Doctor of Philosophy by Columbia University; doctoral dissertation published in Series of Oriental Studies: *The Improvement of the Moral Qualities* (translation from the Arabic and exposition of an ethical treatise of the eleventh century by Solomon-ibn-Gabirol).

1903   Appointed to unpaid post, Commissioner of Child Labor in Oregon; birth of daughter, Justine Waterman Wise.

1904   Attends meetings of Zionist Actions Committee in Vienna and sees Theodor Herzl for the last time.

1905   Candidates at Temple Emanu-El, New York City; rejects overtures.

1906   Sends Louis Marshall famous "Open Letter" on freedom of the pulpit; leaves Portland, Oregon, in fall for New York City.

1907   Founds Free Synagogue in New York City with services in Hudson Theatre; begins branch on Lower East Side with meetings in Clinton Hall.

1908   Starts Social Service Division of Free Synagogue.

1909   Joins with John Haynes Holmes, Jane Addams, Charles Edward Russell, Oswald Garrison Villard, and others in founding National Association for the Advancement of Colored People.

1910   With Holmes and Frank Oliver Hall, inaugurates union non-sectarian services in Sunday evening forums on "Religion and the Social Problem."

1911   Prominent in protests against conditions which led to tragic fire of Triangle Shirtwaist Company in New York City.

1912 Takes leading part in campaign for nomination and election of Woodrow Wilson to the presidency of the United States.

1913 Visits Palestine for first time.

1914 With Louis D. Brandeis, establishes Provisional Executive Committee for General Zionist Affairs.

1915 Joins in programs of the American Union Against Militarism and the League to Enforce Peace.

1916 Encourages Louise Waterman Wise to establish Child Adoption Committee of Free Synagogue; helps form American Jewish Congress in company with Brandeis and Julian W. Mack.

1917 With Brandeis and Felix Frankfurter, aids Woodrow Wilson and Edward M. House in formulation of Balfour Declaration, issued by British Government in support of the establishment of a national home for the Jewish people.

1918 Elected president of Zionist Organization of America; attends Versailles Peace Conference.

1919 Condemns U.S. Steel Corporation in strike.

1920 Helps to establish American Civil Liberties Union; revives the American Jewish Congress.

1921 Lays plans for a training school for the rabbinate in New York City.

1922 Recruits faculty and students in United States and abroad, gathers funds and establishes Jewish Institute of Religion. Visits Palestine for second time.

1923 Effects merger of Free Synagogue with Central Synagogue in New York.

1924 Takes active part in Democratic National Convention, unsuccessfully supporting Newton D. Baker for the presidential nomination; fights Ku Klux Klan.

1925 Free Synagogue–Central Synagogue merger dissolved. Preaches controversial sermon on "Jesus, the Jew."

1926 Aids textile union in Passaic strike.

1927 Opposes execution of Sacco and Vanzetti.

1928   Supports Alfred E. Smith for the presidency of the United States.

1929   Launches attack on Tammany Hall.

1930   Has breakdown in health, intensified by British policy on Palestine question; writes *The Great Betrayal*.

1931   With John Haynes Holmes, heads City Affairs Committee in exposing corruption in New York City; demands action from Franklin D. Roosevelt, governor of New York, to oust Mayor James J. Walker.

1932   Celebrates 25th anniversary of Free Synagogue; supports Norman Thomas for presidency.

1933   Mobilizes both Jews and non-Jews to oppose policies of Adolf Hitler.

1934   Leads American Jewish Congress in boycott against Hitler Germany.

1935   Revisits Palestine; attends 19th Zionist Congress in Zürich.

1936   Effects reconciliation with Franklin Delano Roosevelt and campaigns for his second term as President; founds World Jewish Congress; serves second two-year term as president of the Zionist Organization of America (1936–38).

1939   Attends Round Table Conference of Jews and Arabs in London; protests British White Paper restricting Jewish immigration to Palestine.

1940   As member of President's Advisory Committee on Political Refugees, focuses attention on Jewish refugee problem and urges emigration of victims of Hitlerism to both U.S.A. and Palestine.

1941   Resists isolationists, especially "America First" movement.

1942   Receives from U.S. State Department confirmation of World Jewish Congress reports of Hitler's efforts to annihilate European Jewry; releases information to the public.

1943   Leads in activities of American Zionist Emergency Council, American Jewish Conference, American Jewish Congress, and World Jewish Congress.

1944   Seventieth birthday marked in many nationwide celebrations.

1945   Attends World Zionist Conference in London at end of war; visits European detention centers for Jewish refugees.

1946   Testifies before Anglo-American Commission of Inquiry
        on Palestine. Supports U.S. loan to Great Britain despite
        British refusal of visa to visit Palestine; serves as member
        of the President's Commission on Higher Education.

1947   Presses for adoption of U.N. Palestine Partition Plan.
        Louise Waterman Wise dies, December 11.

1948   Hails establishment of State of Israel, fulfillment of his
        and fellow-Zionists' dream; merges Jewish Institute of
        Religion with Hebrew Union College; re-elected President
        first post-war plenary session World Jewish Congress,
        Switzerland, at which all Jewish communities represented
        except Soviet Jewry.

1949   Celebrates 75th birthday, March 17; dies, April 19.

CHAPTER ONE

YEARS OF GROWTH
(1892-1911)

TO THE PRESIDENT AND MEMBERS OF
TEMPLE EMANU-EL, NEW YORK CITY

> . . . I would not deliver my conscience into the keep-
> ing of the angels. My conscience is my own.
>
> *January 5, 1906*

After Stephen Wise's graduation from Columbia University and his period of study with Thomas Davidson at Glenmore-on-Hudson in 1892, subsequent months of graduate and rabbinical study in Vienna and Oxford, ordination to the rabbinate, and later his installation as spiritual leader of Congregation B'nai Jeshurun of New York City, he began to divide time between rabbinical duties and post-graduate studies at Columbia.

In 1896, his father, Aaron Wise, died suddenly. Now Stephen Wise not only had to assume financial responsibility for the family but was compelled to decide whether he wanted to remain in his rabbinic post at B'nai Jeshurun or accept the invitation to succeed his father as rabbi of Congregation Rodeph Sholom. The specific invitation awaited only his favorable reaction to an inquiry from the board of trustees. He had therefore to reject the feelers without taking too much for granted but at the same time politely indicating a strong disinclination.

November 24, 1896

TO Benjamin Blumenthal*

I take it to be my bounden duty to state here and now that it will be impossible for me to accept such invitation or to preach

---

* *Biographical data of those persons not easily identifiable from the content of the letters will be found in the Biographical Register at the end of the book.*

in your synagogue until after a successor to my sainted father has been chosen. . . .

In the first place, were I to deliver a sermon at your temple, ere yet pulpit arrangements for the future had been definitely settled, it might appear to some that I was a candidate for the vacant position; and, for such a suspicion I must refrain from affording the slightest basis. . . .

I know full well that the honor of becoming one's father's successor in the high place, which is every minister's, comes seldom enough to any man. And I have not considered this weighty matter lightly or hastily. There are many ties which knit my very heart to Rodeph Sholom. My earliest religious instruction I gained while a pupil in your school; it was within the walls of your majestic synagogue-edifice that I first was privileged to give utterance to my hopes and plans, while yet a mere aspirant for the ministry; and, above all, Rodeph Sholom has been my dearly-beloved father's home throughout the largest part of my life . . . I must firmly and finally decline to permit the consideration of my name as a possible rabbi to Rodeph Sholom. You, Sir, will be the first to recognize that this course is the only proper and manly one for me to pursue. My own congregation has in many, many ways placed me, within the past few years, under the most profound and abiding obligations—obligations from which it would be nothing less than basest ingratitude to even ask to be released.

I was a very young man when first I was chosen by B'nai Jeshurun to be the assistant-preacher to my lamented predecessor, Dr. Henry S. Jacobs, and a few months thereafter, upon his untimely demise, I was unanimously promoted to fill his position. Since then, my congregation has given me repeated evidence of the fact that my work is not alone perfunctorily acknowledged but even approved and appreciated far beyond its actual merits and real desert. In a word, I could not forsake B'nai Jeshurun, who are in every sense become "my own people." You, Sir, let me iterate, would be the last to look for any such conduct on my part. Pray accept this, then, as my final decision, and pardon my declination of your invitation for the reasons which I have with sufficient frankness advanced.

Thanking you most cordially for the manifold courtesies wherewith you have honored me in the past, and with very best wishes for God's blessing upon dear old Rodeph Sholom. . . .

To his ministerial duties and graduate studies he now added a third major interest, Zionism. This was to become an all-engrossing activity for the rest of his life. His zeal for a Jewish state and his devotion to that end became a part of his very being. His long-time friend and Ph.D. preceptor at Columbia University, Professor Richard Gottheil, shared his enthusiasm for the Zionist objective, as did the professor's distinguished father, Dr. Gustav Gottheil, rabbi of New York's fashionable and essentially non-Zionist Temple Emanu-El. Shortly after Richard Gottheil had visited Dr. Theodor Herzl, author of the widely circulated tract of 1896, THE JEWISH STATE, *and convener of the 1897 Zionist Congress in Basle, Richard Gottheil encouraged Stephen Wise to keep in close touch with fellow-Zionists in Europe, especially Herzl, and to seek converts to the Zionist cause, particularly among Reform rabbis.*

June 26, 1898

TO Theodor Herzl, Vienna

I know that you are informed on many sides concerning the doings of American Zionists, and I presume that you will have nearer information from the presence of Prof. Gottheil in Europe at this time. Nevertheless, I write you in order to acquaint you with the fact that the New York Federation of Zionist Societies, composed of thirty-six constituent societies with a membership of about five thousand, has finally resolved to hold a conference of American Zionists on the 4th and 5th of July, 1898. The accompanying circular will give you the fullest information concerning our plans. . . .

We have a hard, up-hill fight for Zionism in this country. The Jewish press is almost unanimous in its opposition, and I am half ashamed to state that the fewest of the American Jewish ministers, who should have been first to forward this great movement, are lending it any support whatever. . . .

I hope, *Deo volente,* to be at Basle at the end of August, and may possibly visit you at Vienna before that time.

September 29, 1898

TO Thomas Davidson, Hurricane, Essex County, N.Y.

Let me thank you for your sympathetic lines concerning the great Zionist cause, which is so dear to the hearts of all of us. Do you know, I too have thought, and still think, that nothing but good can event to the Jewish people of all lands from the proposed Anglo-Saxon alliance? Concerning this, however, and kindred Zion affairs, I hope to have an opportunity to chat with you in the near future. . . .

October 26, 1898

TO Theodor Herzl, Vienna

. . . I desire to congratulate you with all my heart upon the magnificent defense of Zionism made by you at London a fortnight ago. The powerful and eloquent manner in which you urged our noble cause makes us all the more anxious to have you come to our country, knowing as we do that your presence and your speech would give a mighty impetus to our movement. . . . No more thankful work could be undertaken by you. The poor Jews have already flocked to our standard. We now require such help as will bring to our side and support the rich and better educated Jews among us. These are the people whom I believe a personal appeal on your part could reach and win over to us.

Professor [Richard] Gottheil and I have not been idle since our return [from the Second Zionist Congress at Basle]. We have addressed meeting after meeting in our city and elsewhere, and within the next few weeks expect to journey to a number of distant cities in order to speak on the Congress and win new recruits

for Zionism. Inasmuch as not one of the American-Jewish newspapers is outspoken in favor of Zionism, I have undertaken to
edit a department in *The American Hebrew,* perhaps the most
influential Jewish weekly in America, which is given over ex-
clusively to the affairs of "Zion and Zionism." I send you herewith a copy of this paper. . . . I have begun to act as regular
correspondent for *Die Welt* [publication of the Zionist move-
ment]. In addition, I write for the *Jewish World* of London and
naturally give a good share of my "space" to the aims and doings
of Zionism.

. . . I have within the last few days met a gentleman who is intimately acquainted with one [Solomon Hirsch of Portland,
Oregon; U.S. minister to Turkey, 1889–92] who in turn enjoys
the highest confidence of the *Porte* [Ottoman Turkish govern-
ment]. . . . I have every reason for thinking that this may prove
very important to us all.

December 21, 1898

TO S. Joseph, Minneapolis

In reply to your letter, I beg to say that I shall send you herewith a circular recently issued by the Federation of American
Zionists. It would certainly be best for the Zionist societies of
Minneapolis to join and work with our national Federation. As
you will gather from the circular, the Vienna Central Committee
[of the World Zionist Organization] does not recognize any American societies unless they are connected with the Federation. You
will also see from the circular that you are expected to pay a
shekel or twenty-five cents a year for every member, as well as
twenty-five cents to cover the general expenses of conducting the
bureau of the Federation. This is all that is expected of you, and
in return for this small amount, the Federation is enabled to
make the Zionist work of this country very much more effective
than it would otherwise be.

I am very glad to hear of your good work in Minneapolis and
was delighted to learn of the presentation of a Zionist flag to you

by a Christian lover of Zion. I send you at the same time a sample badge.

San Francisco, August 2, 1899

TO Simon Blumauer, Solomon Hirsch, Charles Kohn, Portland, Oregon (Special Committee on Notification for Congregation Beth Israel)

I have your communication of July 31, 1899, informing me that at a special meeting of the Congregation Beth Israel of Portland, Oregon, held Sunday afternoon, July 30, 1899, I was unanimously elected rabbi of the congregation for a term of five years, beginning August 1, 1900, at an annual remuneration of five thousand dollars. I am rejoiced to think that, if after searching and prayerful deliberation, I determine to accept the proffered charge, my lot will be cast with a community, upon whose good will and friendly cooperation in all that makes for congregational solidarity I may safely rely. I expect to return to the city of New York after the expiration of another fortnight, in order to resume my pulpit and pastoral work. Soon after my return I shall acquaint the "Heads" of my congregation [B'nai Jeshurun] with the fact of the call; and after engaging in counsel with some members of my family and some honored friends, I shall make known to you my final decision. . . .

San Francisco, August 2, 1899

TO Solomon Hirsch, Portland, Oregon

Let me thank you most heartily for your kindness in communicating to me by telephone on Sunday evening the fact of my election as the rabbi of the Portland congregation. . . .

. . . I expect to return to New York shortly and, after consultation with friends both within and without my congregation [B'nai Jeshurun], will forward my decision. You will readily understand that it behooves me to make known to my people the nature of the "Call" and the spirit in which it was tendered prior to my definite acceptance of the charge, without reservation, because, if God spares me, I am fully and finally resolved to make my future home in Portland. I have considered the matter in its every bearing; and now the feeling is become mine that in undertaking the labor among the Jewish residents of Portland, I shall be doing that to which the hand of God points as my nearest and holiest duty. I am hopeful, moreover, that, with God's help my services may prove of value and benefit to your community, in upbuilding congregational life, in strengthening the ties of loyalty to our undying race and our deathless religious cause, in winning the adherence of the young through careful and approved methods of instruction, in fostering above all things the life of truth and purity and righteousness for the spread of which Judaism elementally stands. I shall strive to merit the friendship and regard of all my people, even as I pledge to devote to the welfare of my flock such gifts and energies as may be given to me in the pursuance of my life's calling. . . .

October 3, 1899

TO The President and Board of Trustees, Congregation
B'nai Jeshurun

On the 1st day of August, 1899, I informed your President that I had been honored with a unanimous call as rabbi of the Congregation Beth Israel, of Portland, Oregon [and] I would reserve my decision until October 1, inasmuch as I could not accept any call before I had conferred with my present congregation.

. . . I have given to this weighty and solemn subject my searching and prayerful deliberation, and have been led to the conclusion that it is my duty to accept the call of the Portland Congregation, and thus enter upon the enlarged field of ministerial work which awaits me. . . .

. . . In accordance with this resolve, I shall this day notify the Portland Congregation of my acceptance of their call, with the understanding that I shall not begin my services with them until the termination of my engagement with you—September 1, 1900.

I trust that the good-will and kindness which you have shown to me ever since you have called me to your pulpit may be continued in the future.

November 28, 1899

TO Theodor Herzl, Vienna

Again and again, I have been tempted to write to you, but have been moved to refrain, because I knew how overburdened you are with the correspondence which comes to you from all parts of the world, and I did not wish to add to that already large burden. I trust, however, that you do not misconstrue my personal silence for inactivity in the matter of Zionism. The fact is, that while I resigned my secretaryship of the American Federation of Zionists, I believe that as a result of being released from that onerous work, I am in a position to be of much more service to the movement in general.

This year, we have inaugurated a plan which I believe is very much better even than conducting our own personal organ; under my special supervision, a budget of Zionist news from all parts of the world, but especially America, is compiled and arranged and then sent out every week to 15 or 20 Jewish weeklies in this country. Even the anti-Zionist organs print the news, although they do not agree with us.

We have asked the Secretary to send a copy of this weekly budget to *Die Welt* in the place of the letters which I formerly addressed to *Die Welt*. I have discontinued my correspondence with *Die Welt* because several of my letters failed of publication, and I do not wish to go to the trouble and expense of preparing them unless I am sure that they are to be printed just as I send them.

I send you by this mail an interesting souvenir program and journal of the Young People's Union of the Northside Hebrew Congregation of Chicago. You will notice that the souvenir contains a symposium entitled "Is There a Jewish Question?" It is certainly interesting and significant that a number of the contributors to this symposium, although personally opposed to Zionism, are yet compelled to take account of our movement as the outcome of an attempt to solve the very real and very terrible Jewish question, which is weighing us down. The first two contributors are Rabbi Gustav Gottheil, the father of the Professor, and dear old Dr. [Bernhard] Felsenthal of Chicago, the two venerable and beloved leaders of our movement in this country.

Lately, I have been making a number of trips in order to deliver Zionist addresses at comparatively remote places. Thus recently I addressed a very large meeting under the auspices of the Young Men's Hebrew Association at Wilkes-Barre, Pa., about 200 miles away; and last Sunday, November 19, I travelled to Worcester, Mass., speaking in that city before a joint meeting of the four Zionist societies—the Maccabees, the Daughters of Zion, the Lovers of Zion, and the Boys' and Girls' Zionist Club. In the near future, I expect to go to Syracuse in New York State, and other places in behalf of Zionist propaganda. Altogether, I may safely report that the movement is progressing very favorably in our country, despite the sharp opposition of the anti-Zionists and the lethargy and indifference of the well-to-do American Jews.

I presume you have heard that, in the summer of next year, I am to take up my residence at Portland, Oregon, which is on the Pacific Coast some 3,000 miles away, so you can see for yourself that I am beginning to travel eastward, though in rather a roundabout fashion. One of the reasons which induced me to accept the very kind and flattering call of the congregation in Portland was the hope, as occasioned by my experience in the West, that I may be enabled to be of great service to our cause in the western part of our land. I really and truly believe that I shall be able to win many men for the movement, and also to gain much material help for the cause in the West.

It is certainly interesting that about a fortnight ago, the Honorable Solomon Hirsch, former United States Minister to Turkey, whose sympathies are with the Zionist movement, has been elected president of the congregation of which I am the minister, he having consented to accept the place largely for my sake. You may remember that in the summer, I wrote to Professor [Richard] Gottheil prior to his departure for Basle, mentioning to him some important facts concerning affairs in

Constantinople, as told to me by former Ambassador [i.e., Minister] Hirsch, which I believed you ought to know.

I shall not continue any longer at this time, but close with the wish that I may hear from you in the near future. Pray remember at all times that the American Zionists stand behind you to a man, everyone of them loyal to you personally, as the Commander-in-Chief of the Zionist forces. I pray that you may enjoy health and strength with which to continue the leadership of our great and glorious cause.

December 4, 1899

TO Maximilian Heller, New Orleans

Let me thank you at the outset for your kindness in sending me your fine sermon on Zionism. I wish that all our opponents were as reverent and respectful and as earnest as are you. Unfortunately, however, the "antis" have been very profuse in their mud-slinging; and it does seem, as you imply, a most unworthy manner in which to treat a great and noble cause.

You say in your sermon that you always wished that you could be persuaded by some of your honored friends in the Zionist ranks. I venture to count myself as one of your friends, and would point out to you, using merely your own argument, that no century has seemed more important for the building up of national ideals, than this century of ours. You do well to instance the Greek nation, the German Empire, the Italian Kingdom and the Slavonic Confederation, all of which have been built up in our own time. Why not the Jewish?

As for the need of Zionism, there can be no question, and you know that well. Anti-Semitism is becoming worse and worse every day, more daring and unprincipled with every hour. In a way, it would seem, as you indicate, that political Zionism is a product of despair; but on the other hand, it cannot be doubted, as you finely point out, that the movement is upborne by a wave of optimism. We Zionists are pessimists, respecting the hope of securing justice from without. We are optimists in that we have the deepest faith in ourselves and our God-given powers to build up a country of our own. You yourself share that optimism in saying that the obstacles, though towering, are not insuperable, and that the "absurdly impossible may become the marvelously opportune."

How can you possibly say that suffering and injustice should be the true Fatherland of the Jew? Permit me to say that such a sentiment is unworthy of any Jew, and most unworthy of you. Pardon my adding, at this place, that that is a very pretty piece of rhetoric, but very poor sense, and certainly very, very wrong to our brethren who are the victims of that injustice and that suffering with which we are but little acquainted, if at all.

I wish to heaven you could be with us [in the Federation of American Zionists], as I know you would like to be, and I somehow feel that we yet shall have your valued cooperation and support. I think that failure is impossible; but even if failure were certain, and certain failure in a just and glorious cause, it is better than the passive indifference and the cowardly lethargy of millions of the world's Jewry today.

March 19, 1900

TO Solomon Schechter, Cambridge, England

It is quite likely that you will have forgotten the writer, who, however, has not forgotten you, and who treasures in remembrance the day it was his privilege to spend with you and your family in the summer of '95 at your Cambridge home. In common with many, many more friends of Jewish learning, I have been deeply interested in the plan of the Jewish Theological Seminary of this city [New York], looking to your assuming the leadership [presidency] of the Seminary. I am a member of the advisory board of the Seminary; and although no such assurance on my part is required, I have always maintained that a new epoch in American Judaism would begin the day you set foot on these shores, the leader of the Seminary forces. I have always been hoping that you might come to the Seminary, in which event I would be so happy to place myself under you, and be as one of the many disciples who would crowd around you.

We have all been more than disappointed lately to learn that it was not certain at all that you would come to our shores. As you may have seen for yourself, the American Jewish press and all those who are truly interested in the furtherance of the highest Jewish interests, were jubilant at the announcement made some months ago, of your prospective coming; but now this jubilation has been converted into the deepest disappointment, since it has been rumored that your university would not permit you to depart. I am writing, not to tell you of my personal disappointment, but to bring to your attention a matter which I hope may yet be of some weight in the ultimate shaping of your decision. For some time past, I have been endeavoring to interest Mr. Leonard Lewisohn, the head of the firm of Lewisohn Bros., who is a member of my congregation, in the affairs of the Seminary. Some months ago, he had subscribed a comparatively small amount to the fund which was being raised in order to make possible a call to you; but after I had told him something of what you had done in England during the past decade and what you may reasonably be expected to do in the future in this country, he authorized me to state, and on Saturday afternoon at the Seminary, I repeated to Mr. Joseph Blumenthal, the president of the institution, that he was more than willing to give the sum of $7,000, which he understood was needed in order to complete the fund. Mr. Lewisohn has asked me to write both to you and to Judge [Mayer] Sulzberger. Mr. Lewisohn says that you may remember him, as the brother-in-law of Mr. [Eli] Bernays, upon whom you frequently called while in London some years ago. If you desire to know anything respecting Mr. Lewisohn, you might inquire concerning him (Mr. Lewisohn asks me to state) of Sir Samuel Montagu, the Sassoons, or Mr. Alfred de Rothschild. Mr. Lewisohn has requested me particularly to say to you that if you come to this country and undertake the leadership of the Seminary, he pledges himself to do all he can to further the Seminary interests. Mr. Lewisohn is a man, let me say by way of parenthesis, given to deeds rather than words, and his enthusiasm in this matter means that, as occasion arises, he will be a most generous supporter of the Seminary. I furthermore believe that he will bring others to lend their cooperation to the Seminary, and that altogether, if you could but accept the Seminary call, the Seminary would stand upon an entirely new footing.

One thing let me add in closing, and I am done. I have understood indirectly that some of your American friends have urged you not to come to this country until the Seminary is reorganized and placed upon a sound financial footing. I remember that you told me five years ago in Cambridge that it was your highest ambition to become the teacher of the American Jewish youth. I say to you in all earnestness that I not alone believe, but I know, that if you come to this country and undertake to guide the Seminary, its material prospects will be at once assured; and there can be no question whatsoever but that your personality will rally to the support of the Seminary many of the best and finest Jews in the country who have heretofore held aloof for reasons into a statement of which I cannot enter at this time. . . .

P.S. If it were not for my keen desire to serve American Jewry, I should not write to you as I am writing, because even if you should come to this country, I would not have the benefit of your companionship or instruction. I have accepted a call to become the rabbi of Portland, Oregon, some 3,000 miles away, for a term of five years. Still I am of the hope that, after some years, I may come back to New York. . . .

March 26, 1900

to Solomon Hirsch, Portland, Oregon

I have been deliberating for a day or two whether I ought to write to you, but feel that it is my duty to do so, in order to prepare you for a possible contingency. Let me lead up to the real point of my letter by saying that during the past few weeks an extraordinary pressure has been brought to bear upon me by the members of my congregation, and many others of the Jewish community of our city, to reconsider my determination to accept the call of the Congregation Beth Israel of Portland. I have all along maintained that such a thing as reconsideration is out of the question, inasmuch as I have formally and definitely accepted the call, and that therefore the matter was closed, but my dear good friends in the synagogue are not satisfied with this, and are most persistent in their requests and appeals for reconsideration. For several days, things have been hanging in the air; and, yesterday, the matter came to a climax when a committee representing the board of trustees laid the matter before me in the following way: they merely desire my consent to write to Beth Israel, petitioning my release. They maintain that they know very well that I could not break my contract, but they at least thought that I might have no objection to their addressing you in this way. They demanded an immediate answer, which I was prepared to give them to the effect that I was absolutely and unalterably opposed to their writing to Portland in these terms. They mean to be very kind and friendly to me; but they did me the injustice of imagining that because they were willing to elect me now for a term of five or ten years at the annual remuneration of $6,000, I might be moved to listen to their pleadings. Finally, after much persuasion, I promised them that I would take 48 hours in which to consider the matter—that is to say whether they might write to you to ask for my release. The promise was only a perfunctory one, as they must needs well understand, because I indicated very clearly to them, as I have all along, that, on the one hand, the duty devolves upon me of following the call that I have accepted, and, furthermore, I still believe that more service is in store for me in the Northwest of this country than I could perform at this time within the precincts of my own city. I have already given my reply to the spokesman of the board of trustees, addressing him in a letter, a copy of which I enclose to you. I know that my decision will meet with your fullest approval.

One thing more remains to be said: I take it for granted that Beth Israel would not under any circumstances consent to my release—that is to say, I am of the hope and conviction that Beth Israel cares sufficiently for my pledged services to be unwilling to release them under any circumstances. I might not have written to you at all in this matter, but I fear that the trustees or some members of the congregation may write to you without my consent or knowledge. In that event, pray understand that you have my fullest permission to reply to any requests which may be made to you or to the congregation to the effect that release is out of the question, for neither the congregation nor I desires to be released.

July 27, 1900

TO S. Joseph, Minneapolis

It has just occurred to me that on my way out to Portland [to begin work at Temple Beth Israel], I may stop at St. Paul and Minneapolis for a day or two. I think, if you desire it very much, I would arrange to deliver an address at a combined meeting of all the Zionist societies of your city. I am not certain as yet that I can make these arrangements, but I believe I can do so. If I decide to stop over in your city, it would probably be for a day in the last week in August, or the first few days in September. Will you let me know at once whether you desire to arrange some meeting, which necessarily should be a meeting of all the Zionist societies of your city, in order that a fine, large mass meeting may be held, etc.?

Portland, Oregon, Autumn, 1901

TO Jennie and Leo Waterman [sister and brother of Louise Waterman Wise], New York City

I am almost too tired to write. I have not recovered from the weariness resultant from an hour's address last night to a gathering which more than crowded the temple, in answer to the minister who dubbed me "Caiaphas." I took up the challenge and told why I reject the Divine Messiahship of Jesus, without any attempt at concealment of my attitude towards the idolatrous features of orthodox Christianity. . . .

Portland, Oregon, February 7, 1903

TO Jenkin Lloyd Jones, Chicago

Immediately upon receipt of your letter, I called a meeting of the (possible) "Liberals" of Portland, to arrange for an invitation to you & your fellows. But *they* seem afraid of you and yours, so that what I had hoped might be a gathering of all or nearly all of the religious forces of our city in welcome of the Apostles of Liberal Religion is not to be.

And yet you must come to Portland. We need you most, because we want you least.

Portland, Oregon, March 17, 1903

TO Jenkin Lloyd Jones, Chicago

I am somewhat discouraged about your prospective visit to Portland. Dr. [G. C.] Cressy [Unitarian] and I find it so hard to move our brother-ministers, even the unorthodox, to join with us in extending to you and Dr. Hiram Thomas [associate to Jones] the hearty welcome which the cause of Liberal Religion and its valiant representatives deserve. We met yesterday; W. G. Eliot [William G. Eliot, Jr., field agent in Oregon for the American Unitarian Association] will be out of town on the day of your visit, Dr. [Albert Alexander] Morrison of the [Trinity] Episcopal Church is rather fearful of "coming in," though at heart—*or in his mind*—he is a "liberal." We were almost tempted to ask you to omit Portland from your itinerary, but I, for one, feel that just because Portland appears loth to welcome the Gospellers of Liberal Religion, it becomes our duty to enable the benighted to see some light. . . .

Portland, Oregon, August, 1903

TO Jennie and Leo Waterman, New York City

If once I tell my people [at Temple Beth Israel] that I will not stay any longer, as I may soon be compelled to do, I must be ready to face every possibility of the situation, including the possibility of remaining in New York without a position, for as you

know, there are no more than five or six positions in the whole
country that I would take. I wish my people would not compel me to announce my decision for the present, that is to say, for
another year, but they may so act that I shall be under the
necessity, morally, of making an unreserved announcement of
my plans. It is a ticklish, not to say, trying situation. . . . I want
to go away after two years. Louise thinks I ought to seek a
broader sphere of activity; and you both, I know, heartily desire
to have Louise and the children in New York. Still it will not be
an easy matter to make an announcement so far in advance which
will involve a considerable loss to me.

I am too far away from the center of things now. . . .

Heidelberg, April 21, 1904

TO Richard Gottheil, New York City

I am writing these lines at the earliest possible moment after
my return from Vienna [from the meeting of the *Grosse Aktions
Komite* or "G.A.C.," the Larger Actions Committee of the
World Zionist Organization]. . . . The confidence in Herzl, rightly
or wrongly, seems shattered. There is no peace, but merely an
armed truce [with reference to the Zionists' debate about Kenya
in East Africa as an alternative to Palestine as a national
home]. . . . One thing I do know—that I am resolved to terminate
my membership in the G.A.C. I have thought of resigning my
membership and of informing Herzl and the G.A.C., but I do
not wish to evoke any comment in the American Jewish press
touching the resignation of one of the earliest of the American
Zionists. I must stipulate—and I take it for granted that my
stipulation will find ready assent—that, at the forthcoming convention of the Federation, *my name be not considered in connection with the American membership in the G.A.C.* . . . I cannot
and will not work with men who refuse to place in me their
fullest confidence. That Herzl and his colleagues fail to take
counsel with the only American member of the G.A.C. then

present in Vienna, touching the status of affairs in America, constitutes an indignity to which no gentleman can submit with honor. I shall not fight, nor even protest. I merely withdraw. But in the matter of my refusal to remain a member of the G.A.C., I am inexorable. I am as much a member of the G.A.C. as Herzl or any man. It was and is his duty to deal with me, with us, frankly and honestly—I am not a Russian underling nor yet a Turkish land-owner who must be kept in the dark as to the real purpose of things. . . .

One thing I must add by way of explanation. Personally, I was treated by Herzl and his colleagues with every possible consideration and courtesy.

Heidelberg, May 6, 1904

TO Theodor Herzl, Vienna

I write to say that I feel in duty bound to accept the explanation of my "chief" with reference to what seemed the exclusion of myself from the proceedings anent American Zionist affairs. That there was such a *Besprechung* [understanding] you admit, and the accidental circumstance that you were not present does not materially affect the situation. But enough of that, as well as of the question of my unavoidable absence from New York [in Portland, Oregon] for some years, the fact of which was not sufficiently borne in mind. . . .

On one point, however, I must insist, in order that no similar misunderstanding may arise in the future. I cannot longer remain a member of the A.C. [Actions Committee]. . . . I do not wish to be, nor do I desire to be held, accountable for the conduct of the American Zionist Federation, seeing that my residence in Oregon, 3000 miles from New York, precludes the possibility of any real participation in the management thereof. I have made that mistake long enough; I shall not make it over again.

. . . I need not assure you of my unalterable devotion to the Cause, which it will be ever my privilege to serve, nor of my personal loyalty to its leader.

Heidelberg, June, 1904

TO Jacob de Haas, Cleveland

For the third or fourth time I am, to my very great regret, unable to be present at an Annual Conference of the Federation of American Zionists [meeting in Cleveland].

My home being on the Pacific Coast, I have been too far West to attend our annual meetings for some years; this year matters are reversed, and I am too far East to be at the Cleveland Conference. . . . Perhaps fortune will favor me another year and enable me to realize the long cherished hope of sitting around once again with my American fellow-Zionists. Only six years have passed since the founding of our Federation; and yet what a far cry it is from the inconspicuous and meagerly attended and occasionally stormy first meeting of our Federation at East Broadway Hall in New York on the 4th of July, 1898, to what, I am certain, will prove to be the harmonious and far-reaching deliberation of the Cleveland gathering of the American Federation.

I bid you give my fellow-Zionists cordial greetings on my behalf. Having been to the Vienna Conference of the *Grosse Aktions Komite* last month, I can send the cheering message that our beloved chief and his associates are striving in the integrity of their hearts and with the strength of their hands to carry out the mandate implied in the Basle Platform. The recent conference at Vienna, you may assure the delegates to the Cleveland Convention, is bound to be productive of lasting good to our cause, for though opinion yet remains honestly divided as to the duty of the hour and the matter of the "East Africa" offer [Kenya] of the English government, the so-called *Neinsager* ["no-sayers"] made no denial at Vienna of the truth borne in on them with irresistible force by reason of the presentation of irrefutable facts; but Herzl and his supporters are loyal to Zion, whatever their attitude may be . . . to any subsidiary colonization project. . . . In the working out of our plans it behooves us to remember that Dr. Herzl is the leader of a movement international in scope and range and that he must be trusted and followed so long as no action of his is violative of the principles of our movement. And of such violations he will never be guilty. . . .

Engelberg, Switzerland, July 11, 1904

TO Richard Gottheil, Bad Wildungen

. . . I have felt nearer to you than ever in these days of our common loss and grief [following Herzl's death on July 3, 1904]. You were, in some measure, prepared for the worst; I, not at all. . . . Your wire was a thunderclap. It almost prostrated me. I was in no condition to go to Vienna [for funeral rites], for I was sick at heart; and when I reached Zürich, "gave out." I had to return. I am not able, even after the lapse of a week, to think calmly of it all, so swift, so tragic, so catastrophic. Saddest of all, to think that noble heart was grieved, almost broken, by the bitterness of the Russian opposition [at the recent meeting of the Actions Committee].

A smile, friendly and almost grateful, lighted up his face when I bade him goodbye [in April at Vienna], after having promised to do everything possible, in compliance with his wishes, to arrange a meeting between him and [Jacob] Schiff. I wired and wrote to Schiff, after having failed to meet him at Frankfort [-am-Main]. Schiff replied that, as an American citizen, he could not meet with Herzl and discuss Zionism. This is the tenor of his dispatch, which it became my duty to transmit to Herzl. I have the original in my possession. It does little credit to Schiff's judgment. All his gifts to Jewry—from above—cannot make good, in my judgment, the unrighteousness of such an attitude. In truth, the position of the leaders (?) of American Israel with reference to Zionism and Herzl will fill an inglorious page in American Jewish history. [Kaufmann] Kohler's nonsense about the Zionist peril almost follows Herzl to the grave; his interview in the [*Jewish*] *Chronicle* [of London] faces the obituary of Herzl. [Solomon] Schechter, fearful of Schiff, advocates "Moral Zionism," and Kohler palavers about the "perils of Zionism." "These be thy gods, O Israel!" . . .

. . . Poor Herzl was surrounded by pygmies. *We* cannot have a cabinet made up of Herzls; but we ought [to] bend every effort in this hour to win, by any and every art that is honorable, the men of leading in every great Jewry, [Lionel Walter] Rothschild and [Claude Goldsmid] Montefiore [of England], N. [Narcisse]

Leven and Baron Edmund [de Rothschild of France], [Mayer] Sulzberger, [Nathan] Straus and [Jacob] Schiff in our own country. This may be the hour. "There is a tide," etc. . . .

Portland, Oregon, January 5, 1906

Open Letter to the President and Members of Temple Emanu-El, New York City

On the first of December I received a communication from Mr. Louis Marshall, chairman of a committee of the board of trustees of Temple Emanu-El [stating that the pulpit had always been and would continue to be "subject to and under the control of the board of trustees"].

On December third I addressed to him the following reply:

Mr. Louis Marshall,
Chairman of Committee of Board of Trustees, Temple Emanu-El.

Dear Sir:
If your letter of December first be expressive of the thought of the board of trustees of Temple Emanu-El, I beg to say that no self-respecting minister of religion, in my opinion, could consider a call to a pulpit which, in the language of your communication, shall always be subject to, and under the control of, the board of trustees. I am,

Yours very truly,
STEPHEN S. WISE.

While my position in the matter under question is thus explained in unmistakable terms, I feel that it is become my duty to address this open letter to you on the question of the freedom of the Jewish pulpit.

I write to you because I believe that a question of supereminent importance has been raised, the question whether the pulpit shall be free or whether the pulpit shall not be free, and, by reason of its loss of freedom, reft of its power for good. The whole position of the churches is involved in this question, for the steadily waning influence of church and synagogue is due in no small part, I hold, to the widespread belief that the pulpit is not free, and that it is "subject to and under the control" of those officers and members of church or synagogue who, for any reason, are powerful in its councils. The question, therefore, "Shall the pulpit be free or shall it not be free?" is of infinitely greater moment than the question of the occupancy of your pulpit by any man whosoever, and it is the deep conviction that this is so that has impelled me, now that any thought of a direct relation between us is definitely set aside, to address you in earnest language as men equally concerned with myself in the well-being and increasing power of our beloved religion.

When a committee of five, constituting a majority of the board of trustees of the congregation, came to me for the purpose of ascertaining whether a call to occupy your pulpit would be accepted, and, if accepted, upon what terms, I stated that I had but one stipulation to make with respect to the terms of such call, and that I was ready to leave everything else to the judgment of the board of trustees and the members of the congregation, merely adding that a written contract ought not to be deemed necessary between a congregation and its minister. The one stipulation I made in the following words: "If I am to accept a call to the pulpit of Temple Emanu-El, I do so with the understanding that I am to be free, and that my pulpit is not to be muzzled." I made no other stipulation; upon this I insisted. Counsels of prudence, which were urged upon me, suggested that I should have taken this freedom for granted, but viewing the manner in which my stipulation was met by the members of the committee, I deem it most fortunate that I anticipated the situation which has arisen. My stipulation that, if I were to occupy the pulpit of Emanu-El, I must be free, was met by the statement of the committee since formulated in the appended letter, "the pulpit shall always be subject to and under the control of the board of trustees," which statement of the committee was not disavowed at either of two subsequent meetings of the board of trustees, held December 4, 1905, and January 2, 1906. Between this position and my own conception of the pulpit, as laid down in my stipulation, there is an irreconcilable difference. It was indeed held by some members of the committee that the phrase, "the pulpit shall always be subject to and under the control of

the board of trustees," was "an empty formula," or "a mere
figure of speech," which interpretation, however, the chairman
of the committee at once emphatically disavowed. Even though
this phrase were admitted to be an empty formula, I would still
be under the moral necessity of refusing to maintain a fiction, of
making a compact in terms of falsehood to teach in a place dedicated to truth. But how can a form of words so threatening to the
liberty of a minister of religion be regarded as a mere figure of
speech? The very fact that it was insisted upon is evidence that it
was not intended as a formula, and, if it be intended seriously, as
it clearly is, I have only to repeat that no self-respecting minister
of religion could consider a call to the pulpit of a church or
synagogue on such terms. Such a formula, taken under any con-
struction that may be put upon it, is not chiefly humiliating to
me, who unequivocally reject its terms, but much more humiliating to the congregation in the name of which such terms are
offered.

For let us consider the obvious meaning of the words "the
pulpit shall always be subject to, and under the control of, the
board of trustees" in the light of the paragraph of the communication appended, which reads: "The logical consequence of
a conflict of irreconcilable views between the rabbi and the board
of trustees is that one or the other must give way. Naturally, it
must be the rabbi. It goes without saying, therefore, that at such
a juncture he should have the privilege of resigning. His failure
to exercise that option necessarily implies an acquiescence by
him in the views of the board of trustees." It is not said that
in the event of a conflict of irreconcilable views between the
rabbi and a majority of the members of the congregation the
rabbi must give way, but that the acceptance of the terms
"the pulpit shall always be subject to, and under the control
of, the board of trustees," implies acquiescence on the part
of the rabbi in the views of the board of trustees in the event
of a conflict of irreconcilable views between him and them,
or the necessity of exercising the "option" or "privilege" of
resigning. The board of trustees thus assert for themselves in the
last analysis the custodianship of the spiritual convictions of the
congregation. When I asked the members of the committee to

define the terms, "subject to, and under the control of, the board of trustees," the same thought was expressed by them in saying that, if some members of the congregation should differ from my views as expressed in the pulpit, and should make representation to that effect to the board of trustees, the latter would expect me either to alter, or to be silent touching, the views to which objection had been raised. Stated more simply, the rabbi, whose whole life is given to the study of and preoccupation with religion and morals, must always hold his views subject to revision or ratification at the hands of the board of trustees, or of any number, howsoever small, of the members of the congregation having sufficiently formidable influence with the board of trustees. In other words, the mere fact that a certain number, not necessarily a majority, of the members of the congregation or certain members of the board of trustees, might object to his views is to compel retraction, silence or resignation, without the slightest guarantee that reason and right are on the side of the objectors. The mere statement of the case is its own severest condemnation.

A fundamental error underlies the position set forth in the communication herewith appended with respect to the office of the ministry. The chief office of the minister, I take it, is not to represent the views of the congregation, but to proclaim the truth as he sees it. How can he serve a congregation as a teacher save as he quickens the minds of his hearers by the vitality and independence of his utterances? But how can a man be vital and independent and helpful, if he be tethered and muzzled? A free pulpit, worthily filled, must command respect and influence; a pulpit that is not free, howsoever filled, is sure to be without potency and honor. A free pulpit will sometimes stumble into error; a pulpit that is not free can never powerfully plead for truth and righteousness. In the pursuit of the duties of his office, the minister may from time to time be under the necessity of giving expression to views at variance with the views of some, or even many, members of the congregation. Far from such difference proving the pulpit to be in the wrong, it may be, and ofttimes is, found to signify that the pulpit has done its duty in calling evil evil and good good, in abhorring the moral wrong of putting light for darkness and darkness for light, and in scorning to limit itself to the utterance of what the prophet has styled "smooth things," lest variance of views arise. Too great a dread there may be of secession on the part of some members of a congregation, for, after all, difference and disquiet, even schism at the worst, are not so much to be feared as that attitude of the pulpit which never provokes dissent because it is cautious rather than courageous, peace-loving rather than prophetic, time-serving rather than right-serving. The minister is not to be the spokesman of the congregation, not the message-bearer of the congregation, but the bearer of a message to the congregation. What the contents of that message shall be, must be left to the conscience and understanding and loyalty of him in whom a congregation places sufficient confidence to elect him to minister to it.

In the course of the conferences held between the committee and the writer, it was urged that the pulpit has no right to demand exemption from criticism. The minister in Israel does not regard his utterances as infallible. No minister will refuse to correct an opinion—though he will take the utmost pains to achieve correctness in substance and form before speaking—when reasons are advanced to convince him of his error. Nor will he fail to welcome criticism and invite difference of opinion to the end that truth may be subserved. "The pulpit shall always be subject to, and under the control of, the board of trustees," in the light of the interpretation afforded by the subjoined communication, implies something radically different from the view that the minister is not above criticism. Namely, the teacher of religion and ethics must bend before the brute arbitrium of any opinion, which the majority of the board of trustees or any chance group of members of the congregation may hold, providing it be in irreconcilable conflict with his own. To declare that in the event of a conflict of irreconcilable views between the minister and the board of trustees, it is the minister who must yield and not the board, is to assert the right not to criticise the pulpit, but to silence its occupant, and, above all, to imply that the board of trustees are always sure to be in the right, or else that the convictions of the board of trustees shall stand, whether right or wrong, and that the minister must acquiesce in these convictions, right or wrong, or else exercise the "option" and "privilege" of resigning.

The Jewish minister, I repeat, does not speak *ex cathedra,* and his views are not supposed to have a binding force upon the congregation to which he ministers. He is to express his convictions on any subject that comes within the purview of religion and ethics, but these convictions do not purport to constitute a creed or dogma to which a congregation must in whole or in part subscribe. But the board of trustees asserts the right to define and to formulate the views in which the rabbi must acquiesce, or, failing to acquiesce therein, resign. Let us assume for a moment that it were possible for the board of trustees to come to an agreement with respect to its convictions upon Reform Judaism for which Temple Emanu-El may fairly be said to stand, though these convictions cannot be ascertained and reduced to unity save in the broadest sense. Let us, furthermore, assume that my convictions are substantially in accord with those held by the present board of trustees. Is it not clear that under the terms, "the pulpit shall always be subject to, and under the control of, the board of trustees," the rabbi may in time be called upon to acquiesce in views of the board of trustees at variance with those held by them today? Not only is the rabbi expected to sign away his present independence, but to mortgage his intellectual and moral liberty for the future. Stated in briefest possible terms, the rabbi is asked to subscribe to a statement of present and future convictions of the board of trustees. The demand is put forth that he subscribe to a blank page the contents of which are to be determined, not on the basis of his understanding of and loyalty to the teachings of his religion, but by "the views of the board of trustees." This is indeed to attempt to rob the pulpit of every vestige of freedom and independence. I am asked to point the way, and my hands are tied; I am asked to go before and my feet are fettered.

It is idle rhetoric to say, as does the communication appended, that the words, "the pulpit shall always be subject to, and under the control of, the board of trustees," "do not mean that the board of trustees will call upon any incumbent of our pulpit to sacrifice or surrender his principles or convictions," in the face of the

menacing declaration immediately following that, in the event
of a conflict of irreconcilable views between the rabbi and the
board of trustees, the rabbi must naturally give way, his failure
to exercise the option of resigning necessarily implying acquiescence by him in the views of the board of trustees. If I could
bring myself to accept a call to the pulpit of Emanu-El upon
such terms, and this is unthinkable, the board of trustees would
never find it necessary to call upon me to surrender my convictions, for assent on my part to the stipulation, "the pulpit
shall always be subject to, and under the control of, the board
of trustees," would involve such a sacrifice of principles as would
leave me no convictions worthy of the name to surrender at any
subsequent behest of the board of trustees. It is equally meaning-
less to declare that "in the past this has never led to any friction
between our rabbis and our board of trustees." Where a rabbi is
reduced to the choice of acquiescence in views, right or wrong,
because held by the board of trustees, or of silence, friction is
impossible. The absence of friction in the past between the
rabbis and the board of trustees of Temple Emanu-El proves that
either the pulpit has been circumspect or that it has been so
effectually muzzled that even protest was impossible on the part
of an occupant who had subscribed to such conditions. A third
possibility obtains—that the board of trustees has had the forbearance of the angels with the occupants of the pulpit insofar as
they have not abused the power which they claim as their own.
As for the forbearance of angels, which has possibly been theirs,
I wish to make clear that I would not deliver my conscience into
the keeping of the angels. My conscience is my own.

Finally, to hold that the subjection of the pulpit to, and its
control by, the board of trustees is a written or unwritten law
of the congregation is to maintain that the pulpit of Emanu-
El never has been free, and this, I am sure, does not accord with
the memories that still remain alive in me and in others of high-
minded, independent, revered teachers who have occupied that
pulpit. One of the former occupants I have intimately known,
and were he living today he would repudiate the claim that he
had for many years been the occupant of a pulpit which was not
free.

I have sought to do you the justice of helping you to realize the seriousness of the situation which you face. This situation, I believe, you have not planned; into it you have, however, permitted yourselves to drift. That this appeal to the spirit of my people at its highest shall not have been made in vain is my hope, for the sake of our religion, which a free pulpit alone can truly serve.

Portland, Oregon, January 20, 1906

TO A. J. Dittenhoefer, New York City

. . . Permit me to quote a sentence from each of your three letters to me. January 3, you write: "The [Temple Emanu-El] trustees continue to favor you, but still insist upon their prerogative [that the pulpit 'is subject to, and under the control of, the board of trustees']." January 9: "For that reason you were justified in showing to the public that you had declined the offer on the terms and conditions on which it was made." January 13: "I cannot help regretting—regretting deeply—that you could not see your way clear to accept an election as minister to the temple, even with the obnoxious condition annexed."

I have cited the above statements of your three communications to me, because I wish to say to you that you have done me a great wrong, in so far as you and your fellow-trustees have permitted Mr. Marshall to give out through the New York press the uncontradicted statement that a call to me to the pulpit of Emanu-El had never even been under contemplation. Mr. Marshall, as you know, made one misstatement after another, each of which aimed to cast doubt upon my veracity. . . . You and your fellow-trustees knew that when Mr. Marshall addressed his communication to me, it was written as the official expression of the thought of the board of trustees. Was it manly and honorable in you and your fellow-trustees to permit this misstatement in this matter to go uncontradicted?

Mr. Marshall stated that I had insisted upon the right to preach politics from the pulpit of Emanu-El and therefore the trustees had found it necessary to limit the freedom of the pulpit, which it was proposed to tender me. You and your fellow-trustees knew that I never stipulated for the right to preach

politics, but that I stated in definition of my demand, "the pulpit
be free and unmuzzled," that I claimed the right to speak upon
any question in which a moral issue was involved, and that I
added that I would have supported Jerome in his candidacy
[for the office of mayor of New York City] because I believe him
to be the leader of an issue which involves civic liberty and civic
righteousness. Was it manly and honorable in you and your
fellow-trustees to permit Mr. Marshall's misstatement that I
threatened to preach politics from the pulpit, to go uncontradicted?

. . . What shall be thought of a body of men, made up of you
and your fellow-trustees, who remained silent while one of their
number was permitted to give publicity to a series of misstate-
ments, calculated to assail the character of one, whose offense, as
you know, lay in the circumstance that he had too much man-
hood and self-respect to accept a call to a muzzled pulpit, and in
his earnest desire to free the Jewish pulpit by an appeal to the
public conscience?

. . . Not for my sake, but for your sake, and the sake of your
fellow-trustees, am I unutterably saddened at the thought of the
board of trustees engaging in a conspiracy of silence in order to
save themselves and the Temple from the shame and humiliation
to which their failure to repudiate Mr. Marshall's communication had brought it and them, even though such conspiracy might
do an irreparable wrong to one, whom, but a few weeks before,
they proposed to call to their pulpit.

You close your letter of Jan. 9 by asking, "Is it true that
you are coming to New York?" In answer to your question, I
wish to say that it is true that I am coming to New York. I will go
to New York in order to organize an independent Jewish religious
movement, by which I mean a free synagogue, with a free pulpit,
preaching a free, vital and progressive Judaism.

Portland, Oregon, January 20, 1906

TO Oswald Garrison Villard, New York City

. . . I gather from your editorial that you understood that the
trustees of [Temple] Emanu-El had not the hardihood to meet

the question which I had raised and that they found it necessary, through the agency of their inventive Secretary, Mr. [Louis] Marshall, to attempt to raise a number of spurious issues in the hope of diverting attention from the real one.

I feel it my duty to make clear to you that no question was raised as between the board of trustees and myself with respect to the doctrinal position of Emanu-El. The trustees understood perfectly that I was in substantial agreement with them with respect to the teachings of Reform Judaism, for which Emanu-El stands.

I made the sole stipulation that the pulpit be free and that I be not muzzled, not merely because I knew the temper of the gentlemen who announced their intention of extending a call to me, but because I felt and feel that one of the chief reasons for the endangerment, if not the loss, of the moral supremacy of the churches is due to the wide-spread and largely justifiable belief that the pulpit is not free. . . .

Rockport, Mass., July 10, 1907

TO Jenkin Lloyd Jones, Chicago

The Free Synagogue is planning a series of addresses to be given one Sunday morning in the month, October, 1907—May, 1908, on the theme "Some Social Problems of Our Age." Among the subjects to be considered under the general title are "Utilization of the Immigrant," "Constructive Charity," "The State and the Wrongdoer," "Child-Saving," "Industrial Peace," "International Arbitration." I write to ask that you have the kindness to make an address on "The Outreaching Church."

I trust that you may feel moved to render this important service to the Free Synagogue. . . . You *must* render this service, Brother & Friend. It is *your* cause as well as mine. Yours is *the* Outreaching Church [newly founded Abraham Lincoln Center]. Tell us how you did it, & help us to do likewise. The Free Synagogue is to "outreach" as does the Abraham Lincoln Center.

One word more—& you will understand & forgive. We have boundless faith, but our funds are limited. You, invincible idealist, know what that means. I am afraid that the Free Synagogue cannot afford to pay your expenses. I shall for the present take next to nothing. Can you, will you, not come just the same?

May 6, 1908

TO John D. Long, Brooklyn

I have been thinking of the Third Annual Conference of the Christian Socialist Fellowship at which I promised to speak for you on "The Social Message of the Prophets," and I feel that I ought to write the following. You know, of course, that the Christian Socialist party in Germany has actively espoused the cause of anti-Semitism, in fact Christian Socialism is almost synonymous with anti-Semitism in German-speaking countries. When your invitation first reached me I felt for a time that I could not accept it, seeing that your body had adopted the title which is odious to Jews by reason of the most un-social and un-Christian attitude toward Jews of the Christian Socialist party in Europe. I concluded, however, to accept your invitation because I knew that you and your colleagues were as far from being in sympathy with the anti-Semitism of the Christian Socialist party in Germany as I am.

I have come to feel, however, that I could not speak upon your platform unless the anti-Semitic attitude of the Christian Socialist party in Europe were clearly and vigorously repudiated by you, not only because it is not a part of your own creed but because you believe it to be, as I do, anti-Christian and anti-social. What is more, since the question has come up, it seemed to be a most fitting thing for your Conference to pass resolutions urging the leaders and members of the Christian Socialist party to renounce the anti-Semitism which is in contradiction to the profession of Christianity and Socialism alike. I had thought of offering this suggestion, preliminary to my address; and unless you take some action prior to my address, you will understand that it remains my purpose to ask the meeting to send a message by its representatives to the heads of the Christian Socialist party in Germany and Austria of the tenor indicated above.

June 21, 1909

TO Louis R. Ehrich

I am delighted that you are to speak for us . . . on Friday evening, February 25, at Clinton Hall. I know we shall have a fine address from you [on the subject, "The Ethics of the Business Man"].

Yes, I did think that the letter in the [N.Y. *Evening*] *Post* written by "Indignant" was of your authorship. The press reports of my address at the Wednesday night meeting were, as you say, miserably inefficient. Possibly you may have noticed that the *Evening Post* contained a fairly accurate and full report of the address.

I do not like the way things are going. Incompetency and inefficiency threaten to characterize the action, or inaction, of the erstwhile Committee of Nineteen now attenuated, or shall we say magnified, into the Committee of One Hundred. If things are not taken hold of more vigorously by this Committee, it may become the duty of those of us who are in earnest in the matter of redeeming New York from Tammany Hall to deal in uncompromising fashion with the situation, and to demand that the men who are now dealing in an uncertain fashion with the problem shall yield the lead to firmer hands.

October 26, 1909

TO Richard Gottheil, Jerusalem

. . . I am very eager to learn about your first impressions as you settle down to the year's work in Jerusalem [as director of the American School of Oriental Research]. What an enviable, rich and full year it ought to be, and best of all, far from the madding crowd of New York and its trivial engrossments. In the world Judean, there is nothing to record except that the Central Conference of American Rabbis is to hold its meeting here [in New York City] next month . . . I have tried to bring about the election of [Emil] Hirsch as president of the Conference, but the Lilliputians appear reluctant to be led by a giant. . . .

November 12, 1909

TO Maximilian Heller, New Orleans

. . . You seem to labor under the impression that I, personally, have, in what you call an underhanded way, sought to undermine your candidacy of office of President of the Central Conference of American Rabbis. Nothing could be farther from the truth; and, if you cared about the truth, you could have learnt that and, therefore, could not have written to me in the strain in which you did.

For several months, a number of men, including Doctor [Maurice H.] Harris, Rabbi [Charles] Fleischer, and myself, have felt that at this time the Presidency of the Conference should not be lodged in a man who has, for what he considers adequate reasons, chosen to place himself in the forefront of the Counter-Reformation movement [in Reform Judaism]. . . . Seeing that the Conference of this year was arranged in order to synchronize with the centenary celebrations of [David] Einhorn and [Samuel] Adler, it seemed to a group of us that, however friendly we personally were to you, it would be most unwise to elect to the Presidency a man who is considered one of the leaders in the movement which makes for the undoing of the Jewish Reformation.

. . . As you know, I have never met you face to face, but I have always believed in your honesty of purpose. True enough, it was shocking to find your readiness, some four years ago, to lend assent to the dictum of certain people in New York that the pulpit need not be free. But I forgave you then, as I had occasion to forgive many who did not and do not understand, even now, the tremendous importance of the fight I made for the entire Jewish ministry in America. Nothing could have been more disheartening at that time than your word written in the *American Israelite* to the effect that a strong man need not stipulate for freedom and that a weak man has no right to expect it— namely, only the strong may be free and the weaker man must be satisfied with the chains. . . .

April 26, 1910

TO Richard Gottheil, Jerusalem

It is a great pleasure to have your letter, and more especially to read your almost hopeful judgment upon the future of Palestine from a Jewish point of view. Your Jewish loyalty is most admirable and serves me as an apt illustration of the validity to our claim that adherence to the Reform movement need not impair one's loyalty to things Jewish. . . .

It is good to learn that you have had leisure for study [while serving as director of the American School of Oriental Research]. What an enviable privilege from the viewpoint of one who is hurried from one address into another, and to whom is denied the needed privilege of that quiet which alone can make steady and concentrated thought possible.

. . . The English experience [of a visit to Great Britain] was deeply interesting. . . . What a rare company of men and women in the leadership of the Jewish Religious Union!

. . . We have no summer plans, except that we are going to the Adirondacks where we have built a little camp [Buck Island on Lake Placid]. Some day, we shall perhaps see you there. . . .

July 4, 1910

TO Richard Gottheil, Paris

It is a great delight to have had your two letters from Florence and Paris, although I was sorry to note that you were somewhat perturbed over the newspaper report of Professor [Felix] Adler's address at the [Free] Synagogue. It is good that you suspended judgment, for you would have done Adler a grave injustice if you had accepted the newspaper reports as truthful. Nothing could have been further from the truth than that Adler sought to cast ridicule upon any Jewish rite or observance. On the contrary, his address was a presentation of his own deeply reverent attitude toward the realities and sincerities of the passing order. If anything, his word was calculated to give aid and comfort to the "enemy," within the camp of the Counter-Reformation. Illuminating and stirring as his address was in many respects, it would almost have given more delight to a [Solomon] Schechter than it did to me, possibly because he seems to find no middle-ground between Orthodoxy and Ethical Culture. He did not state this as crudely and baldly as I have put it, but that appeared to be in his mind—*aut aut,* perhaps I ought to have put it, "in or out."

I have carefully considered what you have said concerning the need of a new attitude toward Jewish settlements in Palestine, and I shall be prepared most heartily to second any plans that you may formulate upon your return that shall look to the betterment of the Jewish status in Palestine. It is incontrovertible, as you say, that Jews will persist in going to Palestine and that it would be spiritually suicidal to rob a multitude of Jews of their Palestinian hope. But, as you say, you will give me the *Parush* [full explanation] in September.

As you know, [Claude G.] Montefiore has been here for a month and returns tomorrow [to Great Britain]. I need hardly tell you that everyone is delighted with him. His address at our [Free] Synagogue was a beautiful plea for the mystic element in religion. I saw an advance copy of the address which he was to give at the Central Conference [of American Rabbis]—a simple, earnest, courageous, and withal temperate statement of his own liberal position. Have you seen his little volume on *The Religious Teachings of Jesus,* containing some addresses which he gave at Manchester College and Oxford [University] while we were in London [in the late winter and early spring of 1910]? I think I shall review the book for the *Century* magazine.

The resignation of [Judah L.] Magnes [as rabbi of Temple Emanu-El], as you know, has made a tremendous stir. He could not have remained in Emanu-El without forfeiting the respect of American Israel. Many of us wondered that he could have remained as long as he did. It is believed by many that Magnes and [Louis] Marshall did not imagine that he would be taken at his word when he made his rather tentative suggestions to the congregation [to alter the rites and broaden the program]. Strange to say, the board [of trustees of Temple Emanu-El] actually ventured to take issue with Marshall and refused to consider the proposals. Mr. [Jacob] Schiff told me that Magnes would probably undertake a work similar to my own, possibly under the name of the "People's Synagogue" and with the [Solomon] Schechter *Plomba* [seal of approval] affixed.

In making up our plans for the year, I came upon the enclosure, the proposed program of addresses on "The Conflicts of Judaism" which you were to have given for us the first year. I now feel that I would very much like to have you give this course for us—that is to say, under the auspices of the [Free] Synagogue. In fact, I have a rather ambitious plan in view, and I am hoping I may secure your cooperation. Could not some of us get together in New York with a view to training men for the Jewish ministry —that is to say, men who have had a college education—not unbred nor underbred boys, but educated men? We must consider this carefully upon your return. . . .

Lake Placid, August 5, 1910

TO Richard Gottheil, Bad Wildungen

. . . Your response to my suggestion with respect to the course of lectures ["The Conflicts of Judaism"] is not altogether heartening. I have no right to object to your asking for remuneration, to which you are entitled, but I cannot help wishing that this factor in the problem were not made to obtrude so sharply.

As to the dream of founding a school for the training of rabbis, I hope in time to do the work along the lines laid down by your father [Gustav Gottheil], namely, to get a few earnest worthwhile men and direct them, not enslave them, nor run them all into a mold, and what a sorry one it is, as does Cincinnati [Hebrew Union College], but to give some hopeful, promising men an opportunity to prepare themselves, under the guidance of men who are in earnest, for the high task of the ministry. . . .

As your long-time pupil and all-time friend, I ought perhaps be grateful for the compliment implied in your suggestion, "Temple Emanu-El ought to take you in place of [Judah L.] Magnes." But are you in earnest or is this a *Kurwitz* [a health resort jest]? Emanu-El take me? Do you happen to remember

some words in *Coriolanus?* "You banish me! I banish you!" . . .
Seriously, our work [at the Free Synagogue] is only begun; but
it is begun, and we are alive and we have a work to do. . . .

November 9, 1910

TO Israel Zangwill, Worthing, England

I have not heard from you for a long time, and have no word
concerning the Australian project [for the Jewish Colonization
Association] which seemed so big. But I send the enclosure, which
may have escaped your attention. It contains an interview with
one Governor [John Green] Brady of Alaska, whom I had occasion to meet lately, and who seemed anxious that you should
know more about this. Perhaps you have already discussed the
matter with Daniel Guggenheim, who would be likely to know
more about the Alaskan situation, although I hardly believe that
he is familiar with that section of the country to which Brady
particularly refers. I have been in Alaska and know something
of the richness and beauty of the land. It seems at first glance a
noble plan and well worth considering [as a place for colonies
of East European Jews].

August 3, 1911

TO Israel Zangwill, London

In the first place, let me thank you for your most generous
hospitality to my friends, Mr. and Mrs. [Julius] Rosenwald. In
America, we should say you gave them the "glad hand." . . .

But my special reason for writing at this time is to tell you
that I have read and re-read with great delight your paper ["The
Jewish Race"] before the [Universal] Races Congress [convened
in London]. It is magnificent and it is war [against assimilationist
views]. I have just heard from Professor [Edwin R. A.] Seligman
that Felix Adler [founder and head of the Ethical Culture Society]
was profoundly impressed by your statesmanlike utterance, and
your addendum [supporting "the creation of a Jewish state, or

at least a Jewish land of refuge upon a basis of local autonomy, to which, in the course of the centuries, all that was truly Jewish would gravitate"] was delightful. . . .

Your reference to the gateless Ghetto in America ["Even in America, with its lip-formula of brotherhood, a gateless Ghetto has been created by the isolation of the Jews from the general social life."] reminds me of my own experience with the Lake Mohonk Peace Conference which invited me to make an address before it in May. Ordinarily, the Lake Mohonk Hotel gives the Jews no quarters, so I turned around and gave them no quarter. I am sorry to say that Oscar Straus and other Jews went there despite my protest, but that is all a part of what you have rightly stigmatized as the protective mimicry of the Jew, which incidentally does not protect the Jew, but exposes him to superadded contempt. . . .

September 27, 1911

TO Woodrow Wilson, Trenton, N.J.

I had meant to call upon you some day this week in order to discuss a matter which I believe you would agree with me is of great importance. But I hesitate to encroach upon your time, seeing that you are on the eve of an arduous political campaign in your own state. Upon several occasions during the past few months, I have been tempted to write to you concerning certain matters of common interest; but I have forborne because I know how heavy are your duties and that it is the part of kindness to forbear trespassing upon the time of a man occupied as you are. I therefore mean to leave the discussion of the particular matter to which I referred in an earlier letter until the New Jersey campaign is over, when I shall venture to call upon you, if I may.

For the present, however, I mean to bring another matter to your attention and earnestly to invoke your interest and help.

Last year, the Church of the Divine Paternity (Universalist), the Church of the Messiah (Unitarian), and our own Free Synagogue united in a series of public meetings on Sunday evenings at which the great social, industrial and civic problems of our time were considered with special reference to their religious bases. Among the speakers at these meetings were Hon. Ben B. Lindsey, Francis J. Heney, Professor John Graham Brooks, and Jacob A. Riis. This year, our churches plan to have a second series of meetings beginning Sunday evening, January 7 and continuing for six weeks. Among those who are to speak for us are Washington Gladden, Bishop [Charles] Williams of Michigan (probably) and Gifford Pinchot. The general theme of the addresses for 1912 is to be "Social Justice."

My associates and I turn to you and extend a most cordial invitation to give the opening address on the evening of Sunday, January 7, such an address to view the problem of social justice on the political side. I know, my dear Governor Wilson, how many are the invitations which come to you, and yet I do feel, apart from my own personal desire to have your message brought to us, that the occasion will be worthwhile.

With most hearty regard and looking forward to seeing you after a triumphal campaign in your state.

October 6, 1911

TO Theodore Roosevelt

I have just learned from Mr. [Abram I.] Elkus, who is counsel to the New York Legislative Commission on Public Safety, that he has invited you to appear at the hearing of the Commission to be designated by you, in order that the Commission may have the benefit of your thought with respect to conditions in industry, with special reference to the work of women and children.

I do hope, my dear Colonel Roosevelt, that you will find it possible to accept this invitation. It will, as you know, be difficult, if not impossible, to enact needed legislation unless the attention of the community be directed to the evils which obtain, and that can best be done through a strong and earnest word of your own, fortified as it would be by your own leader-

ship, it may truly be said, of the cause of children in industry
for many years.

December 19, 1911

TO Ward Baking Company

Some men have come to me representing the Bakers Union,
and have made the statement that your establishment is expelling
any man who is found to belong to a labor union. They have
asked me to protest against such an unfair and discriminating
attitude on your part, and I told them I would seek to ascertain
from you whether the facts be as stated by them, that you are
trying to drive all union men out of your employ, even though
there be no union organization among the ranks of the men in
your establishment.

CHAPTER TWO

THE NEW FREEDOMS
(1912-1919)

TO MAXIMILIAN HELLER

> We must cease our negative attitude. "Cease your
> negatives; nerve us with affirmatives." There are great
> and commanding affirmations to be made by Liberal
> Judaism; and we must get away, as those of us who
> are alive have gotten away, from the purely negative,
> largely rationalist positions of the earlier phase of
> Liberal Judaism. It may be a good time to protest
> against the use of the Bible in the public schools, but
> it does seem that there should be something better
> and bigger for which we should stand. . . .
>
> *April 7, 1915*

Lake Placid, July 8, 1912

TO Henry Morgenthau, Sr.

. . . Having extended to you my congratulations and patted myself upon the back for my prescience in the matter of the [Woodrow] Wilson candidacy, I want to take up with you a matter which I think of very great importance. I do not like the Democratic [party] platform, and I hope Governor Wilson doesn't. . . . I want to urge a plan which ought to win to the support of Governor Wilson a considerable number of Progressives, such as the writer, who in many ways are tempted to join the Third party movement because, or in despite, of [Theodore] Roosevelt. They believe in Wilson as I do. They believe that it may be possible for Wilson, because of his great personality and power of leadership, to win back the Democratic party to the furtherance of the people's cause. Governor Wilson ought to say something about this, say it strongly and clearly as he so well knows how to do.

I have written by this mail to George Foster Peabody and to John Haynes Holmes, asking whether they and you and I cannot get together with a view to uniting upon a statement to be presented to Governor Wilson before the date of the notification, in the hope that he may be moved to make some allusion to the more obvious omissions of the Democratic platform; but, after all, he is the platform, and, therefore, it appears to me an extraordinary opportunity is presented to him of presenting in his own terms and formulation a vision of democracy which we know to be his own. . . . I had thought of writing either to Dr. [Henry] Moskowitz or Miss [Lillian] Wald, but, unless you have won them over, I presume they will continue to use their influence on behalf of Roosevelt. Jane Addams said to me in Washington that Wilson was her choice after [Robert] La Follette; and I wonder whether we ought ask her to meet with us.

Lake Placid, August 7, 1912

TO George Foster Peabody, Lake George, N.Y.

. . . I hope with all my heart that Governor Wilson will in today's address show that he is committed to a program of social democracy with all that that term implies. I have the deepest confidence in him, as you have, but I cannot overcome my distrust of the men who are behind him—I mean, of course, the old ring-leaders, the Murphys and Sullivans and Taggarts. A very good test of the Governor's independence will come in the matter of naming a candidate for the governorship of New York. . . . He has the right and upon him is the duty of saying to the Democratic [party] leaders of New York that they must not weigh down the presidential ticket with a man who represents Tammany Hall. . . .

Yes, I had a good and satisfactory talk with Governor Wilson [at the summer home, "Shadow Lawn," at Sea Girt, N.J.]. We are at one in our complete confidence in him. At the same time, I urged upon him that he must not even seem to be too near to Tammany Hall. He must not permit himself to be surrounded by its representatives and . . . on the question of the governorship he must speak out. . . . I rather think that his superb utterance of Thursday may have reflected in part our common feeling touching the necessity of tearing himself loose from the men who have put the Democratic party to shame in our great state. . . .

September 16, 1912

TO Jane Addams, Bar Harbor, Maine

. . . I do not know whether you have heard from any member of the committee who waited on the President [William Howard Taft] that he, and not we, mentioned your name in connection with the [Industrial] Commission, and that of his own volition he expressed a desire to name you as a member. You will pardon my saying that it is almost too good to be true, and I think, irrespective of your willingness to accept the appointment if offered you, it is highly honoring to the President that he should take such a position at this time, in view of what is upon fairly creditable evidence believed to be your own sympathy with the Progressive party and its nominee [Theodore Roosevelt].

It may interest you to learn that I have had a long talk with Governor Wilson within the last few days and am surer than ever that he is absolutely dependable as a Progressive. If [he is] elected, you will see that the Progressives who are now supporting Roosevelt will have a much larger share in the determination of the policies of the administration than have any of the old line Democrats who have no understanding of and sympathy with the fine purposes of Woodrow Wilson.

September 28, 1912

TO Woodrow Wilson, New York City

The Civic Forum has arranged for a meeting at Carnegie Hall on Saturday evening, October 12, at which "Social Progress through Political Action" is to be considered. Jane Addams is to speak on behalf of the Progressive party and I have been asked to speak on behalf of the Democratic party. . . .

In order to make that presentation as strong and convincing as possible, I am taking counsel with a number of men within the party ranks, such as Mr. [Louis D.] Brandeis and Mr. Peabody, whose judgment on this question would be of value. I feel that my statement at this meeting, which is likely to be of importance, would be greatly enhanced if I might have a few mo-

ments' talk with you on the question before you leave for the
West. . . .

I could meet you at any place by you to be named at almost
any hour after Sunday noon—or late this afternoon.

P.S. I regret that I am under the necessity of saying that I could
not call at the University Club. No self-respecting Jew can cross
its threshold.

October 5, 1912

TO Thomas M. Osborne, Auburn, N.Y.

I wish I could tell you in person how tremendously I admired
the position you took at Syracuse [at the state convention of
the Democratic party]. It was fine from beginning to end, and
you have rendered a great service to your party in the state
and in the nation.

I wanted to go, and it was terribly hard for me not to do
so; but the representatives of [Woodrow] Wilson at the national
headquarters importuned me not to, and adjured me to stay
away from Syracuse. They knew I would go only for one reason
—namely, to wage the hottest kind of a fight against the evil
of the Tammany Hall system—and they feared that, as a personal friend of Wilson . . . my word might hurt him. But it
was a very hard choice to make.

One other consideration weighed with me to some extent.
Even the editors of the [N.Y.] *Evening Post,* with whom I took
counsel, said that, as a very recent convert to the party, I would
have no standing in the Convention, even though nominally I
had the right to the floor; and in view of what they did to you,
I am very certain that the Tammany Hall gang would never
have heard me out.

Another opportunity will come, and I want you to know that
I am in the party not for fun but to fight with you and at
your side for better things and for the new order in democracy
of which you and I alike dream.

December 18, 1912

TO William E. Borah, Washington, D.C.

Let me tell you how much I appreciate your kindness in tele-graphing, as you did, to inquire concerning our own feeling with regard to the Industrial Commission appointed by the President [William Howard Taft] and your telegram in which you say, "There will be no confirmation until after you have heard from us." We had a meeting on Wednesday afternoon, attended by a dozen of the men and women most active in pushing the project; and we decided to give out a statement to the press in protest against the personnel of the Commission. The points we espe-cially made were, first, that there was no woman on the Com-mission; second, that there was no political economist; and third, that the three representatives of the public were not men who would bring to the Commission that equipment, experience, and expert knowledge which would enable the results of the Com-mission to be of real value. It is rather significant that President Taft has named no one of the thirty or forty people who first brought the matter to his attention and who conceived and earnestly labored at the whole project.

The question is, what is to be done? Professor [Samuel Mc-Cune] Lindsay, Dr. [Edward T.] Devine, Mr. [Henry] Morgen-thau, and others of us are very anxious to have a conference with you in the near future. We thought possibly you would be in New York during the Christmas holidays and we could see you here. If not, we are prepared to go to Washington, whenever con-venient to you in order to go over the question carefully. Some of us think that the President may be moved to withdraw some of the appointees and name three representatives of the public who would be more satisfactory and fitting. It is the opinion of most of us, and I concur therein, that if possible the Senate should withhold its confirmation of the appointment of the Commission and leave the matter to Wilson. I hardly know whether you will agree with us. In any event, we wish to have your judgment and counsel and you will be good enough to tell us when we may see you in New York or in Washington.

January 27, 1913

TO Frank Walsh, Kansas City, Mo.

I lunched with Governor [and President-elect] Wilson at
Trenton on Monday and talked with him at some length among
other things about two matters—namely, the Industrial Commission and the formation of a Social Service group.

With regard to the former, you know, of course, that the
President [William Howard Taft] appointed such a Commission,
and we are not at all satisfied with its makeup. We think we
have succeeded in getting Senator [William E.] Borah and others
to hold it up . . . and have it go over to Wilson's administration.

With regard to the Social Service group, my thought was
this: I urged the President to meet with a small group of his
own friends and supporters who were active in Social Service.
I mentioned your name and also the names of [Edward] Devine,
[Adolph Bernard] Spreckles, Dr. Lee K. Frankel and Homer
Folks (Mr. Folks was a Roosevelt man, but I think he would be
valuable in this matter).

My thought, as expressed to Governor Wilson, was that this
group of men meet together in the near future and subsequently
meet with the Governor and submit to him a tentative social
program. It seems to me, as it must seem to you, that there are
certain things with which the President ought take the initiative
in dealing in the next two months.

I am persuaded that a Federal Commission on the minimum
wage would be of great value. I know that national legislation
on this subject could not be enacted, but the educational value
of a national and authoritative investigation of the minimum
wage problem would be of great value.

I think the problem of social insurance ought to be considered.

But these are only my tentative suggestions, which I want to
lay before such a group.

What do you think of the plan?

I said to the Governor that this group ought to consider
itself authorized to pass upon such social measures and proposals

as might come up from time to time with a view to reporting
to the President with some measure of authority upon them.

If the plan appeals to you and you agree with me touching
it, why not write to the Governor and give him your thought
about it? It may be that you will not agree with me at all. If
that is the case, say so frankly, although it will hardly be necessary to write to the Governor adversely. I don't know that I
have brought my thought home to you because I am writing
this line hurriedly and under great pressure, but you will be
able to glimpse what I mean.

February 3, 1913

TO William Naumberg

. . . I note your statement that in your own shop, wages
have been going up, hours have been shortened, and sanitary
conditions improved. You will pardon my saying, however, that
you have failed to deal with the fundamental question, which
is the right, as the men see it, to deal with the employer
through the process of collective bargaining. In this fundamental
right of the workers, as I see it, in any industrial democracy,
I am at one with them. I know quite as well as anyone could
the evils which are attendant upon trade unionism. I know
of the corruption that has obtained and continues to obtain
among some of its leaders, but trade unionism as a whole is
not to be judged by the blunders, even though they be moral,
of the men who represent the cause. I would as little condemn
trade unionism because of the unwisdom of some, or even many,
of its leaders as I should be moved to condemn municipal self-
government because of the evil conditions which have obtained
in many American cities.

I am glad to have your point of view, although I cannot
help believing that the time is not far distant when men will
be unable to maintain the position of organized antagonism to
the right of the workers to collective bargaining.

February 5, 1913

TO George W. Coleman, Boston

I learn that on Sunday, Feb. 23, the fifth anniversary of the
Ford Hall movement [an adult education program and forum]
will be celebrated by special exercises. I want to be one of a
multitude of friends of the Ford Hall movement and well-wishers
of its founder [George W. Coleman] who will send birthday congratulations in honor of the day.

I may say to you now for the first time what I have been saying
about you and behind your back, as it were, for a number of
years, that I think you are doing one of the most finely serviceable
and constructive pieces of work in the social life of the nation. I
think, dear Coleman, that your very special, if not unique,
achievement lies in showing forth, as you do, with earnestness
and power what I venture to call the practicability of religion—
the realizableness of our ideals. It is good for us teachers and
church leaders to know that we can count upon the fellowship
and furtherance of a man like you, who has the firmest of grip
upon our business affairs and yet knows that business, like everything else in life, must be touched by the spirit of holiness.

I give little to the Ford Hall meetings, but they give me much;
and I cannot help feeling that they reflect your own spirit in large
part. They are you projected and magnified into the life of your
community.

God bless you and Ford Hall!

Jerusalem, April 23, 1913

TO Gertrude Wolf

. . . Jerusalem is glorious beyond words. We saw Bethlehem
today, and the Hill [Mount] of Olives and my grandmother's
grave. We are entranced. . . .

Shanklin, Isle of Wight
August 7, 1913

TO Henry Morgenthau, Sr., Venice

I cannot tell you how happy your letter has made me. I was
hoping and hoping that you would see your duty in the matter,
which, to me, seemed very clear. For a moment I was tempted to
telegraph to you, so that you might, if necessary, revise a cable
message which I have already sent the President; but, in view of
your letter, I felt that I could exercise my own discretion, such
as it is; and so I cabled to the President as follows:

> Have earnestly urged Morgenthau to accept your offer of the Turkish
> Embassy earnestly urged Morgenthau to accept your offer at this time.
> I would suggest immediate renewal of invitation to serve which I
> believe he would now accept. Could forward message to him.

. . . But the important thing is that you have reached a decision,
and I can only say again in tritest fashion, that I am more than
happy. I see great possibilities of usefulness. If the thing goes
through, as of course it now will, I hope you will go to London
and Paris at once, for there are some people whom you must
see, and whom you could at once see, in just the right way
through [Francis] Montefiore and others. The two men I have
in mind particularly are Baron Edmond, as Rothschild is fa-
miliarly known in Paris, and Lord [Lionel Walter] Rothschild in
London. . . .

(later) August 7, 1913

I cabled to the President about 10 in the morning on Wednesday, and at 7 in the evening I had the answer, which I forwarded
to you by wire. Let me confirm it by sending it.

> Cable received. Please forward following to our friend. Can you not
> reconsider declination Turkish Embassy?
>
> Woodrow Wilson.

. . . Even though the matter is concluded, I don't suppose you
can go to Constantinople before receiving your credentials from

Washington. In any event, seeing it would be necessary for you to go to New York and close up a lot of things, it would be well to postpone the first visit to Constantinople until after you have been home and prepared yourself a little more fully in some directions for the duties of the post. If your plans do not change, and you mean to return by the S.S. *Cecilie,* will you spend at least a week or ten days in London? We would have a week together, and there are certain persons in London with whom it would be highly desirable that you should get into touch, outside of the men we have already spoken of—certain men I have in mind particularly well-informed on Near Eastern questions.

September 16, 1913

TO John Howard Melish, Brooklyn

I hope to see you soon and to learn that you have had a good and restful summer. We have had a rare experience— namely, that of travelling through Egypt and the Holy Land, as well as seeing much of Europe, for nearly half a year.

I want to see you, if possible, very soon about a matter of very great importance. Your Episcopal Congress, I understand, is soon to be held in this city; and I hope it will not be necessary to do more than suggest that it deal with a matter of world interest which bears very horribly upon the lot of my own people.

At present, there is a Jew named [Mendel] Beilis under indictment for murdering a Christian in Russia for ritual purposes. I need not point out to you that this charge was made against Jews time and time again and that churchmen of all creeds have again and again denied and given proofs of the denial of this terrible accusation. Your [Episcopal] Church, and more especially the English [Anglican] division of it, is in some sort of relation to the Russian [Orthodox] Church, which is in large part responsible for this vile and barbaric charge.

It would indeed be significant if the Episcopal Convention should pass a resolution earnestly imploring the churchmen of Russia to use their influence to the end that so grave and terrible a charge should not be made against a son of the House of Israel to which Christendom owes so much.

I would like to show you a memorial, signed by some of the greatest men in England, including representatives of your own Church, in protest against the horror of this ritual murder charge.

Will you think about it for a few days and then we can arrange to talk it over? I take it for granted that it would be easy to secure the earnest cooperation of such men in your Church as Bishop [Charles] Williams, Bishop [Charles P.] Anderson, and perhaps even Bishop [David H.] Greer.

P.S. Of course you understand, dear Melish, we are not concerned about the fate of an individual Jew; but, as has been clearly pointed out, the accusation does not alone affect one Jew but is a charge preferred against the whole Jewish race and its religion. It is a blow dealt at every individual Jew, whatever his citizenship and whatever the exact color of his religious conviction.

September 26, 1913

TO The Editor of the *World,* New York City

Will you permit me to express my earnest approval of your editorial in this morning's issue entitled "A Shocking Decision." It seems impossible to explain the decision of Chief Justice [Isaac F.] Russell and his associates [of the Court of Special Sessions, City of New York] in inflicting nothing more than a minimum fine upon the owner of the Triangle [Shirtwaist] Company factory as a penalty for committing an act which led to the slaughter of the workers [147 deaths] at the Triangle fire disaster [on March 26, 1911]. You do not wish any more than do I that a vindictive spirit shall be shown to Mr. [Max] Blanck or any other misdemeanant, but I agree with you that nothing less than jail terms will put a stop to this infamous practice; and, whether they are conscious of it or not, when justices impose minimum penalties, which happen to be ridiculously inadequate, upon acts of this kind, not alone is the future violation of the law invited, but the law and the courts are brought into disrepute which, alas for American institutions, is deepening every day.

October 16, 1913

TO John Howard Melish, Brooklyn

I want to tell you how deeply grateful I am to you for your action in bringing about the passage of the resolution at the Joint Convention. I knew I could count upon you. I know how broad and catholic are your sympathies; and I know, too, how earnestly and genuinely you are laboring to translate Christianity into life. Such an act as that of the Convention in passing these resolutions does infinitely more to make Christianity understood of the Jew than do all missions to Jews.

I am truly glad, for the sake of your Church, that the resolutions have been passed.

Would you be good enough, at the earliest possible moment, to have the secretary of the Convention send me an official transcript of the resolutions, together with a line so that I may forward it to the leading Jewish papers of Europe, where the publication of the resolutions would do a maximum measure of good?

December 25, 1913

TO Richard W. Montague, Portland, Oregon

I want your help, want it immediately, and want it badly. . . .

About a month ago, I was in Washington, having an appointment with the President, to discuss the Russo-American Treaty and other matters of importance with him. I saw our friend [Senator Harry] Lane first, and he told me he had known nothing about the appointment of S_____ as Minister to Siam. . . . He felt it was an outrage that the appointment should be made. I never knew S_____ well, but nothing I knew of him was very flattering to him. . . . Lane was insistent upon S_____'s absolute unfitness, telling me that a large part of S_____'s practice at the Bar had consisted in the defense of owners of houses of assignation, and Lane went so far as definitely to maintain that he was personally and pecuniarily interested in one or more of these himself. . . . Lane went with me to the President and . . . immediately brought up the question of S_____, and told the President in Lanesque lingo that the latter had been buncoed. The President seemed amazed, and was astonished to learn that Lane had known nothing of the appointment; and Lane said—Mr. President, Dr. Wise knows S_____ and believes as I do that he is absolutely unfit. The President . . . evidently knew little or nothing about S_____, and it was obvious that the appointment was one made altogether by [William Jennings] Bryan and after little or no consultation with the President, in order to pay off one of the old 1896 debts. Lane hinted at things, rather than said them very clearly, until the President insisted again and again—But Mr. Lane, you must tell me, you must tell me; you disturb me deeply. And in answer to the straight question of the President, I told him that, having lived in Oregon, I was distinctly of the impression that S_____ was not quite the type of man that ought to represent the administration in a ministerial post. . . . Wilson at once said—We shall see to the matter, and I suppose it meant that the appointment had been held up and that S_____ is not going to be confirmed. Lane then left the President and me, and the President asked me again my impression, which I substantially repeated. . . .

. . . You know me well enough to understand, my dear Montague, that while I am willing to hit any man hard if he ought to be hit, I would not consciously do a man an injustice. I have hit some men pretty hard in public life, but events have always proved that I have never attacked a man unless it was really necessary to do so in the public interest. . . . I want you to write to me at once and tell me whether I have done right or wrong. If you should say that S_____ is fit, if you say that my impression has been erroneous, if you say that S_____ in the years since I have left Portland has been a good citizen and a member of the Bar in fine standing—if, in a word, you write to me that I have done an injustice, I am going to do the thing that any decent,

manly man ought to do—namely, write to the President and
withdraw my objections; I will, moreover, if you permit me to
do so, send him your own letter, if you decide that I have done
wrong. . . . No friendship for Lane would keep me from making
a manly apology if, depending upon your word, I did wrong. On
the other hand, no friendship for any man on earth would move
me to withdraw my statement if what I believe about S____ be
true—namely, that he is unfit for the office of minister of the
United States to a foreign land.

February 5, 1914

TO Richard W. Montague, Portland, Oregon

. . . I feel more strongly than ever, as a result of your communication, that it is not the sort of appointment which Wilson
ought to make.

. . . We are having a tough winter of it here with an awful
lot of unemployment. I think we shall be coming pretty soon to
some sort of unemployment insurance. That would not be the
best way out, but some way must be found. The seasonal arrangements which doom men to long terms of idleness are an accursed
thing.

March 15, 1914

TO Otto Wise, San Francisco

. . . I look forward to the 26th [of March] with great misgiving.
Brandeis insists upon my acting as permanent chairman [of the
preliminary meetings in preparation for the formation of a pro-
Zionist American Jewish Congress] and I believe I ought not do
this. In the first place, I am a clerical; in the second place, I am
an ultra-Liberal; and in the third place, I am a New Yorker.
Even assuming that I possess all the other needed capacities for
chairmanship, I believe we ought to have a non-New Yorker and
if possible one who is not as pronouncedly, though as really,
Zionistic as I am.

April 10, 1914

TO Israel Zangwill, Worthing, England

As 1/12,000,000 of the world's Jewry, may I not send you my congratulations with all my heart upon the close of the first half of your centenary? . . .

I want you to know—what you must understand—that, while some of us Jews have not given up the habit of murmuring and even rebelling against our best, Jews everywhere are at one in their recognition of and gratitude to you as one of their truly noble and faithful sons. God bless you and Mrs. Zangwill and the precious children.

Lake Placid, August 31, 1914

TO George Foster Peabody, Lake George

Often and again I have been thinking of you during these sad days. I know that you are unhappy as I am over this desolating war. It is too sad and too terrible for words. If only Europe had had a Wilson to guide its affairs! And still I feel that Sir Edward Grey made every honorable effort to avert war. Do you not feel that it is Germany that is morally responsible for this devastation? This war shows one thing—that we anti-militarists must more than ever have the courage of our convictions. We must not suffer any compromise hereafter. Whether men like it or not, we must oppose the big navy policy, and it will not be easy to do that after all that will now be said by the big army and big navy advocates. . . .

November 18, 1914

TO Maurice Leon

I have your letter of the 16th in which you call attention to a report of my sermon of Sunday morning in the New York *Sun,* a report which, incidentally, I may observe I have not yet seen.

As for the diversity of opinion among American Jews, my

reference was not to the war but to an explicable want of unity of judgment and solidarity of action among Jews. With regard to the present war, while personally I am strongly on the side of the Allies because I believe their cause to be just, I can understand, however much you or I might regret it, the attitude of those American Jews who cannot hope that the victory of Russia will redound either to the advantage of civilization or to the betterment of the Jewish status. Those of us who side with the Allies are taking it for granted that England and France will be able to exert a liberalizing influence upon the Russian government, although our hope is not securely founded. Some of us are deeply disquieted by rumors which reach us of recent Jewish massacres in [Russian] Poland. What right have the Allies even to expect the sympathy of any American Jews with their cause as long as Russia fails to make any pronouncement with regard to the Jewish question and, moreover, as long as the Jews have reason to dread the Polish order of things that is promised in the place of the old Russian order after the war?

If you are really concerned about your fellow-Jews declaring themselves unequivocally on the side of the Allies, there is only one thing to be done: namely, to make French and English ambassadors to this country understand that Russian must speak out and speak out promptly with regard to her Jewish subjects. Unless things are speedily bettered in Russia, I look for a very considerable deflection of opinion from the side of the Allies, not only on the part of Jews in America but on the part of many non-Jews whose reluctance to commit themselves to the cause of the Allies arises out of their hesitation in siding with Russia.

December 9, 1914

TO Henry Morgenthau, Sr., American Embassy,
Constantinople

Your letter of the 13th [November], which has been forwarded through the State Department, has just arrived and gives me very great pleasure. I had a long talk with Maurice [Wertheim, Morgenthau's son-in-law] yesterday, and he told me a great deal of the

inward workings of the Embassy—everything, of course, being
fascinating to one who is as interested in all you are doing as
I am.

I cannot quite agree with you that it was "a great piece of luck"
that you should be where you are at this time. I wonder whether
you will not recall how deeply I felt at Dijon [in July of 1913]
that somehow an opportunity for service would arise, and I cannot help feeling that there was a wisdom much higher than my
own which was bidding me speak to you in terms of utmost
urgency and appeal that day. . . .

. . . On Wednesday, Nov. 25, I went to the Rockefeller
Foundation and had a conference with Jerome Greene, who is
virtually its head, with respect to the possibility of sending a
shipload of supplies to Palestine and Syria. I pointed out to him
the moral and irenic effect which such a gift on their part would
have, more especially seeing that the bounty would be shared by
Mohammedans, Christians and Jews alike. He seemed to think
favorably of it and urged me to get in touch with the leading
representatives of the missionary groups with a view to submit-
ting a common proposal. . . .

December 14, 1914

TO Henry Morgenthau, Sr., Constantinople

The enclosure will interest you seeing that it makes mention
of the address which Maurice [Wertheim] is to give at [the Free
Synagogue service] at Clinton Hall on Friday night on "Impressions in Palestine." It is a perfect joy to note how deeply impressed he is by all that he saw and what a new and wider per-
spective he has of Jewish life. No man can truly be said to have
looked on Jewish life steadily nor to have seen it whole until
after having been in the Holy Land. It seems to me that his visit
to Palestine and what he did there will make a permanent difference throughout his life. We had the delight of seeing Alma
[Morgenthau Wertheim] as well as Maurice yesterday and those
three lovely little girls. As Barbara [Wertheim Tuchman] said to
me, "*We* have no boys—only three girls."

You will be interested to learn that we had a further conference today with Jerome Greene of the Rockefeller Foundation. The Christian Missionaries were represented by Dr. Arthur [Judson] Brown [of the Presbyterian Board for Foreign Missions], Dr. John R. Mott [of the Student Volunteer Movement and the World's Student Christian Federation], Dr. [Edward L.] Smith of the Congregational Missionary Board, and Dr. [James] Barton. On behalf of Jewish interests there were three of us: Professor [Richard] Gottheil, Oscar Straus, and myself. . . . The claims of the Balkan states and Eastern Europe are being urged upon the Foundation so that they may limit themselves to furnishing a ship which we are to fill with breadstuffs. The plan is to try to bring some relief to Palestine, Syria, and Asia Minor—in other words, to try in some measure to cover Asiatic Turkey. . . .

We of the Provisional Zionist Committee invited Mr. Straus to cooperate with us because the American Jewish Committee, unwisely in my judgment, gave out a statement to the effect that they hoped to send a boatload of supplies to suffering Jews. Any such racial or religious discrimination would be exceedingly unwise, and I think it will be possible to counteract it if we succeed in prevailing upon the Rockefeller people to do this important and needed work. For my part, I am as deeply concerned in succoring the starving Moslems as I am in helping the suffering Jews and Christians. . . .

December 28, 1914

TO Nathan D. Kaplan, Chicago

I deeply regret that it will be quite impossible for me to give myself the pleasure of attending the Eighteenth Annual Convention of the Knights of Zion at St. Louis on Friday morning, January 1. I rejoice to think, however, that the Conference will be enriched by the presence of such men as Louis D. Brandeis, Dr. Schmaryahu Levin and Professor Horace M. Kallen.

In the despite of the burdens and the new hardships which have become the portion of our brothers in the war zones, I yet feel that we ought to meet together in the spirit of hopefulness and confidence. For one thing, the war has already shown that if Jewish interests are to be served anywhere, they must be served chiefly by ourselves. We would not, if we could, nor could we if we would, rely upon help from without. It is the business of strong and self-respecting people to help themselves, and that is perhaps the first lesson which Zionism teaches.

In the next place, we are come to feel today not only that self-respect must be the order of the new Jewish day but that such self-help must be based upon a real unity within Israel—not the nominal unity of that type of organization which organizes chiefly its own aims and ambitions, nor yet that spurious uniformity which is as far removed from unity as are divisiveness and discord, but that unity which springs out of the united and determined resolve of a people to work out their own destiny and to do it in no mean and paltry spirit, but in that spirit which rests upon ennobling self-determination.

Above all, I would congratulate my fellow-Zionists throughout the country upon the new and inspiring leadership that is become our own through the accession to Zionism of the life and personality of Louis D. Brandeis. It is sometimes said of a great leader in warfare that he is worth a corps of men. Genuinely and passionately democratic though he be, Louis Brandeis is, by virtue of the gifts of his mind and the nobleness of his character, uniquely qualified to serve as a leader of the Jewish people. He brings to the Zionist movement the prestige of his own great service to the American people and, more than everything else, a devotion to Zionism which is indeed a precious asset at this time. Under his leadership, may we not come together and serve together in the interest of Zionism. His presence at your Convention ought to spur you and your associates on to a new devotion to our common cause.

March 2, 1915

TO Henry Morgenthau, Sr., Constantinople

. . . Things are moving very slowly in the matter of the foodship. [Herman] Bernstein did, through his personal friendship with [Secretary of the Navy Josephus] Daniels, secure permission to place nine hundred tons of (in part, Passover) food which is to go off in about a week, but of course the food-ship project remains the same. The matter of hiring a ship has been left by the American Jewish Relief Committee to [Judah L.] Magnes who finds most difficulty in securing a bottom. Our Christian friends of the non-sectarian committee have raised only thirty thousand so far and at least another hundred thousand must be raised, if the three hundred thousand which the food-ship of three thousand tons of supplies will involve are to be gotten. . . .

It may interest you to learn that we are having splendid services [for the Free Synagogue] at Carnegie [Hall] this year, the average attendance being twice as large as it was two years ago—practically two thousand. It is encouraging in a way, but the membership does not grow as fast as it should. Next week we shall have Jane Addams and, of course, we shall have a great crowd of people eager to hear her. . . .

April 2, 1915

TO S. M. Fechheimer, Cincinnati

I have been giving a great deal of thought to the matter of our recent conference in Cincinnati. It was a very real pleasure to have had an opportunity to confer at length with you and Judge [Julian] Mack as well as with Mr. [Max] Senior. The more I have pondered over the matter, the more deeply I am persuaded of the wisdom of Mr. Brandeis' decision. You surely understand that Mr. Brandeis is not unmindful of the courtesy and hospitality of you and your associates in urging him to come to your city, but as I go over the situation and upon the basis of our conference, I am led to agree with him that, in the light of conditions in Cincinnati, it might be viewed as divisive at this time to carry to your city the Zionist propaganda. It is indeed unfortunate that the question has arisen—that is to say, that Dr. [David] Philipson and those under his leadership should have been unwilling not only to permit the Zionist side of things to be heard, but virtually to make it impossible for Zionism to secure a hearing in the important and influential Jewish community of Cincinnati. But that, as you know, is the fact. The time may come when Mr. Brandeis will feel that he ought to reconsider his decision, but in any event I agree with him that for the present his decision should stand.

It is the part of leadership to unite and to heal differences, never to deepen and intensify them. Mr. Brandeis, I feel I have the right to say, will be prepared to go to your city and plead the cause of Zionism whenever he may feel that his word will be helpful in the direction of unity.

November 4, 1915

TO Horace M. Kallen, Madison, Wisconsin

. . . You forget one thing which unhappily is true—namely that I have hardly any access to the men of large fortune. They are the special preserve of [Judah L.] Magnes. [Jacob] Schiff and I have no relations whatever, and as a result of that I cannot touch any of the really rich men. Moreover, they do not like me and the things for which I stand—and there you are. When Mr. [Henry] Morgenthau [Sr.] is here I can get a little money from him; and sometimes Mr. [Adolph] Lewisohn gives, but he rarely gives to a cause of which Mr. Schiff does not approve. I really can promise nothing for [Pinchas] Ruttenberg or his work [to found the Palestine Electric Corporation]. I wish things were different, but the fact is the burden of our work must be borne by all of us. The one thing that makes me fearful of the outcome of Zionism is the failure of the people to have any part in the bearing of the burden. We object to a subsidy from above and yet our own followers do little or nothing to render such subsidy unnecessary. . . . What a pity it is that we cannot count on [Julius] Rosenwald's help. It is really a crime on the part of some of those men, Schiff, Rosenwald and others, to let this unsupportable burden rest upon us. It is their business to bear it and it is our business to say so. I should be perfectly willing with you to address a letter to Mr. Rosenwald and lay down the law to him, pointing out his obligation to his people and to the supreme

interest of Israel at this time. Suppose you draft the letter, and
you and I send it to him. . . .

November 12, 1915

TO The President, The White House, Washington

From time to time during the last two years, it has been my
privilege to write to you in order to express my agreement with
the things you have said and done. I therefore regard it as my
duty to tell you how deeply I deplore the necessity under which
you have found yourself of accepting and advocating a preparedness program. . . .

It is occasion for profound regret to some of us . . . that you
have seen fit at this time to urge that so-called defensive preparedness, which at other times and in other hands than your own is
not unlikely to be used in the interests of aggression. You will
pardon my pointing out that your program, moderate though
you believe it to be, will not and of necessity cannot satisfy
those advocates of military preparedness who will for a time
purport to assent to preparedness measures.

I should not, my dear Mr. President, have written in this way
nor would I burden you with my thought on this question if I
did not feel in conscience bound to dissent in pulpit and on platform from your position. I regret this not only on personal
grounds but because I believe that issues of deepest moment are
at stake touching which you will not expect even the most
revering of friends should remain silent.

January 24, 1916

TO Bernard G. Richards

I cannot tell you how deeply I regret that I must leave in order
to make a series of addresses in southern cities and therefore am
to be denied the privilege of participating in what I am sure
will be your great meeting [for preliminary organization of an
American Jewish Congress] on Monday night at Carnegie Hall.

The meeting means that Israel is at one with the world in demanding equal rights for all men. The days of philanthropy toward Israel must be succeeded by a period of statesmanship for and by Israel. The meeting is to demand equal rights for all men, excluding none, and the meeting of every Jewish need as it arises.

Paraphrasing the word of Goethe, may we not say that a great work is laid upon our souls to which we are to prove equal? "The people's voice," speaking through the meeting of Monday night, will make so clear that none can misunderstand:

> We are a people yet,
> Though all men else their nobler dreams forget.

February 13, 1916

TO Maximilian Heller, New Orleans

. . . The problem that is still uppermost in the minds of those of us who care most is what we shall do after [the appointment of Supreme Court Associate Justice Louis D.] Brandeis has [been confirmed and he has] left us [as a leader in the Zionist movement]. He is not to leave us absolutely; but even under the best of circumstances, he cannot retain the active and immediate leadership of the movement. He can give us of his time and strength and counsel, but that is all we may ask. We are to have a meeting tomorrow and shall put to him your suggestion that he be the maker of a percedent if necessary, and retain his leadership of the movement, seeing that Justice [David J.] Brewer was ceaselessly active on behalf of religious and missionary interests while on the Supreme Court Bench. Moreover, we are trying to make clear to him that while he could not retain the chairmanship of such an organization as the American Jewish Committee if he were its chairman, it is possible for him to remain in a sense the actual head of the Zionist movement, in so far as none of the questions involved in the Zionist movement can ever come before the Supreme Court for review. . . . We face a difficult problem and a terrible loss. Some of the men [among Zionists] are very unhappy, and some of us even go so far as to say that Brandeis has no right to accept the post. . . . My own sense of loss is tempered by my conviction that he will make a great judge and will win such a name for himself as is sure to redound to the lasting honor of Israel. . . .

March 30, 1916

TO Otto Wise, San Francisco

. . . As for the Convention [of the American Jewish Congress in Philadelphia], there is a great deal to be said, but I shall tell you about it at Chicago [where Otto and Stephen Wise would meet on April 10]. It was really a fine meeting excepting that the high and mighty stayed away. Even Philadelphia Jews wouldn't peep in to see what was happening. From that point of view, it was disgraceful, but the proceedings were dignified and orderly and altogether creditable. At the last moment, it was decided that I should not preside. I did not want to do so, as you felt I should not; and it was much better that I did not. It was important that I should be on the floor. I was not an officer and on no committee; but I served with all committees, and there were a number of snarls that I unravelled.

. . . The Convention resolved itself into a love feast and its members were very generous in their attitude toward me. . . .

You will note you were made a member of the Executive Committee. I told them I would rather have you on it than myself and wanted to resign in your favor because I shall be doing a great deal of work in any event, but they insisted that I serve as well as you.

. . . I am not very cheerful or very happy today because this is the 30th of March [anniversary of the death of their father, Aaron Wise] and it is twenty years ago since that dread and fateful day. But one must live through it and a lot of other things. . . .

April 4, 1916

TO Israel Zangwill, Worthing, England

I was tremendously interested in your meeting last week of the National Union of Jewish Rights. We are trying to do something of the same kind in this country, although we have a pretty hard battle to fight, for the powers [in Jewish life] are against us—I mean by that the money powers. Moreover, a split comes in part over our unwillingness to assent to the pro-Germanism of some of the mighty, including [Jacob] Schiff, who, I think, are pro-German before they are pro-Jewish. I am of the number who feel that as Americans and Jews, alike, we owe our sympathy and, if necessary, our support to Great Britain and France. We regret that Russia is included in the number of the Allies, but we believe that after the war either the government of Russia will deal justly by its Jews or the Russian government will face some very grave questions.

We had a pre-Congress Convention at Philadelphia last week, and I enclose a copy of what I said on that occasion, the address being accepted as the keynote of the Convention. I wish you might know Mr. Brandeis and what a tower of strength he is to us. He is really a statesman, and far and above the biggest man in Jewish life in America today. He has come back to us [as a leader in the Jewish community] rather late—he is soon to be sixty—but he is wholly ours. In a sense, we regret that he is to go on the United States Supreme Court because he cannot be quite as active in things Jewish as he would otherwise have been. Still, even on the Bench, we feel he will lend the immense prestige of his personality and office to the furtherance of every high Jewish interest.

We eagerly await the hour when we may return to England after the war.

April 5, 1916

TO Israel Abrahams, Cambridge, England

. . . Our chief concern at present is with the [American] Jewish Congress movement. We do not know how it will develop. We had a meeting at Philadelphia last Sunday, distinguished by the absence of the mighty [leaders in Jewry]. Mr. Brandeis could not preside because of the proprieties of the occasion which forbade any apearance on his part until after his confirmation or rejection [as the newly appointed associate justice of the U.S. Supreme

Court] by the Senate. He will be confirmed, but a nasty fight has been made against him by the representatives of money and privilege who are rightly fearful of his advent to our Supreme Court.

I send you a copy of the address which I gave at the Conference, which was adopted as the keynote of the occasion. The real difficulty lies in the circumstances that the German Jewish millionaires in this country, led by [Jacob] Schiff, persist in treating the Jewish masses as if they were forever to be in a state of tutelage and incapable of having anything to say with respect to the management of their own affairs. It is a very serious question and must be fought out.

. . . We have never ceased to be hopeful of the ultimate triumph of the Allied Powers. We wish it might come very soon; but we believe that come it must; and though I am utterly opposed to militarism, I cannot help feeling that it were better that peace be postponed until there can be promise of its permanence. It is hard to side with Russia as among the Allied Powers, and yet I believe that the triumph of Germany would be deadly to every moral interest of the human race, and that Jews everywhere would suffer most, as they always do, from the triumph of the wrong.

May 5, 1916

то William G. McAdoo

In the first place, I want to congratulate you upon the great work you have done in the interest of Pan-American comity. It is a very great service to have deepened the relations of goodwill between our own country and the republics of South America.

I want you to know at the earliest moment of that which I am sure will give you great pleasure. A number of men, including myself [Adolf A. Berle, Sr., Amos Pinchot, *et al.*], recently went to the country on an anti-militarist trip [under the auspices of the League to Enforce Peace]. In Kansas City and St. Louis, I made reference to Mr. Brandeis and the President's appointment of him to the Supreme Court. Throughout the entire ten days, there was no such demonstration of enthusiasm and unanimity as marked the mention of his name. It was really magnificent. Back of it, as I later learned, is a deep-seated sense of revolt against, I am tempted to say, the "powers and principalities" who are trying to avert Mr. Brandeis' confirmation, and I rejoice to think that the people understand what lies back of the [Senate's] opposition to him—namely, the dread of him by the predatory interests. While in Washington the other day, it came to me from a United States senator that there is no driving power behind the campaign on behalf of Mr. Brandeis; but I feel persuaded that the Administration and the [Democratic] party will do everything to impress upon the Senate that Mr. Brandeis' confirmation must be brought about. If the Republican senators are to oppose him, so much the worse for them rather than for Mr. Brandeis. And those Democratic members of the Senate who would be ready in bringing about Mr. Brandeis' rejection must be fought from within the party. Mr. Brandeis' election is not a party issue. It is become, as I am sure you clearly understand, a national issue.

I covet nothing better for the Democratic party than its unalterable insistence that Mr. Brandeis shall not be kept from the Bench by those interests which it is the duty and the destiny of the Democratic party always to oppose.

May 31, 1916

TO Maximilian Heller, New Orleans

. . . I thank God, as you will, that the fight against Brandeis has ignominiously failed, and that this great man and Jew is to go on the [Supreme Court] Bench. It appears to me nothing can avert it now. We are not to lose him. He will remain the leader, though of course in view of his position the stress of his service is to be in international affairs.

January 29, 1917

TO Edward M. House, The White House, Washington

It has taken us [Louis D. Brandeis, Felix Frankfurter, and Wise on behalf of the Provisional Executive Committee for General Zionist Affairs] some time to prepare the enclosure [suggested text of an anticipated declaration by the British government concerning the establishment of a national home for the Jewish people in Palestine], but we have necessarily prepared it with great care, and I know, after what you said, that it will be deeply interesting to you.

It is heartening to know of your own good-will touching this great matter that lies so near to our hearts.

February 9, 1917

TO The President, The White House, Washington

I have not written to you during these days of crisis because I know you would be overwhelmed by messages from those who do not perhaps realize the importance of sparing you at such a time as this. I merely write now in order to tell you that I thanked God for your leadership of the nation.

On Sunday morning, in my pulpit, I shall say that the country must stand behind you and will stand behind you. You have kept us in the paths of peace as a result of your high statesmanship and as a result of that infinite patience worthy of the head of a great and free people.

The time has come for the American people to understand that it may become our destiny to have part in the struggle which would avert the enthronement of the law of might over the nations.

Speaking on Sunday morning on "America's Lincoln and Wilson's America," I shall have great joy in saying, not only of the President of the United States but of an honored and cherished friend, that, as Washington was the father of the nation and Lincoln later became its savior, so in this time of world crisis the American people was led by a man whose name is hereafter to be bracketed with the names of Washington and Lincoln, equal to the genius of the spirit of America and worthy to become the champion and servant of humanity.

February 15, 1917

TO Nathan Straus, St. Augustine, Fla.

... The outlook for the [Zionist] cause seems to me to be better and better. It may prove to be the greatest of blessings for our people and our cause that the war should, in the last analysis, take the form of a defense of the rights of the lesser peoples and smaller nationalities...

... I have been thinking a great deal about your own message when the [American Jewish] Congress convenes and among my memoranda I find certain things which may be of interest to you. In *Multitude and Solitude,* one of the less known works of [John] Masefield, he says: "When an Irishman is great enough to escape from the littleness of his race, he becomes a splendid person, but until that happens, he seems to be wanting in any really fundamental quality."

Does it not seem to you that the reverse is true with regard to Jews—namely, when the Jew is little and mean enough to escape from the greatness of his race he becomes a most unsplendid person? I felt that deeply last night at a meeting of the Zionist Society of Greater Boston, called to celebrate the completion of the thousand membership list. A really notable and stirring address was made by Professor Felix Frankfurter, and before him by Dr. [William] Rosenau on "Sanitary Conditions in Palestine." . . . After Professor Frankfurter's address, Dr. Rosenau handed in his application for membership in the Society. It is, of course, a great victory to have won him to the support of our cause. I could not help feeling that he was a bigger man than ever before when, through his newly professed allegiance, he sought, as it were, to enter anew into the greatness of the heritage of his people. . . .

April 9, 1917

TO Jacob de Haas, Boston

I have just had a good long talk with Colonel [Edward M.] House, and I cannot tell you how pleased I am. He understands the situation, and what is better yet, not only is it in his mind and not only did he realize the imminence of the British possibilities, but he said he is keeping our papers before him in order to move at the right moment. He said this that was significant: "Perhaps we can help to get the British government to make such concessions to France and Russia as will make it possible for them to grant the desired concession in Palestine." It is almost too good to believe, and almost too important to put to paper. Of course, you will put this letter away as soon as you have read it.

I left with him the copies of the letters from [Moses] Gaster and [Nahum] Sokolow, which he promised to read at once. Of course, we must trust him in the matter, and we do. He is enlisted in our cause. There is no question about it whatever. The thing will go through to Washington, I think, without delay.

He made this statement that is interesting: "Six months ago, I would have said that a British-American protectorate over Palestine and Syria would be impossible. Nothing is impossible any longer. Everything has broken down, and we can build up again almost as we choose."

April 11, 1917

TO The President, The White House, Washington

. . . I venture to ask the question whether this were not an opportune time, in such a way as may commend itself to you, to appeal to the British government to do that which the best thought of the British people has long been prepared to do—namely, to accord *home rule to the Irish people*. Such an act at this time on the part of Great Britain would not merely answer the question touching Britain's right to stand out as the champion of smaller and oppressed nationalities; would not only end disaffection among the Irish people and the unrest which obtains

Graduated from Columbia and ordained to the rabbinate. (This and all other photos are courtesy of Justine Wise Polier and James Waterman Wise, unless otherwise indicated.)

Louise Waterman Wise at the time of her marriage, November 14, 1900.

Rabbi of Temple Beth Israel, Portland, Oregon, 1900-1906.

Stephen and Louise Wise in Cairo: ". . . The Pyramids were wonderful. We climbed . . . to the top of the least of the Pyramids. One little Arab boy exclaimed, 'Not good for very fat man.' That's me! . . ." (from letter to Gertrude Wolf, April 17, 1913).

A Sunday noon in the summer of 1916 after an interfaith service in Chapel, Lake Placid, N.Y. Stephen Wise with Rev. Newell Dwight Hillis, Congregationalist, Brooklyn, N.Y. and Rev. Charles W. Parkhurst, Presbyterian, New York City.

Theodor Herzl, founder of modern Zionism, Vienna, 1904. *Courtesy of American Zionist Archives.*

David Ben-Gurion, Israeli prime minister, Lake Tiberias, 1948. *Courtesy of American Zionist Archives.*

Woodrow Wilson, president,
U.S.A., 1913-21. *Courtesy of
American Zionist Archives.*

Alfred E. Smith, governor,
N.Y., 1917-27. *Courtesy of
American Jewish Archives.*

Felix Frankfurter, associate justice, U.S. Supreme Court, 1939-63. *Courtesy of American Zionist Archives.*

Franklin Delano Roosevelt, president, U.S.A., 1933-45. *Courtesy of American Zionist Archives.*

With fellow-Zionists: philanthropist Nathan Straus (left) and jurist Louis D. Brandeis (center), after World War I.

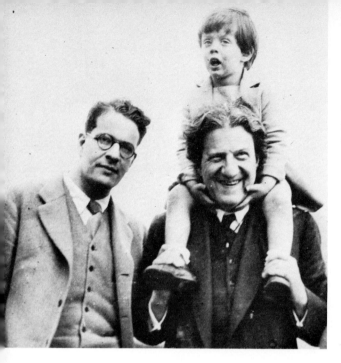

With son, James Waterman Wise, and grandson, Stephen A. Wise, 1925.

With daughter Justine, Atlantic City, 1930.

Speaking at anti-Nazi protest meeting, Madison Square Park, 1933.

Wise testifies at hearing of Board of Estimate, New York City, February 8, 1933, ". . . protesting reduction in payments for widows, old age pensions and contributions to charitable institutions." (*New York Times*, February 9, 1933).

With Chaim Weizmann, president of World Zionist Organization, during negotiations with British Colonial Office, London, summer of 1936.

With Henrietta Szold,
founder of Hadassah,
Women's Zionist Organ-
ization, at anti-Nazi protest rally, New York
City, October 1937.

With Herbert E. Lehman (left), governor of New York State, 1933-43,
and Francis J. McConnell (right), bishop of New York East Conference,
Methodist Episcopal Church, 1930-44, at anti-Nazi rally of American
Jewish Congress, Madison Square Garden, March 15, 1937.

TIME

The Weekly Newsmagazine

Associated Press

Volume XXX

NEW YORK CITY'S LAGUARDIA
He hopes for Kings and Queens and knaves.
(See NATIONAL AFFAIRS)

Number 5

"The Little Flower," Fiorello H. La'Guardia, campaigns for reelection to a second four year term, seeking the votes from Kings County (Brooklyn), Queens, and the remaining three—Manhattan, Bronx and Richmond. *Courtesy of* Time, *Inc. and World Wide Photos.*

With Eleanor Roosevelt at meeting of American Jewish Congress, Washington, D.C., February 1940, before her address on "The Jew and His Status After the War."

With Albert Einstein, Princeton, N.J., May 1945, after V-E Day.

With Philip Murray (left), and Jacob Potofsky (right), at C.I.O. Convention, Atlantic City, 1946.

With orphaned children in displaced persons' center, Camp Zeilsheim, Frankfurt-am-Main, Germany, July, 1946. Brick column, with star of David, erected by "DPs" in memory of the Jews killed in the Holocaust.

On 75th birthday, March 17, 1949, with Jo Davidson's bust of Louise Waterman Wise (who had died on December 11, 1947).

among the Irish elements of the American people; but would, like the self-liberation of Russia, support the position taken by you on behalf of the nation in eloquent terms, that we are battling for the freedom and democracy of the peoples of earth.

April 26, 1917

TO Israel Abrahams, Cambridge, England

What is the matter? I never hear from you. I suppose I have written three or four times since the War began, but never does a word come from you. I regret this and wish I might hear from you, more particularly seeing that [Claude Goldsmid] Montefiore wrote some time ago that you had been ill. I take it, however, that you are better, for I have been reading your reviews and note that you are shortly to preach at the Liberal Synagogue.

. . . Now you can see how wise and great President Wilson has been throughout. Had he gone into the War at any other time, he could not have carried the country with him. Now the country stands with virtual unanimity by his side. The present visit of the French and British embassies is making a very deep impression upon the country, and it was a stroke of genius on the part of Great Britain to send one of its choicest spirits, one of its noblest men, in the person of [Arthur James] Balfour.

April 29, 1917

TO Israel Zangwill, Worthing, England

Boruch Habo! which, for the benefit of the censor, not for you, let me translate as "Blessed be the prodigal son in his homecoming." We are rejoiced to learn of your return to the Zionist movement, which has needed you and has missed you and welcomes you back with all joy. Justice Brandeis and I have frequently spoken of you and wish with all our heart that we might have had the benefit of your help and cooperation during these critical years. We are very, very hopeful. Of course, we count now more than ever, although we have ever counted, upon the help of Great Britain. We know how sympathetic Great Britain has ever been to our people, and Great Britain entering into the war on behalf of small nationalities and her triumphant occupation of Palestine seem to settle our problem for us. It is almost too good to be true that the great hour is approaching. Either we must show as a people that we can live together and translate our ideals into a reality or it were as well that we should pass.

The American people are become one in their support of the President. The Russian Revolution won over those who dreaded the thought of our fighting by the side of the Russian autocracy. I confess I never yielded to that dread. I felt since the beginning of the war that either Russia would free its people or its people would fling away its rulers. The latter end has come to pass, and who knows but that we, the friends and comrades of Herzl, may yet live to see the great day. . . .

The Zionist movement in this country is become another thing since the war began. Brandeis is our leader and in some ways he is the first Jew in the world. He is a great statesman, a great democrat and a great leader. I do not know that you have any Jew in England to match him. I wish you could come over and talk to us and let us see you.

Zangwill replied he could not feel the joy of the BORUCH HABO. *As an "ITOist" (a member of the Jewish Territorial Organization), he had followed Herzlian Zionism and therefore had never ruled out Palestine. He felt, however, that a Jewish state in Russia might now be possible; it might prove to be "far superior to the Weizmann conception of a Palestine state." His greatest concern, however, was that America stood at a critical point in her destiny, for she might "insidiously slide into the Prussianism she had started out to combat."*

May 7, 1917

TO Abba Hillel Silver, Wheeling, W. Va.

It was my very great pleasure to write to you a few days ago to congratulate you upon the honor that has come to you in being called to the service of the leading congregation in Cleveland [Temple Tifereth Israel]. I have had no word from you in reply, but I know you are a very busy man and your word, however deferred, will be welcome when it comes.

I write, however, at this time about a matter which I consider of great moment. I shall write with entire frankness even though you may not like what I am about to say. I am so much older than you and I have felt so friendly and deep an interest in your career that I not alone feel I have the right to speak as I do but that I would not be fulfilling the office of a friend if I failed to speak to you with perfect frankness.

While in Cleveland [recently], I learned, not alone to my regret but to my dismay, that it was understood when you were elected to the pulpit that you were not a Zionist; that as someone put it, you had "passed muster" after consultation with Dr. [Moses J.] Gries with respect to Zionism; that, as it was put, your Zionism was so qualified as to be altogether unobjectionable.

I write, as I do, not for the sake of the Zionist cause, which as you will understand needs no one of us. No one of us, however strong or great, is indispensable to the Zionist movement. But I wish to say to you that, in the first place, I cannot believe that you have suffered such an impression to go out as would on any ground lead anyone to imagine that you would abate your devotion to Zionism in order to secure a pulpit or on any extrinsic ground whatever. I feel that a great injustice is being done you and that you ought to correct this impression at the earliest possible moment. You may feel that it will be time enough to do so when you first occupy the pulpit in the course of your inaugural sermon, and I might be disposed to agree with you. However, I believe that it may be true that you would not have been called to the pulpit of the congregation if it were felt that you were a warm and unequivocal supporter of the Zionist movement and ideal.

I place the matter before you and submit it to your conscience and judgment. I have no counsel to offer you. The matter seems too clear to require any word of counsel even from a man so much older than you as is the writer.

With most cordial good wishes and trusting that you will per-

mit no impression to stand that is bound to do incalculable hurt
to your position and above all to your self-respect.

*Silver responded that he was, and for years had been, a disciple
of Achad Ha'am, the exponent of spiritual and cultural, not
political, Zionism. He shared with Wise the letter he had sent
to his Cleveland predecessor, Moses J. Gries, explaining that a
spiritual and cultural center in Palestine would meet with his
sympathy and approval, and would be a galvanizing force in
Jewish life, while the political aspects of Zionism had always
been of secondary importance to him; now with Russian Jewry
emancipated, they were a negligible consideration. Therefore, he
could not become enthusiastic about establishing "a little Jewish
state in Palestine." Religious apathy and indifference, ignorance
of Jewish life, and a lack of organization were, he felt, problems
which far outweighed Zionism; Zionism was not, he stated, the
vital problem of American Israel at that time.*

June 30, 1917

TO Adolf Kraus, Chicago

I have just returned from Washington and hasten to give you
an account of what happened during my conference with the
President. I had not seen the letter of [Washington, D.C., B'nai
B'rith leader] Mr. [Simon] Wolf to the President, although I
knew its contents as a result of your communication. Having
now seen that letter, I understand that the President made clear
to me why it was that his telephonic assent to Mr. Wolf's statement was secured. The President put it, "If it be true that the
American Jewish Congress, as Mr. Wolf has said, is going to be
obstructive of American interests, I could not avoid the inference
that the Congress ought not to be held."

I need not say, my dear Judge Kraus, that this is written in the
strictest confidence, because I am quoting the President literally,
and you know that this is impermissible. But I must say that the

President told me that he was deeply distressed over the entire situation. I asked him whether he would not give out a statement that would set the whole matter at rest. He looked over the statement and added three words—"wisely and prudently"—signed it and authorized me to give it out. You will see that our good friends in Washington had hoped to hurt the [American Jewish] Congress, and all they have done has been to help it, for we never could have had from the President his word of sanction and benediction, as it were, touching the Congress, if poor, dear, old Simon Wolf had not sought to thwart us. Incidentally, and in the confidence of friendship, I may say to you that Mr. Wolf's measure has been taken and that neither more nor less harmlessly benevolent he, nor his rather more malevolent allies will have an opportunity to be heard hereafter on any Jewish questions without their statements being carefully checked up after consultation with men whom the White House trusts.

With deepest appreciation of your own fairness to us, and your helpfulness in averting the evil that would have come to pass had the statement of Mr. Wolf gone unchallenged. . . .

June 30, 1917

TO Harry Cutler, Providence, R.I.

It will interest you to learn that I had a conference with the President on Friday afternoon, the outcome, insofar as it bore upon the [American Jewish] Congress, being that the President authorized me to issue a statement concerning the Congress, which I think appeared in the public prints throughout the country this morning. I think we can now afford to make light of the suggestion of those who are constantly urging that the President and the Administration are opposed to the American Jewish Congress. The President has now spoken definitely and authoritatively; and I cannot help feeling that it is of very great moment to the Congress movement that the President has not only said that he is "persuaded that the American Jewish Congress will

wisely and prudently serve Jewish interests, but that its deliberations and policies will be in accord with and helpful to the aims
and policies of the American government."

P.S. I should have added in the body of the letter what I must
now include as a postscript. In view of the President's intimation
in the sentence, "While it may seem necessary to the gentlemen
who have called the Congress to postpone it from the date fixed
because of the urgency of the public business," do you not think
it will be necessary for us to postpone the Congress for the
present? I am persuaded that it will, and I would urge that you
call a meeting of the Administrative Committee at the earliest
possible moment to consider ways and means of acting in accordance with the intimation, if not direction, of the President looking to such postponement. . . .

March 8, 1918

TO Richard Gottheil

I beg to return the communication of Dr. [Madison] Peters.
The [anti-Zionist] views of Dr. Peters are not unknown to me.
. . . If we find the attitude of Dr. Peters is characteristic of the
Christian peoples of the world, it would be nothing less than
a tragedy, and that while the loss would be ours, the real spiritual
and eternal hurt would be to the Christian peoples themselves.

I do not believe the attitude of Dr. Peters is characteristic of
Christian peoples generally. I think it will be given to you and
to me to find that most Christians are much more nearly Christian
in their attitude toward Zionism than is Dr. Peters. His own
position is frank but not friendly, it is candid but not fraternal,
it is ecclesiastical but not Christian.

. . . A great disaster, moral and spiritual, awaits Christianity
and Israel alike if the unbrotherly and Christless position of Dr.
Peters herein should be found to be characteristic of any great
number of Christian people, however simple and unenlightened.

August 28, 1918

TO Josephus Daniels, Secretary of the Navy, Washington

I deeply regretted not to have had an opportunity to see you while in Washington yesterday . . . I hoped to have a chance to get a glimpse of you after the Cabinet meeting, before talking to the President; but I must have arrived after the Cabinet had adjourned.

I beg to send you the enclosed memorandum, which summarizes my own findings in the shipyard [where Wise and his son, James, worked as laborers to aid the war effort]. I ought to have added one thing—namely, that yet another reason for the fine loyalty of the workers to the cause of the country and the Allies at this time is to be found in the circumstances that the men who have come to us from the little lands, Servia, Bulgaria, Rumania, Armenia, Poland, the lands that lie under the shadow of German militarism and despotism—that these men feel that the winning of the war means deliverance for the nations from whom they are sprung. The workers know that when the President speaks of the rights of small nations, he has no scheme of commercial exploitation and territorial aggrandizement in the back of his head and that he is frankly stating the highest purposes of the war, which are his own.

November 13, 1918

TO Charles E. Bloch

I beg to acknowledge herewith the receipt of your communication in which on behalf of the Executive Committee of the [Free] Synagogue you inform me of its action in increasing my annual honorarium from ten to twelve thousand dollars per year. I beg you will understand that I am most grateful to the members of the Committee for their generous action. I beg, however, to add that while I am most appreciative of the spirit of good-will that moved the Executive Committee to take such action, I find myself unable and unwilling to accept its terms. For one thing, I do not believe the congregation is so circumstanced as to be able to make this arrangement; but even if it were, I should still be under the necessity of definitely declining it because I feel that the honorarium allowed me is ample and generous and that any increase thereof would deny me the privilege of feeling that I am rendering any unremunerated service to the cause. While I serve the congregation as I can, I am not making any sacrifice on its behalf; and I wish to claim the privilege of feeling that in denying myself that increase of honorarium which the Executive Committee is pleased to offer me, I am making some contribution to the work of our organization.

November 29, 1918

TO Maximilian Heller, New Orleans

. . . I am to leave for Europe in a few days, as head of the Zionist delegation to the Peace Congress—that is to say, we are to serve in connection with the Peace Congress, my special work being to act as liaison officer between the delegates of the American Peace delegation and the Zionist Organization under Weizmann. The Chief [Brandeis] seemed to think I could be of some service in that direction, and perhaps my personal relations with the President and Colonel House, as well as Secretary [of State Robert] Lansing and others, may be of some value in that connection. I earnestly and devoutly hope so. . . .

London, December 24, 1918

TO Gertrude Wolf

Your letter is the first that came to me from the other side, and I may frankly say to you that I wish it had been from the children instead of from you. What you write is not especially comforting, having in mind what you say about [the poor attendances at] the services and the Forum [of the Free Synagogue]. Perhaps you will have brighter reports to send me a little later. . . .

. . . In a day or two I shall prepare a statement which you may use in some number of the [*Free Synagogue*] *Bulletin;* perhaps the two most important things will include references to a brief address I made at the A.J.A. [Anglo-Jewish Association]; my conference with Mr. [Arthur James] Balfour, and my words at the dinner tendered by Lord [Lionel] Rothschild to the Prince [Emir] Feisal of the [Arab] Hedjaz Kingdom. . . .

While Wise prepared to see President Woodrow Wilson in Paris and made plans to leave London, Israel Zangwill urged him and his fellow Zionists not to take any official action without having talked with him, noting that "the naivete with which America accepted the Balfour Declaration was both touching and amazing, but it may be of use to pin the Government withal."

February 4, 1919

TO Maximilian Heller, New Orleans

. . . The political situation is good, but there are grave complications. The most hopeful thing of all is the attitude of our President. I spent an hour with him in Paris just before I left— in fact waited over until his return from Italy in order to have that hour with him. He is our friend and he will stand by us to the end. One difficulty is that he may not feel America is ready to take over a protectorate, say, over Armenia, which would be analogous to the protectorate of Great Britain over Palestine. The situation politically is far better than I had conceived to be possible.

I might put it in one sentence: a Jewish Palestine is taken for granted throughout the Allied peoples in just the same way as a renascent Poland or a reorganized Servia. Surely that is nothing less than a God-given miracle.

[Winter, 1919]

TO Henry Pereira Mendes

. . . I am pained to learn of what you tell me concerning what you call the strained silence without any hearty response that fell

upon the Clergy Club a few days ago [when the subject of a
Jewish national home in Palestine was introduced]. I regret to
say that I am not surprised at this. I do not find among Christian
ministers the right attitude toward the hope [Zionism] that lies
before us. The Christian laity is far more brotherly and generous.
. . . I think the admission of rabbis to the Club is an afterthought,
very much belated, and due, it is not unlikely, to financial
stringency.

March 6, 1919

TO Nathan and Lena Straus, Aiken, S.C.

I have tried to write to you and tell you of our conference with
the President on Sunday. Nothing could have been more satisfy-
ing than that. I saw the President for twenty minutes before our
fuller conference, and he spoke in a manner that would have
rejoiced your heart concerning our own prospects. I wish I could
tell you by word of mouth just what he said about Palestine. I
may say this to you, without committing an indiscretion in the
use of the mail, that the President seems to have no doubt that
Palestine is to be ours. I wish I might be assured that the Jewish
people will be equal to the opportunity as I believe the opportunity will come to them.

After I had been with the President for about twenty minutes,
he asked [Louis] Marshall, [Julian W.] Mack and [Bernard G.]
Richards to join us; and we had a full discussion of the points we
submitted to him. I may say that the President and Colonel
[Edward M.] House, and I dare say, their associates as well, will
fight for everything we want, as they ought to fight, because the
things that we want are things that America wants and things
that are dictated by the spirit of democracy. The real problem
is over minority or group rights; but even here, the President told
us things that led us to believe that he will make a most vigorous
and determined fight for everything we hope for. . . .

Judge Mack left on Thursday [for the final deliberations of the
Paris Peace Conference], and will work together with [Felix]
Frankfurter, who went a fortnight ago. Frankfurter is very astute

and very wise in dealing with men, as you know. [Jacob] De Haas
will remain a few days longer, long enough to hand things over
to Mack, and on Monday Marshall is to leave [for Europe].
Nothing could be finer than the way in which Marshall is working with us. His support of and participation in the [American
Jewish] Congress is beyond praise. It is of enormous value to us
—of greater value than he himself knows.

I suppose you, like all the rest of us, have been half amused
and half irritated by the [anti-Zionist Julius] Kahn resolutions
[presented to President Wilson by California Congressman Kahn
on March 4, 1919]. Of course you will notice that a great many
men have signed it who have really no part in Jewish life. The
really great Jewish figures are not among the signatories. I am
deeply surprised that [Henry] Morgenthau should have done it,
and I believe the day will come when he will regret having put
his name to such a statement. The two moving spirits, as you
know, are [Max] Senior of Cincinnati and [Henry] Berkowitz of
Philadelphia. Senior is a good man and Berkowitz a fine man,
but they should not have done this. We are not going to take any
notice of it. I may tell you that I asked the President, "What
about the Kahn protest?" and his only answer was, "Has the
gentleman protested?" Then I said, "What will you do, Mr.
President, when the protest comes?" His answer was, "I will
accept it." Then I asked, "What will you say, Mr. President?"
to which he replied, "I will say nothing." And you will notice
he did say nothing—although he said exactly what we asked in
speaking of Zionism.

I need hardly say that this letter is written in confidence; and
of course its contents are not to be disclosed to anyone, for I have
dealt in perhaps imprudent fashion with very confidential matters. . . .

June 18, 1919

TO Samuel Gompers, Washington

I learn with very great pleasure that the A.F.L. [American
Federation of Labor] under your direction will attempt to

organize the steel workers. This should have been done long ago and cannot be delayed for a moment. I simply want you to know that if I can be of any help to you, if necessary through making addresses to the workers in the steel district, please remember that I am at your command. Surely the heads of the steel industry will not be idiotic enough to attempt to withstand the organization of their workers. I cannot believe, despite their record, that they will be so Bourbonish.

July 11, 1919

TO Edward M. House, Paris

. . . I want to say to you . . . now that things are nearly concluded, the Jews of America are, and ever will be, grateful to you as the leading associate of the President for all that you have done at and before the Peace Conference to the end that the Peace Treaty terminate the wrongs of the Jewish people. I know, and all Jews shall know, how much we owe to you, who have been a wise and helpful friend. I once said to the President, what I am justified in repeating to you, that the Jewish people have not had many friends who have in serving the cause of justice helped them as, under God, it has been given to the President and to you to serve the Jewish people. Any man who furthers the cause of human liberation is sure to endure in human fame, and any man who like you has not only served the cause of freedom but helped to right the wrongs of an ancient and, at best, a great people, will be remembered in the gratitude and praises of a people imperishable. . . .

Lake Placid, July 23, 1919

TO Julian W. Mack, New York City

I have your letter of July 21 in which you give me further information concerning the [Louis] Marshall dinner and reception. In your previous letter, you will remember that you had said that every member of the delegation of the American Jewish Congress would be asked to speak for five minutes at the dinner. From your letter and the daily press I gather that virtually every member of the delegation is to speak at the dinner excepting myself.

. . . I insisted with utmost vigor that under no circumstances ought any such meeting be held which failed in some way to give you the place to which, as president of the [American Jewish] Congress and president of the Zionist Organization, you were entitled.

I now see that all the members of the delegation [to the Peace Conference as consultants] practically, save for myself, have been asked to speak at the dinner, as well as Dr. Cyrus Adler, the longtime violent and implacable foe of the [American Jewish] Congress.

I wish to tell you that I consider it an entirely unfriendly, not to say, viewing our relations, disloyal thing in you to be ready to speak at the dinner and the meeting from which I, your associate in the Congress and as vice president of the Z.O.A., had been shut out.

. . . Assuming that my name was omitted through ignorance— and the assumption is a very generous one—it was your business to insist that I be asked to be present. But the omission, as you well know, is not accidental. It is dictated by one or another of several circumstances with all of which you are familiar. You know that I have not been invited either because of the malignant enmity felt for me by those who are your friends, [Jacob] Schiff and [Felix] Warburg, or else because more than any one of the speakers I represent the American Jewish Congress ideal, for which I fought and which I served with utmost earnestness at a time when you were indifferent or opposed to the Congress and Mr. [Louis] Marshall himself accepted it only because it was inevitable.

The reasons for the envenomed ill-will toward me felt by Messrs. Schiff and Warburg and their obsequious underlings, I shall not pause to discuss. I know that whatever may have been their feeling toward me prior to the War, their enmity was intensified by reason of my uncompromising adherence to the Allied Cause at a time when they and most of their friends and supporters were as uncompromisingly pro-German.

If the failure to invite me was due to the fact that it was desired to minimize the American Jewish Congress in the matter, it was your business as president of the Congress and loyal to its principles, and not as a matter of personal friendship, to insist that I be asked to be present, whatever might be the personal attitude toward me of those whose very nod directed the content of the meeting. Perhaps the failure to invite me as a representative of the Congress was due to neither of the grounds named, the bitterness toward me of the controlling spirits of the meeting or the reluctance to magnify the Congress ideal or, by shutting me out, to restore to its one-time place hegemony, the American Jewish Committee, but to the circumstance that I had not rendered sufficient service to the Congress to make necessary an invitation to me to take a place by the side of its other representatives at the dinner.

It is not for me to say whether or not I was useful in relation to the Congress. Possibly you know these things—that I had some little part in bringing the Congress to pass and that, owing to Justice Brandeis' enforced withdrawal from leadership in Jewish affairs, a withdrawal that resulted from the malignity of the very people who are responsible for the attitude toward me now, it fell to my lot to take the leadership in the Congress movement at a time when those who were forced ultimately to accept it as inevitable, remained indifferent to it or its unyielding opponents.

If I did not remain for the meeting of the Congress in Philadelphia, you know that my absence was due to the imperative duty of representing the Z.O.A. in London and Paris, when, however, it was also felt that it would become possible for me to establish relationships between the delegation of the Congress, to which it seemed natural that I should be elected, and the authorities in England and in France.

In the third place, I think I have the right to believe that I did represent the Congress delegation in England and France and it fell to me to negotiate those arrangements which at the

time met with the fullest approval of you and Mr. Marshall,
arrangements which, as a result of my personal relation to the
Administration, most happily initiated negotiations between the
American Peace delegation and ourselves.

. . . That you should assent to so viciously insulting an attitude
on the part of those responsible for the Marshall meeting toward
one who has been your loyal colleague and friend is somewhat
but not wholly surprising. I beg you will not take the trouble to
explain; the matter is beyond the need or possibility of explanation. The only explanation that could have been offered was
your statement to Messrs. Schiff and Warburg, with whom you
have consulted touching the meeting, "If Dr. Wise is to be in-
sulted in this way, as his colleague alike in the Congress delegation and the Zionist Organization, it will be necessary for me to
absent myself from the meeting." This explanation you failed to
make, none other is tolerable now. The time to have explained
was when Messrs. Schiff and Warburg firmly decreed and you
infirmly assented.

. . . I have written as I have written not on my behalf but in
the interest of decency—to say nothing of the elementary mandate of loyalty.

October 6, 1919

TO M. Wertheim

I have your letter in which you inform me that not being able
to subscribe to my conception of the trouble in the steel industry,
you desire to take your name from the membership roll [of the
Free Synagogue]. I shall bring your letter to the attention of the
membership committee which I have no doubt will act in con-
formity with your wishes.

There are two things I wish to say to you: in the first place,
are you persuaded you ought not be a member because you cannot subscribe to my views on all questions moral, industrial,
political? In the next place, I desire to say that as a result of a
great deal of comment, public and private, on my address of
Sunday morning ["Bolshevists at Home—Who Are They?"], I

mean to speak this Sunday on "How Ought the Pulpit to Deal with the Industrial Situation?" I should be glad if you were to defer your action in the matter until after hearing that address.

October 7, 1919

TO Daniel Klein

I have had a number of communications from people, some of whom agree, others of whom disagree, with my utterance of last Sunday respecting the industrial situation. I have been able to reply to every communication because they have all been written by gentlemen. I am unable to reply to your letter because no gentleman would have written in the terms you permit yourself to employ.

You say you resign from the Free Synagogue. You have no place therein. The Free Synagogue seeks to minister to those who have some understanding of the meaning of religion and the decencies of life. My own interpretation of the meaning of religion moved me to speak as I did concerning Garyism. No gentleman would permit himself to forget and to violate the decencies of daily intercourse as you have permitted yourself to do.

November 29, 1919

TO Joseph P. Tumulty, Washington

I must let you know something for the comfort it may bring you and possibly to the President, who, I devoutly hope, is growing stronger day by day.

On Tuesday night I was in Holyoke, Mass., speaking at the initial meeting of the Public Forum. Nearly fifteen hundred men and women were gathered at the City Hall. In the course of the discussion, I was asked a question about Americanization, which was my theme in relation to internationalism. I turned to the questioner and said: "Do you really want me to speak

to you with frankness about Americanism and internationalism?"
He answered, "Certainly." I then said: "It is very difficult to
speak in the state of Massachusetts on Americanism and international relations without saying things about the senior Senator
from Massachusetts that may give pain to this audience. I feel
that Senator [Henry Cabot] Lodge has done a very great wrong
to the nation [by leading the Senate isolationists in attacking the
treaty of Versailles and opposing America's entry into the League
of Nations]. He has brought it about that America has for the
present failed to keep its engagement of honor with the European nations. No one could have done a more un-American and
anti-American thing than Senator Lodge has done in making
our international relations and our place in the world a matter
of national politics instead of international principles and ideals.
Let this meeting inform Senator Lodge that we are not electing
a president but adjusting world relationships."

I wish you might have been present and gotten the response.
The audience cheered and cheered in approval. A few persons
took no part in the demonstration, but I should say, as far as I
can estimate, ten to one in the audience were in agreement
with me and shared my own contempt for the mean, petty
politics of Lodge and his group of followers. I wish we had
time to go into Massachusetts and make the fight day by day
against Lodge and [Senator David I.] Walsh. I didn't deal with
Walsh because I think he is beneath notice.

If you happen to tell the President of this, will you not give
him my most affectionate greetings and say to him that the
fight isn't lost yet and that it will be won.

                                             December 31, 1919

TO Nathan Straus, Augusta, Georgia

I know you will be glad to learn that Lord [Edward] Grey, the
retiring British Ambassador, having been invited by me to a
luncheon in order to meet with a group of Zionists, telegraphed
that instead of luncheon, he would come to tea at my home on

Friday afternoon. I wish you and Mrs. Straus could be present on that occasion. We are asking Zionists, just as you would, and none others, for we all mean to tell Lord Grey how we feel concerning the great part which his country has played and is continuing to play with respect to the possibility of restoring Palestine as the national Jewish homeland.

CHAPTER THREE

AMERICA AT THE CROSSROADS
(1920-1932)

TO GEORGE ALEXANDER KOHUT

> If one be a hundred years behind one's time, one may remain blissfully unconscious of belatedness. But if one be a month or three months or a year, as I usually am, ahead of one's time and ahead of events, it is little less than a personal tragedy.
>
> *March 9, 1932*

January 9, 1920

TO Charles Evans Hughes

As soon as I read of the great wrong which had been done in
the [N.Y. State] Legislature the other day [barring five elected
Socialist legislators from being seated in the legislature], I hoped
and said that you might take up the cudgels, not in their behalf
but in behalf of our country and that spirit of democracy which
were threatened by this lawlessness. And you have done it and
done it with courage and with power. It is a very great service
which you have rendered the nation, and all Americans once
again are become your debtors.

January 9, 1920

TO Nathan Straus, Augusta, Georgia

... We had two wonderful [Zionist] meetings on Monday at
both of which Rabbi [Abba Hillel] Silver of Cleveland spoke. He
is a remarkable man and made two extraordinarily fine addresses.
Including your own most generous gift, nearly two hundred
thousand dollars was given and over one million pledged. That
does not mean that we shall actually get that amount, but it
does indicate what is most important—namely, that there is an
intense desire on the part of the Zionist workers in New York to
help all they can. ...

97]

February 26, 1920

TO Nathan Straus, Augusta

. . . Confidentially, I may say to you that I do not think we have suffered any real loss as far as Jewish affairs go through the passing [resignation] of [Secretary of State Robert] Lansing. He did what the President dictated as far as Jewish affairs go, but little more. He never gave himself to the furtherance of Jewish affairs with any zeal or warmth. [His successor, Bainbridge] Colby is a personal friend and I think we shall find he will be helpful. . . .

March 29, 1920

TO Nathan Straus, Augusta

We missed you and Mrs. Straus very much last night and wish indeed that you might have been present [at the 13th anniversary dinner of the founding of the Free Synagogue]. The family was well represented, for it was a great delight to welcome Nathan Jr. and his wife and Judge and Mrs. [Irving] Lehman.

People seem to think that this dinner was a pleasant affair. The addresses in the main were of a high order. [William G.] McAdoo was absent because of illness, but all the others, including Mr. [Henry] Morgenthau who came in as a surprise, appeared. Percy [Stickney] Grant and [Edwin] Markham and [Alfred E.] Smith spoke particularly well as did [Nathan] Krass, who is always eloquent. There were five hundred guests and I think you would have been pleased to have noted the friendly and cordial atmosphere which obtained. An appeal was made for a fund of twenty-five thousand dollars per year for five years with which to do all the special work of which I had written to you, and about half that amount was raised in a few moments at the dinner. I am very anxious to tell you about it and other things, and as soon as I have word from you upon your return we shall meet.

I hasten to enclose a copy of a letter which I addressed to the President a few days ago in view of his forthcoming Turkish pronouncement [urging expulsion of Turks from Europe]. Admiral [Cary] Grayson [Wilson's physician] has written to say that the thing was placed in his hands at once. McAdoo is very helpful in getting things to the President whenever we wish it.

Lately, we prepared an important communication, which was sent in the name of Brandeis, and now we have word from London that the President adopted our views, concurred in them entirely, and that Ambassador [John W.] Davis took those views as of the President directly to the [Allied] Supreme Council. It is of inestimable advantage to have the President at our side and as our warm and helpful friend. If only he were a little stronger, he could yet confound his enemies—I mean those partisan, selfish beings who are fearful that the Democratic party might reap some advantage from the enactment of the League of Nations.

April 22, 1920

TO Nathan Straus, Mamaroneck, N.Y.

. . . The whole of Asia Minor is to be ceded to the Allies and disposition will later be made. In any event, for the present we are freed from the horror of Arab suzerainty, an indignity and dishonor which Jews could not have tolerated.

Is there no prospect of your coming to town? I wish we might see you and particularly that you might come to the service [at the Free Synagogue in Carnegie Hall] of Sunday morning and hear a man who in my judgment is the ablest rabbi in America today, barring no one—Rabbi Abba Hillel Silver of Cleveland— a remarkable youth, only twenty-seven, who, if God give him health and strength, will do great things for Israel. He is a most ardent Zionist and gives of his time and strength to the cause. . . .

April 28, 1920

TO Edward M. House

I know that no one enters more heartily into the spirit of our joy over the conferment of the Palestine mandate upon Great

Britain than do you. As soon as the good news came, I thought, and continue to think, of the important part that you had from the beginning in those negotiations that have now been crowned by the great consummation [voted by Supreme Council of European Powers on April 24, 1920, at San Remo on the Italian Riviera].

The people of Israel owe you a very great debt, and I trust we may feel free upon an early occasion to indicate for the first time with what sincerity and wholeheartedness you played your part in those negotiations that made the Balfour Declaration possible and the San Remo decision the inevitable consummation. It was a great good fortune for the Jewish people and the cause of justice for which they stood that the President and you were the two men placed in a position that offered the opportunity of service to the Zionist cause. You have indeed deserved well of a people which already knows, and will have made clear to it, how generous and unwearied has been your cooperation in the work crowned at San Remo. . . .

May 26, 1920

TO The President, The White House, Washington

I rejoice indeed in your Message to the Congress urging that we take a mandate for Armenia. It would be one of the fine things of American history if Congress were to rise to the height of taking favorable action upon your recommendation. I wish it were possible for you to make clear to the American people how important it is that this service be rendered to the Armenian people by Americans.

October 7, 1920

TO Richard Gottheil, Paris

. . . Things are rather dull and uninspiring in America just now. [Warren G.] Harding [candidate of the Republican party for the presidency] is an impossible person, and yet he is inevitable as President. He is a person without even an elementary understanding of the rudiments of English, to say nothing of the rudiments of national and international policy. His nomination is the greatest insult ever levelled at the American people, the people do not understand that; and they will make him President . . . The country has come round to your state of mind with regard to [President Woodrow] Wilson, failing to understand that his faults are almost wholly those of manner and that, in matter, he is distinctly great and will have a very great place in history. . . .

October 12, 1920

TO Meyer Weisgal

In response to your request, I have the pleasure in sending you an abstract which I have prepared especially for the readers of *The Maccabaean* [official organ of the Federation of American Zionists]. It gives the essence of what I have sought to make clear with respect to the challenge of Henry Ford [whose publication, *The Dearborn Independent,* gave wide circulation to the *Protocols*—or "minutes"—*of the Elders of Zion* which falsely listed schemes of the Jews to gain control of and utterly destroy "Christian civilization"].

It seems to me that if Mr. Ford and the men behind him had any understanding of Zionism, or if the authors of that mass of forgeries, the *Protocols,* had the faintest understanding of what Zionism means, they would not even have imputed the authorship of the *Protocols* to one in any wise associated with the Zionist Organization of America or indeed to any Jew.

The Jew has no secret aims. The Jew has no hidden purposes. What the Jew needs most of all is a complete public understanding of his aims and ideals.

The Balfour Declaration, the San Remo decision [by the Supreme Council of European Powers to award the Mandate for Palestine to Great Britain], the appointment of a British High Commissioner of Palestine together represent the attitude of the reasoning, well-meaning world in the face of the publicly uttered demand of the Jew that Palestine, as I have ventured to call it, the oldest of earth's irredentas [unredeemed territory inhabited by natives who formerly held it and seek to recover it], be restored to the earliest of earth's great surviving peoples.

October 19, 1920

TO Joseph Tumulty, Washington

I do not know whether you happened to see the statement I made with regard to the President's appointment [in 1916] of Justice Brandeis. It had to be made because the Indiana State Democratic Committee made the mistake of appealing to Jews to vote against [Senator Warren G.] Harding because he opposed the confirmation of Justice Brandeis. You will notice the way in which it was done and the reason I gave for his appointment and the reason for Harding's opposition to him.

I am making a number of addresses for the ticket; and I find to my very great joy that while there is a great deal of strange and inexplicable anti-Administration feeling, there is a reaction about to set in; and if the election were a month later, I believe the American people might be moved to understand how false are the issues that have been drawn as against the President. In all my addresses I am saying that [Henry Cabot] Lodge and his associates ought to have been held for treason.

I do not know whether I ever told you that, both in London and in Paris, while the President as President began his negotiations, I found that representatives of both French and British governments had been moved by Lodge and his garbage-distributing agents, such as Judson Welliver, to believe that the peace had to be made not with the President but with the Foreign Relations Committee of the United States Senate.

I get a tremendous response when I urge that Lodge and his associates ought to have remembered that the President represented the United States and that he was entitled to their loyal support while dealing with foreign nations, even though of course they were free to oppose the ratification of the Treaty when it came before the Senate.

Please present my most cordial greetings to the President; and tell him, if you care to do so, that wherever I speak, I accept the challenge of the Republican party and say that if the President failed to get all that he might have gotten at Paris, it was because of the treasonableness of the Republican gang, and that what he did get was a mighty tribute to his own personality and the power which he exercised as the representative of America, and accepted as such by the people.

January 31, 1921

TO William T. Manning

May I not be permitted, as one of your older colleagues in the ministry of New York, to tender you my heartfelt congratulations upon the very great honor which has come to you in the call to serve as Bishop of the [Protestant Episcopal] Diocese of New York.

I look back with deep satisfaction upon the personal relations which I have enjoyed with your last three predecessors, all of whom I have been proud to consider my personal friends. I rejoice, too, to think with what fineness of spirit Bishop [Henry Codman] Potter, Bishop [David Hummell] Greer and Bishop [Charles Sumner] Burch spoke for their great Church whenever it was well that a word of sympathy and helpfulness should be spoken on behalf of my people.

I trust that we may often serve together, and I know that whenever it shall be needful, the word of goodwill and understanding will be spoken by you as head of the Diocese of New York, and you will not fail to maintain the high tradition of the Diocese. . . .

March 7, 1921

TO Israel Abrahams, Cambridge, England

I am delighted to hear from you. I thought you had forgotten that I was alive, for you have owed me answers to a number of letters for some years. But I forgive you. . . .

Some day in the very near future I shall write to you at great length and tell you about a plan that has been maturing in my mind for a long time, to found a Jewish Institute of Religion—this institute to be a training school for men in the Liberal Ministry. Emil Hirsch [is] to be its honorary president, and I am to be the directing head, with Hirsch giving us a month of the year for day-to-day teaching. We are not to compete with Cincinnati [Hebrew Union College] but to complement its work. I have and shall have access to university men. No man is to be admitted to our school who is not a university graduate. In New York we have the largest Jewish community in the world. . . . Do let me hear from you with regard to many things and let me have your judgment on my undertaking. Do you want to come to America and settle down with us and be the dean of the college I am to found? The place is yours, though I have taken it for granted that you would not now exchange the dignity and distinction of a Cambridge Readership for the pioneering task of teaching in an American seminary.

April 18, 1921

TO Felix Frankfurter, Cambridge, Mass.

I wish you could have been present at the meeting [of leaders of the Zionist Organization] of yesterday. You were with us at the beginning, so you ought to have been with us at the end. You were with us during the stages of the controversy that touched the lowest mark. You should have been with us yesterday when it was lifted up by L. D. B. [Brandeis] I have never seen or heard him when he made the impression upon a group of men that he did yesterday. He took the meeting in the hollow of his hand and lifted it up, enabling all of us to see the thing anew, steadily, and whole. I shall never forget his words: "Our aim is the kingdom of heaven, paraphrasing Cromwell. We take Palestine by the way. But we must take it with clean hands; we must take it in such a way as to ennoble the Jewish people. Otherwise it will not be worth having."

April 27, 1921

TO Richard Gottheil, Strasbourg

. . . We are going on apace with our plans for our own [Jewish] Institute [of Religion]. I am getting money, and the time is soon coming when I shall begin to think of getting men. . . .

May 9, 1921

TO Israel Abrahams, Cambridge, England

. . . I rejoice in your word and approval of the program [of the planned Jewish Institute of Religion]. . . . The fact is there are fifty to one hundred congregations today without a rabbi— I mean Reform congregations. And what is worse, congregations cannot get a man unless they are able to pay a minimum of three thousand [dollars] per year. . . .

I need hardly point out to you, dear Abrahams, the advantage of having a Liberal Institute in the midst of the largest Jewish population in the world, where, to borrow a scientific phrase, there is the greatest amount of clinical material upon which to draw. In Cincinnati, there are no real university facilities for the men at the College. We can give our men post-graduate opportunities, including the doctorate work at Columbia and New York University.

May 11, 1921

TO Richard W. Montague, Portland, Oregon

Your letter of the 6th is at hand together with its truly generous contribution to the work of the Synagogue, for which I am truly grateful.

As for my views about [Warren G.] Harding and the Administration, I am surprised you should ask them. I think America has gotten exactly what it deserves. Harding is a perfectly good man. There probably is not a bigger man on the Common Council of Portland than the President. His English style may not be quite as good as President Wilson's, but then these things do not matter. I really feel that America is entitled to all that it has in the President and his administration. It repudiated the best because of minor faults. It now has the worst because of minor virtues. I believe Harding's style is good. It amuses us; it has a certain robustness that shows the American people that they have elected a big man to the Presidency. No, indeed, you shall not get me to say or write, least of all write, what I think about things today—with Colonel [George] Harvey, one of [J. P.] Morgan's lifelong pups, as the American Ambassador at London and sent over to undo whatever little has been left undone that Wilson did.

Henry Morgenthau, Sr. differed with his rabbi on Zionism, which he described as the "blackest error . . . the most stupendous fallacy in Jewish history." In widely quoted interviews, well-publicized speeches, and autobiographical reflections, he called Zionism "wrong in principle and impossible of realization . . . unsound in its economics, fantastical in its politics and sterile in its spiritual ideals." He contended that "where it is not pathetically visionary, it is a cruel playing with the hopes of a people blindly seeking their way out of age-long miseries." When Stephen Wise met these accusations with the counter-attack of a sermon on the subject, Morgenthau objected even more: he withdrew his membership from the congregation of which he had been a founder and a long time president (1907–17).

January 13, 1922

TO Henry Morgenthau, Sr.

I do not quite understand what has happened in the matter of your correspondence in writing and by telephone with Mr. [Frederick] Guggenheimer, and I should really like to know just what is the situation that has arisen. Have you really resigned your membership in the Free Synagogue because of my recent address on "Zionism: Solution Not Surrender"? I do remember that you asked me to send you a copy of the address about a month ago and I thought I could; but it has not yet been printed.

As soon as it is (i.e., in the near future), you will of course receive a copy if you continue to be a member of the congregation; and, if you have ceased to be, I am sure Mr. Guggenheimer or I will send you a copy if you desire to have one.

I cannot quite bring myself to believe that because I deemed it my duty to reply earnestly and vigorously to your terrible arraignment of Zionism and Zionists last June you should wish to end your connection with the Free Synagogue.

The thing that I cannot understand is this: I had long imagined you really believed in the freedom of the pulpit and that it meant something to you. I founded the Synagogue upon pulpit freedom as upon a rock, and long assumed that you shared my conviction with respect to its importance. Now you resign your membership in the Synagogue because I have spoken out of the depth of my conviction in reply to your own word against Zionism wherein you made the gravest charges against the leaders of the movement.

It is all inexplicable to me and will so remain until you are good enough to enlighten me.

Morgenthau replied that, in his mind, free speech, a free press, and a free pulpit entitled everyone "within the bounds of decency" to free expression without subjecting themselves or others to a personal attack such as that which his informants said Wise had made on him. Since his request for an unedited transcript of the address had no response he could only infer that the reports of an abusive, personal attack against himself were accurate. It would be "a wrench" for him to sever relations with the Free Synagogue; but he "would be totally devoid of all self-respect" if he did not resign: "Hence my telephone message to Mr. Guggenheimer that my resignation must stand, and my interest in the Free Synagogue cease."

January 20, 1922

TO Julian W. Mack

You will remember I told you some time ago about Judson Welliver. He is the man who wrote the article in glorification of [Henry] Ford. Note the enclosure from the *Times* of the 17th

which speaks of him as "Chief Clerk of the White House" and
reading a letter before the Reading [Pa.] Chamber of Commerce
on behalf of the President. He has probably established the connection at the White House with [Warren G.] Harding for Ford,
and is the man who day by day cabled those scurrilous things to
the *Echo de Paris* of which, I may say to you confidentially,
[French Premier Georges] Clemenceau spoke to [Colonel Edward]
House, asking that they be discontinued. . . . I venture to predict
that Welliver may yet move Harding to say something unwise
and even disastrous about the Jews. I am told by [former] Secretary of the Treasury [David F.] Houston that Welliver is a
miserable and particularly venal creature. It is well to be prepared against him.

February 1, 1922

TO Felix Frankfurter, Cambridge, Mass.

. . . On Thursday and Friday there came telephone messages
. . . saying that [Arthur James] Balfour would try to see Brandeis
and the rest of us but that he could not definitely fix a time nor
even say he was sure he could meet with us because Saturday
might be given over to an important meeting of the Armaments
Conference. . . .

As soon as I got to Washington in that awful storm, I learned
. . . that L. D. B. and I were expected at 5:30. We met with
Balfour at that time. . . . We had a chance to drive home some
of the things that needed to be said, though of course our
particular object was to help Balfour to understand that our
own interest was unlessened [despite the split in the Zionist movement in America and on the world scene]. L. D. B. steered things
with quite characteristic wisdom. It seemed to me from time to
time as if Balfour were a bigger man than Brandeis, but Brandeis
is a greater spirit than Balfour. The one is a full-orbed personage,
and the other a luminous personality. . . .

March 20, 1922

TO Maximilian Heller, New Orleans

. . . I have been busier than usual this winter owing to the circumstance that I have had two big jobs on my hands, though I have done less travelling than for many years.

One of the jobs has been the securing of funds for the new [Free] Synagogue House, which we are about to build, the architects' plans to be submitted this week. And that is a pretty big enterprise. We have about three hundred and fifty thousand [dollars] in hand, but we need another fifty or seventy-five thousand. We shall have a fine five-story building adequate to every purpose of the Synagogue, excepting of course the Sunday morning and Holyday services which we shall continue to hold perhaps for some years at Carnegie Hall.

Over and beyond that, there is the work of the Jewish Institute of Religion, and it is about that I want to write more particularly. Things have moved and have now reached a certain stage; and I want you to know all about it, for the problem may in some way come before you, and I want you to be informed.

You may recall the letter which we addressed to the Union [of American Hebrew Congregations], a copy of which I enclose to refresh your memory. We have been having a series of meetings with the New York representatives of the Union—[U.A.H.C.] President [Julian] Morgenstern participating in one of them— and they have been pressing us for terms of cooperation. At our last meeting held last Friday and attended by Messrs. [Daniel] Hays, [Ben] Altheimer, [Ludwig] Vogelstein, and Rabbi [Jacob] Pollak on behalf of the Union, we submitted a method of co-operation, Judge [Julian W.] Mack and Dr. [Lee K.] Frankel being spokesmen for our group. I wonder what you will think of the arrangements as planned by us.

You will note the important things are that we place ourselves squarely and unreservedly under the aegis of the Union [of American Hebrew Congregations], and are to become an activity thereof coordinate with the H.U.C. [Hebrew Union College], but expressly stipulating that we shall have absolute freedom and autonomy in every sense—namely, for board of trustees, faculty, and student body alike. The Union [of American Hebrew Congregations], of course, is to have representation on our board of trustees, which, as in all academic institutions, is to be a self-perpetuating body. The Union is to supply a minimum budget of forty-five thousand dollars per year. In return, I am to place my services and those of my colleagues unreservedly at the disposal of the Union, in New York or anywhere in the country where the Union may wish to use me on behalf of the funds for the two colleges.

. . . I should greatly appreciate your judgment. I may say to you that I believe the New York representatives will strongly urge the adoption of the proposals upon the Union. Whether they are to be adopted I do not know; but in any event I shall require a definite reply by April 15, by which time I must begin to go out and secure funds if this arrangement is not to be perfected.

We are almost ready to make some very important announcements with regard to faculty. We are to have some outstanding Jewish teachers, for we shall insist upon high standards of Jewish scholarship. The students are to give us three years and we are to have every moment of their time. They must know the sources of Jewish literature and history and command the technique of scholarship which is all that an academic institution can give a man.

April 12, 1922

TO Edmund I. Kaufmann, Reading, Pa.

. . . Now the important thing is this: We have been flatly and irrevocably turned down by the Union [of American Hebrew Congregations in response to a request for support of the projected Jewish Institute of Religion, due to open in September, 1922]. This is not to be wondered at, but the fact is it has come to pass. We must now mind our p's and q's and do whatever can be done and needs to be done. The first thing of all is to arrange for a meeting of the Directors of the J.I.R. to be held almost immediately.

May 6, 1922

TO Maximilian Heller, New Orleans

. . . I am not surprised that you should take the position that you do with respect to the Union and its negotiations with the J.I.R. You speak of your surprise at the J.I.R.'s placing before the Union a plan which called for so large an appropriation and promised in return so small a measure of control. As for the large appropriation, nothing more was asked than for a term of three years. All had to be asked for that was needed, because the adoption of the plan would not have left me free to ask for a penny outside of the appropriation. Moreover, evidently you do not quite understand that had the Union made the appropriation and had the rabbis of America cooperated with us in the right spirit, I could have gotten for the Union toward the support of the [Hebrew Union] College and the Institute two or three times as much as would have been appropriated by the Union for the Institute.

As for the small measure of control, you must remember, dear Heller, and I speak with utmost frankness, that the one thing we could never permit would be the infringement of the freedom of the faculty and the student body alike as you have known to obtain for a number of years at Cincinnati. The trustees of the Institute must be and will be free, the faculty must and will be free, and the student body likewise. I do not believe that has always been true, nor do you believe that has always been true, with respect to the faculty and student body of the College.

The big and generous and catholic thing would have been for the Union to have supported two widely different institutions, each of them doing its work as best it could.

But I do not desire to enter into any further arguments respecting the Union and the Institute. We have presented our case and we refuse to enter into further discussion any more than we desire to have any quarrel. We purpose to remain friends and to support alike the Union and the College. We shall not compete with the College or try to rival it. Our work is to be our own under auspices that will in time make it enormously significant to the well-being of American Israel.

Within the last few days, we have received thirty thousand dollars as a beginning for an endowment fund for the Institute, and the [Free] Synagogue at its executive meeting the other night voted fifty thousand dollars for three years as its contribution toward the support. How does that compare with what has been done in the past by the rich temples in Cincinnati and elsewhere on behalf of the College? . . .

London, June 26, 1922

TO Julian W. Mack, New York City

. . . I can see that [Chaim] Weizmann is greatly disturbed and apparently very fearful. At the same time I must say at once that the real difficulty as far as being of help in a critical time is in question, arises out of the fact that W. is unchanged, purporting all the time to be frankness itself, and yet if anything less frank than he was a year ago. I cannot know, for example, whether he is worrying about the vote in the House of Commons or whether he is worrying about the danger to his own position as leader. . . . I am going to try today and tomorrow to get at [Arthur James] Balfour, [Winston S.] Churchill and Lord Robert Cecil and learn as far as I can how the matter stands.

. . . The tragedy is that, as a result of setting out to stand alone through the years, he [Weizmann] is now alone and deserted. . . . I do not trust him and I can never tell what is really in his mind. The only thing I see anew is that he is not a man with whom one can work and upon whom one may build; and the other thing I see is that it is unutterably sad that he alone should be at the helm, and Brandeis and you and Felix F. [Frankfurter] and the rest of us outside of the range of service.

I know I am taking a risk and a great risk, a risk of being in at the débâcle, and perhaps even of being held in some part responsible therefor, but that risk must be faced. . . .

London, June 28, 1922

TO Julian W. Mack, New York City

. . . After thinking matters over very carefully, I . . . let Major de Rothschild secure an appointment for me with [Colonial Secretary] Winston Churchill, from whom I imagined it would be possible to learn exactly how things stood, and to whom it might be possible for me as an American to convey the depth and breadth of feeling in my country respecting the matter [of empowering the World Zionist Organization to form a Jewish Agency for Palestine to cooperate with the British Colonial Office in administration of the League of Nations Mandate for Palestine].

In the meantime, I had met [former President William Howard] Taft, to whom I stated that Lord Robert Cecil was very anxious to have a talk with him. They had never met, and [Oxford University Professor] Gilbert Murray and Robert Cecil alike had stated to me that it was highly desirable that Taft should have from one of them a clear statement with respect to the League of Nations. I went back to the House of Commons, Tuesday 27th, and told Robert Cecil of the appointment which I had made for him with Taft. We then had a good talk about the whole situation. . . . He seemed to think . . . that the decision finally did not rest with Churchill, for whom I should say he had rather limited respect, but with Balfour. . . .

Immediately thereafter, Major de R[othschild] 'phoned that he had made an appointment for me with Churchill for Friday afternoon at 4:45 at the Colonial Office. . . . I met de R. at the Reform Club, and we went over the ground very carefully. . . . de R. said to me right off the bat, "You must not be too truculent with Churchill, as you have been with our Ambassador in Washington upon several occasions." I don't know to what he referred, unless it be my fairly sharp reply to [Rufus Daniel Isaacs, Lord] Reading when the latter refused to attend the Zionist Convention. . . .

. . . Now comes this letter of [Richard] Gottheil's, written obviously at the instance of Weizmann. It is in one sense a warning; in another sense, it is a threat. In the circumstances, there is nothing for me to do but to cancel my appointment with Churchill, and I have done so. If there were any integrity of motive or conduct in Weizmann, I would stay on, knowing as I do that I meant to give him loyal support. In the light of the warning of Weizmann that I might spoil things, nothing is left for me but to withdraw. He would either fasten upon me the blame for failure, or else spread broadcast that more and better might have been done if I had not intervened. I am writing to Mr. Churchill conveying to him my—that is our—views, and such letter will have to serve. I should not have permitted Gottheil to act as go-between, but I was acting frankly, with a desire to co-operate with Weizmann. . . .

I am forced to leave London for just the same reason that we were forced to leave the [Zionist] Organization a year ago: the character of Weizmann, who is so untrustworthy, that cooperation with him is not only most difficult, from the moral point of view, but actually impossible.

. . . Perhaps I ought not to have seen him at all. I waived my very deep disinclination to see W., because the cause seemed to demand it, and I was truly sorry for what I believe to be his plight. . . . He is the same old Weizmann.

If we had a week or ten days, and were still at the head of the Z.O.A., and could, moreover directly and immediately bring pressure to bear through our govt., something might yet be done with Churchill and Balfour. In the circumstances . . . it is too late to do more than I, with entire loyalty to the cause, have asked you to do.

Paris, July 1, 1922

TO Sidney Goldstein, New York City

No word as yet from you. Hopeful still! (1) [Professor] Kirsopp Lake, with whom Jim [James Waterman Wise] and I had a wonderful hour in London, will come first term or second [to the Jewish Institute of Religion]. Theme: "Beginnings of Christianity." Two weeks in November and two in December.

He will send you syllabus in July or August from Harvard. (2) Got Theodore Reinach and Louis Germain-Levi for visiting staff. (3) Am on the trail of [Simon] Dubnow, said to have been expelled from Kovno [Lithuania]. (4) Preach at French Synagog Sunday A.M. (5) Leave for Berlin tonight. [Chaim] Tchernowitz is out of it—leaving for Palestine.

You move over to your new home today. God bless you and yours to it and it to you.

Berlin, July 4, 1922

TO Sidney Goldstein, New York City

. . . Of one thing I am persuaded, . . . namely, that my coming to Europe ought to be richly productive of good to the J.I.R. for years to come. I am enabled to make my program clear, *Lehrfreiheit* [academic freedom] as the atmosphere of Jewish study and Jewish loyalty. I have the feeling that before another week I shall have most of the great scholars of the four seminaries [Berlin, Vienna, Budapest, Breslau] enrolled as members of the visiting staff and perhaps some of the best of them as our permanent teachers; they seem to like the plan of trial visits.

Aboard the S.S. *Semiramis,* July 15, 1922

TO Sidney Goldstein, New York City

One or two things I must add to my letter of yesterday [from Trieste], a copy of which I do not possess. If you make any public announcements [concerning the opening of the Jewish Institute of Religion], don't forget to mention:

[Emil G.] Hirsch,
[Harry A.] Wolfson,
[Israel] Abrahams,
[Felix] Perles,

Travers Herford and
the Hochschule men:
Prof. Dr. I[smar] Elbogen,
   ″   ″ Leo Baeck,
   ″   ″ Harry Torczyner,
   ″   ″ Julius Guttmann

. . . Now to two or three other, if other they are, matters:
(1) Has the building actually been begun?
(2) What is more urgently important, I have begged [Joseph] Levine to move promptly re 40 West 68th [Street]. We must have a house for the J.I.R. at once—offices for faculty, ourselves, students, and library.
(3) And what of applications from students? Are there no more? We must have classes preparatory. Berlin and Breslau both have them.
(4) I am most keenly and impatiently awaiting report of your [survey of West Virginia coal] mines visit. . . .
I have still much to do in Vienna, Budapest, and Berlin en route home. I never was more keen to begin work than today in relation to J.I.R. We can make it a truly serviceable work in and for and through Israel. Cable then before 30[th of July] to Trieste, Banque Commerciale Italienne, or after that to Vienna, Anglo-Austrian Bank, writing, however, as before, to Paris or London address.
Affectionate greetings to you, Mrs. Goldstein and the girls from all of us.

Vienna, August 3, 1922

TO Bernard G. Richards, New York City

I have just returned from Palestine, where, I need hardly say, my family and I had a most glorious time. There is much, very much, to say; but I can sum it all up in one sentence: Things are hopeful in Palestine, and they are hopeful nowhere else. Not that I have visited Eastern European lands; but I have heard a great deal, and think I have come to know.

... The Harvard situation [concerning proposals to establish a quota system on admission of Jewish students to the University] is distinctly disturbing. All of Europe knows about it, and is talking about it. In many ways, it is much more serious than the [Henry] Ford campaign [to circulate the discredited anti-Jewish *Protocols of the Elders of Zion* in *The Dearborn Independent*]. ...

Vienna, August 9, 1922

TO Gertrude Wolf

... All sorts of bundles, barrels and bales will soon be coming from Vienna, containing antiques, from a rib of Noah's Ark to a vertebra in Jonah's whale. Don't have anything unpacked. The things are much too precious and much too sacred to be touched by the Vandal hands of unappreciative and un-understanding secretaries. ...

The one most interesting thing to report is that we have made the pilgrimage through Hungary, including Budapest, Totis and Erlau; and I had one of the most fascinating sessions of my life with [Admiral Nicholas] Horthy [regent of Hungary], who invited Jim and me to his castle, where we spent two hours with him.

Congratulations to you upon the prospective nomination of your Christian rabbi, John [Haynes] Holmes, as candidate for the U.S. Senate [on the Socialist party ticket].

September 14, 1922

TO Martin Meyer, San Francisco

... We went to Palestine, having nearly a fortnight there. We did pretty nearly everything with the help of good motor cars, which everyone now uses, and I am enormously encouraged by what I saw. The Arab question, despite newspaper rumors and statesmen *à la* [Henry] Morgenthau, is not insoluble. There will always be Arab difficulties. There are always difficulties everywhere in relation to all problems. The important thing is that Jews are standing on their own feet and want nothing more than economic opportunity. That the Jews of the world must give them. . . .

December 10, 1922

TO Jacob Billikopf, Philadelphia

. . . I feel deeply that [Judah] Magnes has it in him to do a great work for Palestine [as president of the Hebrew University in Jerusalem], and I mean to render all possible service to him. I have started several things going, which ultimately are bound to be fruitful. . . .

It is just a matter of getting funds quickly enough to enable Magnes to shape his plans while yet he is young enough and strong enough to move forward. I think he has the most thrilling opportunity in the world. . . .

December 22, 1922

TO Richard W. Montague, Portland, Oregon

. . . Will you accept from your Rabbi for his Gentile lamb the affectionate greetings of the Season? We poor Jews have neither Jesus nor Christmas, and the Gentiles have both, though for the most part they have perverted the one and are gradually spoiling the other.

January 17, 1923

TO Edmund I. Kaufmann, Reading, Pa.

. . . So happy you are to come for the Jubilee [50th anniversary of founding of Union of American Hebrew Congregations]. You ask me to advise you as to what day I speak. I have not been invited to do as much as offer a prayer or read a Psalm, let alone to make an address. I am always singled out in that way by the Union [of American Hebrew Congregations].

I am to speak this Sunday morning, immediately before the Convention, in connection with our Memorial Service [of the Free Synagogue] for [Emil] Hirsch; and the following Sunday I shall give what I trust may be one of the most important addresses of my life—namely, "Liberalism That Is True and Liberals Who Are False."

January 22, 1923

TO Julian W. Mack, Belleaire Heights, Florida

I went to Philadelphia last night and Billy [Jacob Billikopf] had his usual great pow-wow [fund-raising event]. Julius R. [Rosenwald] spoke briefly and well, but the address of the evening was made by [Albert D.] Lasker. It was a Jewish stump speech of the heartiest kind. If his wife had heard it, she would have perished. It was his frank, sincere, virile expression of loyalty to things Jewish as he understands them. I think they got half a million, but the more I see of those drives, the more I feel L. D. B. is right. They are the undoing of things Jewish in America. There is something vulgar about them and the way in which they put a premium upon giving by those who do nothing but give a part of the superfluity of their gains. If ever Billy asks me again, I shall ask to be excused.

February 2, 1923

TO Jacob Billikopf, Philadelphia

. . . Ought not a community like Philadelphia, which can do what you have moved it to do within a fortnight, envisage Jewish needs in a large and statesmanlike way, not merely spasmodically raise one and a half millions for local charities, but face the problem of Jewish need within and without Philadelphia and raise its annual budget accordingly? Europe has needs, Palestine has needs, Jewish schools of learning throughout Europe have needs. Why don't you take the next step and have Philadelphia call a group of Jews from a number of cities in America into conference so that they may together plan out the budget of their contribution to local and extra-local needs? . . .

February 10, 1923

TO Julian W. Mack, Tampa

. . . I went to the Storrs luncheon [Sir Ronald Storrs, civil governor of Palestine], amusing in one sense. All the swell Jewish members of the English-Speaking Union were dragged thither— Felix and Paul Warburg, James Speyer, Sam Lewisohn—it doubtless being taken for granted by former Ambassador [John W.] Davis, who presided and who together with [John] Finley [of the New York *Times*] runs the show, that any reference to Jerusalem would thrill the hearts of those devoted Jewish patriots. Finley spoke in his usual semi-attractive style, he being of the very essence of insincerity. Davis spoke a few words and then Storrs. I suppose, owing to the presence of half a dozen or more of us, including [Israel] Abrahams, [Abraham] Flexner, [Elisha] Friedman, myself, etc., he made no anti-Jewish reference, but there was not the faintest hint at the Balfour Declaration or a Jewish situation in Palestine, and of course Finley used his wearisome old figure of speech: "Palestine must be a religious reservation for all peoples." Storrs will, I fancy, publicly not dare to do us hurt, limiting his views to private circles where he can let loose. [Paul] Cravath gives him a dinner at the University Club next Wednesday night. For once I wish I might be within the shades of the Club.

February 16, 1923

TO Julian W. Mack, Tampa

We had a corking good luncheon for [Israel] Abrahams [1922– 23 visiting professor at the Jewish Institute of Religion] yesterday, and how I wish you might have been present. . . . [F. J. Foakes-] Jackson and [Arthur Cushman] McGiffert of the Union [Theological] Seminary were really felicitous. . . . McGiffert said that the Seminary in one hundred years had not brought as many great scholars to America as have we [of the Jewish Institute of Religion] in the first year.

March 8, 1923

TO Julian W. Mack, Tampa

. . . [Rabbi Nathan] Krass' synagogue [Central Synagogue, East 55th Street and Lexington Avenue] is now trying to join us [Free Synagogue]. What do you think about it? They have half a million and a membership of six hundred. If we do not have to make any compromise, such as fixed dues and pews, we might be able to do it. Let me have your thought about it.

March 15, 1923

TO Julian W. Mack, Tampa

. . . The Central Synagogue plan is moving, and now looks as though we might really get together. You are right in saying, "Only if it can be done without compromise." This afternoon there is to be a meeting of the two groups, and I have laid down the fundamental principles: Freedom of the pulpit, including real leadership of the rabbi or rabbis, as attested by membership in the Executive Council; unassigned pews; and voluntary dues. If a stodgy old group such as 55th St. can accept this, I think we are reasonably safe. For the transition period, we would go on as we are now with separate funds and organizations, and perhaps no more than a joint committee helping to run both congregations, with a Sunday service at 55th St., and the community and social work of both, including the School, at the new Synagogue House. . . .

March 19, 1923

TO Julian W. Mack, Tampa

. . . The 55th Street plans are maturing swiftly and I think that the thing will be almost settled by the time you return.

There is to be no compromise and no surrender on our part but an enormously important stabilizing and strengthening of our own power. My proposal is that the Central Free Synagogue—that is to be the new corporate name—shall give $25,000 a year for three or five years, which would mean that we have to double that throughout the whole country, and that ought to be fairly easy [as a contribution to the Jewish Institute of Religion]. . . .

April 18, 1923

TO Ismar Elbogen, Berlin

. . . There is nothing that I feel free to say concerning your declination of the offer of the chair in Jewish History of the Jewish Institute of Religion. It is occasion for real sorrow to me that circumstances at home make it impossible for you to accept our invitation. It would have been a great joy to have had you with us in the work from the very beginning, and I know that your service to the Institute would, in truth, have been invaluable. I must, however, admit that I understand the circumstances which, for a time in any event, debar your accepting our invitation. I am truly sorry to think that your wife is so unhappy, and I have wondered whether coming to America might not even help her in this time of sorrowful memories.

Things are moving well at the Institute. [Israel] Abrahams, as I have written to you in several previous letters, continues to do finely. He has a literary touch and grace in dealing with learned themes which stand him in good stead. [Julian J.] Obermann is meeting our expectations as scholar and man. He will give a summer course on mediaeval Jewish philosophy, and by that time, I trust, have been enrolled as a permanent member of the faculty. The arrangement with [Harry A.] Wolfson has finally been concluded, Harvard accepting our proposal submitted with so much foresight and understanding by Judge Mack.

Speaking of America and Harvard, I presume that you have read of the outcome of the Harvard [Jewish quota] problem. Most of us are satisfied. Our young friend [Louis] Newman feels that the victory is nominal and the defeat material. I think that a great thing has been done, insofar as a faculty committee has been moved to report against a suggestion of the University's president. . . .

Just one thing more. We are on the verge of consummating the merger of the Central and the Free synagogues. As I wrote to you in an earlier letter, the best thing about the merger or federation is that I have moved two congregations together to contribute the sum of $25,000 annually for the Institute. I am really proud of this fact—the fact that the two congregations are giving one-fourth of the entire amount given by the three hundred con-gregations of the Union of American Hebrew Congregations for the Hebrew Union College. There is a great deal of talk of the Institute going under the aegis of the Union of American Hebrew Congregations. We shall always be ready to consider fair and honorable proposals as they may be made. Personally, I believe, as you do, that a great blunder was made in the failure of the U.A.H.C. to include the Jewish Institute of Religion from the beginning within the range of its activities. . . .

July 5, 1923

TO Edith Bolling [Mrs. Woodrow] Wilson, Washington

I do not know whether you ever saw an address made by a former President of the United States, entitled "The Present Task of the Minister," delivered, I believe, during his presidency of Princeton [University]. It is a noble utterance, an utterance so inspiring that I want at least part of it always before the eyes of the students of the Jewish Institute of Religion. . . . If, after looking over these lines, Mr. Wilson approves of them with something of the warmth with which I love them, then I mean to have them beautifully engraved in the hope of sending them to you and to him so that he may affix his name thereto, perhaps with a word of greeting to the men. . . .

The excerpts which Stephen Wise sent to Woodrow Wilson and his wife read as follows:

We live in an age when a particular thing cries out to be done which the minister must do and there is no one else who can do it. . . . Who shall show our soul the tracks of life? Who shall be our guides to tell us how we shall thread this intricate plan of the universe and connect ourselves with the purpose for which it is made? . . .

The world offers this leadership, this intellectual mediation to the minister. It is his if he be man enough to attempt it; man enough in his knowledge, man enough in the audacity and confidence of his spirit, man enough in the connections he has made with the eternal and everlasting forces which we know to reside in the human spirit. . . .

I congratulate young men who are looking forward to the ministry that this is their high and difficult function in life. . . . Do not go about, then, with the idea that you are picking out here and there a lost thing, but go about with the consciousness that you are setting afoot a process that will lift the whole level of the world and of modern life. . . .

If you have something to say to these people that fills you as with a living fire, it will not be necessary to have any music or any cooking classes or any bowling alleys or any gymnastics in order to bring men to the source of the things for which they must long. If you feel this, you can preach in such seething syllables as to make them feel it; and unless you preach in that wise I advise you to go into some more honest occupation. This work in the modern world is assigned to you by invitation and if you decline the invitation then you have shown that there was some mistake in the address on the envelope. It was not intended for you. It was intended for you only if when it meets your eye, your spirit leaps to the challenge and accepts it, as these do who accept the obvious lesson of every impulse that is in them, every dictate of their conscience.

And so, standing outside the ministry, longing to see it come to the relief of those who undertake the imperfect processes of education, longing to see the modern world given the privilege of witnessing a day when the human spirit shall come unto its own again, I congratulate all young men who are looking forward to the ministry, in taking their part in giving to the world the vision of God.

December 29, 1923

TO C. D. Van Horn

I hasten to repeat that I am deeply interested in any movement which looks to the abolishment of capital punishment.

July 7, 1924

TO John Haynes Holmes, Kennebunk Beach, Maine

Thanks enormously for your letter! My speech [before the Democratic National Convention] was not worth talking about; it really was not. It came in a repetitious and rather anti-climactic fashion after what was perhaps the greatest address I have ever heard on any platform, that of Newton Baker! Baker was so tremendous that he and I agreed that no one else was to speak. But nevertheless the chairman called upon me before the Secretary of the Convention communicated with him.

[William Jennings] Bryan was a tragic spectacle at night. I used to think that he was an honest man. I know now that he is not. He is a time-server and a compromiser. He seemed the prophet of Baal as compared with Baker, a prophet of the Lord.

I have as yet reached no decision with regard to the Third party, but I may tell you in confidence that I am sorely tempted to give it my support. I, however, feel that I can reach no decision until after its platform shall have been shaped . . . If that proves a true social platform, I do not see how any of us can stay out of it. . . .

Lake Placid, July 26, 1924

TO Julian W. Mack, Paris

. . . I am becoming increasingly disinclined to support [John W.] Davis, but the [Robert] La Follette splash is almost as unattractive. I am a little disconcerted by the whole mixed character of La Follette's supporters, pro-Germans, anti-British, anti-Leaguers, pro-Sovietists, anti-Socialist Liberals and illiberal

Socialists, all temporarily standing together not on a platform but for a man, with the likelihood of another drive for a man as in 1912 rather than a cause. I am, as you see, thinking aloud and hardly doing that. . . .

Lake Placid, August 18, 1924

TO Richard W. Montague, Portland, Oregon

I have been thinking of you a great deal notwithstanding the fact that I am plugging away up in the Adirondacks at my long-deferred book [eventually to emerge in 1949: *Challenging Years*]. I am working hard at it, but it is not going as well as it should. I ought to have a year to do nothing else but the book, instead of which I have a hectic, hurried six weeks, starting those six weeks in wretched physical and mental condition, but the latter statement is not the reason for my thinking of you!

My daughter has been going through my files for weeks and she finds that yours are the most interesting and, as she puts it (not I!), the most beautiful letters, excepting for John Haynes Holmes', in my possession. . . .

. . . I'd like to send you a good part of the manuscript of the book. You write English and I don't! My children always say that mine is the most perfect example of Manhattanese-Yiddish! If I could write English as you do, I would not write to you at all but sell it outright to the [*American*] *Mercury*, the *Nation* and other approximately pestiferous journals! Just by way of sample I shall enclose two or three chapters. Will you red-pencil or blue-pencil them mercilessly? . . .

Discussing somewhat less immediate personal things, did you emit a horse-laugh when you read that I was named delegate to the Democratic Convention in succession to Murphy? What could be lower excepting to hire out as a helper in your friend Erickson's gambling halls [in Portland]? It was a great Convention, as Mr. Dooley ought to say—two weeks of it; and I really believe that the bosses knew from the beginning how it would end. Are you satisfied with Davis? I like him personally. He is a fine, high type of man, but I loathe his clients. His acceptance speech was

magnificent, and I really think he means it. If he is licked, as he
probably will be, I suspect that he will not go back to the employ
of the interests. I want a Third party in the hope that the Third
party and the Democratic party together may promote a great
liberal, progressive party and lead the unblessed South out; but
I cannot endure La Follette's European policy and I am still
more intolerant of the gang which surrounds him. . . .

October, 1924

TO Newton D. Baker, Cleveland

I have had a week in bed with sciatic rheumatism, or I would
have answered your letter before this. Your word helps me somewhat; still my doubts are not at rest. I assume that [John W.]
Davis is genuinely in favor of our entrance into the League, and
of making it a living instrument of peace; but can Davis do what
[Woodrow] Wilson could not do—so liberalize the Democratic
party as to make it the instrument of politico-economic progress?

Speaking in utmost confidence to you, as I know I may, there
is a great deal about the [Robert] La Follette following [in the
Progressive party] which is repellent to me. I don't like the airy-
fairy socialists in the group. I like still less the anti-Wilsonians in
it. I appreciate your feeling that there is no present bond of coher-
ence within the group. But I do see, on the other hand, beneath all
the differences, that there is a measure of common devotion to
the end of wresting the control of our country's affairs from the
two groups that have ineptly at best, and criminally at worst, mis-
managed [them] for many years. I am loth to vote against Davis,
for I respect him and I like him, and to vote against him will, I
suppose, prove to vote for [President Calvin] Coolidge. On the
other hand, may it not be that this is the time and the hour in
which to lay the foundations of a new party? Even if I should
vote for Davis, I would be most sorely tempted to leave the Democratic party the day after, for I derived little comfort and hope
from the Madison Square Garden affair of July.

Believing in the need of a party of true liberalism as I do, I
am deeply troubled by this question: have I the right to hold

aloof from the group and thus fail to exercise that influence which it might be possible for me to exert on behalf of those things in which I believe, things which it might be possible successfully to urge upon the discordant and yet plastic elements which together make up the La Follette following?

My indecision is contemptible. I know it and I deplore it more than any one else could, for it is mine! My political soul may not be worth saving; but won't you as my cherished friend, try it once again?

October 22, 1924

TO J. R. Gilbert, *Lancaster New Era,* Lancaster, Pa.

I am very grateful to you for your kindness in sending me the issue of the *New Era* of October 18, containing the full page Klan advertisement, and also your editorial comment.

I desire, as an American citizen, to express to you my profound gratitude for the courage and the power with which the *Lancaster New Era* has faced the problem. The *New Era* is entirely right in saying that the one thing to do is to unmask the Klan, and I think it is more important to unmask its purposes than its membership. The membership gradually but surely peters down to the roughnecks and the hoodlums and rowdies of the community, but the purposes must be laid bare. To unmask the Klan is to destroy it. Do you realize that not one member of the Klan had the courage to stand up at the National Democratic Convention and defend it? I, for my part, always feel that the Klan is not so much a menace to America, which is secure, or can be made so by the spirit of its citizenship, as it is blasphemous in the Christlessness of its repudiation of all that is fundamental in Christianity.

February 11, 1925

TO Sigmund Goldschmidt

... As for the terminating of the merger [of the Free Synagogue and the Central Synagogue], I think it is best from every point of view. We really had no choice in the matter. Our good friends would not move forward in the matter of a building program, and we could not possibly go on in this way. We had to centralize things and have one home rather than three [East 55th Street, West 68th Street, and Carnegie Hall]. In parting, however, I am glad to tell you, as a friend of the Synagogue and of myself, that the relations are to continue to be really of the happiest type; and I believe you will find that the [Jewish] Institute [of Religion], in any event, will continue to have the earnest and helpful support of the Central Synagogue.

March 18, 1925

TO Richard W. Montague, Portland, Oregon

. . . You were very generous in the matter of your gift—so generous, that I clove the gift in twain, devoting one-half of it to the [Jewish] Institute [of Religion], which is really moving forward splendidly. By the way, I may be out in your part of the world rather soon, making a very hurried visit to the four or five big cities of the Coast in the interest of the Institute. I will have to point to you from the platform as the one far western contributor. . . .

March 28, 1925

TO Rebekah Kohut

The more I think about it, the more definitely I am persuaded that it would be unwise at this time to arrange for the kind of meeting of which you spoke [to protest persecution of Jews in Poland]. It is well sometimes to protest even though one knows in advance that protest will be unavailing; but I cannot see the value of protest at this time, when, after all, the chief fact that stands out in Jewish life is not so much the indifference of the world to injuries done to the Jew, but the indifference of the Jew to the welfare of world Jewry. I am ready to have part in any protest meeting against the sodden, I had almost said damnable, indifference of Jews to Jewish problems, however important. The sins of Jewish omission are greater by far at this time than the sins of Christian commission. It is far more important now to arouse the Jewish consciousness than to stir the conscience of Christendom.

October 8, 1925

TO Abba Hillel Silver, Cleveland

I learn with delight of the vigorous [United Palestine Appeal] campaign [of which Wise was national chairman] which is being prosecuted in Cleveland under the inspiring leadership of yourself, Rabbis [Solomon] Goldman and [Barnett] Brickner, on behalf of the Keren Hayesod [Palestine Foundation Fund]. Ours is not the only claim, nor is the claim of Palestine by any means the only claim upon the Jewish people, but it is a prior claim, a claim of the first importance, because whatever is done in Palestine means the building of a future, as you well know, for the Jewish people.

I know that Cleveland meets its responsibilities with generosity. If you bring this responsibility to the heart of the noble Jewry of your community, it cannot fail Palestine. I bid you and your associates Godspeed in their noble cause.

October 15, 1925

TO Julian W. Mack, New York City

Welcome home [from vacation in Europe]! I shall be mighty glad to see you, for there are so few with whom one can take counsel in time of trouble. I must not use quite that word, trouble, seeing that Louise and the whole shooting match, including even me, are very, very happy over nice, little Stephen Wise [first grandchild] who arrived on the eve of the Atonement Day, and although a Stephen Wise, he really is a very attractive, intelligent, thoughtful little fellow. I am sure that Lady Jess will love him when she goes to see him and his parents. He is now three weeks old. . . .

. . . There is a very serious situation developing, the assurances coming to us on all sides and principally from [Abba Hillel] Silver who saw David Brown [chairman, committee raising funds to settle Jews on land in Russia], that everything for Palestine will be put off now, perhaps for some years, until after Russia is out of the way. That is exactly what we feared and why we fought.

You know, of course, that poor [Israel] Abrahams died very suddenly, and I had to break the news to [daughter] Phyllis who was here and to send her home the next day. I think you will approve of my setting out to get a fund of about $2000 a year which the Institute will present to Mrs. Abrahams for a term of five years as pension. She has next to nothing and everyone whom I have asked has been perfectly lovely about it. I wrote to J. R. [Julius Rosenwald], but I expect a coldly negative reply from his secretary.

October 15, 1925

to Charles H. Parkhurst, Lake Placid

. . . Yes, I know the little volume *Stranger Than Fiction*. It is written by one of my young friends and students [Lewis Browne].

As for Zionism, concerning which you make inquiry, I am glad to tell you that in the last four years the Jewish population has doubled from 65,000 in 1921 to 130,000 in 1925. I think it safe to say that the population will increase in the next ten years at the rate of 30,000 to 40,000 per year. It is not possible at this moment to say just how large a population Palestine can take care of. That depends upon developments in coming years. If there is to be an urban as well as a rural population, there is no reason at all why Palestine, not counting Trans-Jordania, should not come to have a population running into two or three million within twenty to forty years. . . .

December 21, 1925

TO Richard W. Montague, Portland, Oregon

... I am going to be in for a hell of a time because the New York *World* in scare headlines says today that I urged the Jews to accept Christianity. I never said such a thing at all. What I did say was—well, you know all the things I did say and ought to say and don't say.

The sermon on "Jesus, the Jew," preached in Carnegie Hall the Sunday before Christmas, focused on the newly published book JESUS OF NAZARETH, *by Joseph Klausner of the Hebrew University in Jerusalem.*

In the New York TIMES *of December 21, 1925, Stephen Wise was quoted as having said, "For years I have been led to believe, like thousands of other Jews, that Jesus never existed. 'Jesus was a myth' is the common belief among many Jews. I say this is not so. Jesus was."*

The address had four points: (1) Jesus was man, not God; (2) Jesus was a Jew, not a Christian; (3) Jews have not repudiated Jesus; and (4) Christians have, for the most part, not adopted and followed Jesus, the Jew. As Wise had said many times for more than 30 years and as many other rabbis had often stated, Jews were urged to accept Jesus as an outstanding prophetic contribution to the ages, a great moral and ethical leader, a Jew of whom they might be proud because of his teachings. The Union of Orthodox Rabbis demanded Wise's resignation as national chairman of the United Palestine Appeal, a demand in which the Mizrachi, the Orthodox Zionist group, joined. In order not to jeopardize the Appeal, Wise tendered his resignation. In the first week of the new year the executive committee of the United Palestine Appeal met and overwhelmingly rejected Wise's resignation.

December 30, 1925

TO Isaac Landman

Many thanks for your note. I am not surprised to learn that you mean to stand with both feet at my side. You know how woefully one can be misunderstood. I tell you, and this is the first time that I have made mention of this to an editor or a publisher, I did not give out one word of the address to the press. It was late Sunday night, while I was in the midst of a conference with [Louis] Marshall, [Julian] Mack and the Roumanian Ambassador, that I was apprised by the [N.Y.] *World* that they would publish excerpts of the morning address which they had evidently gotten. They insisted upon publication, though I begged them not to do so. It is interesting to find that one does not have to be great to be misunderstood. All one needs is to be exposed to the daily press.

But, in all that has happened in the last ten days, I have no complaint to make against the Orthodox rabbis who, I really think, have for the most part erred in darkness. My pity, which almost rises to contempt, goes out to those pseudo-liberals who will not stand by their own guns, but will strike at a man whom they do not like, though he march under their banner and do their work. You know whom I mean and I am sure you agree with me. For the most part, the liberal rabbis have stood out splendidly.

December 31, 1925

TO Edmund Waterman

I am deeply touched by your word. As you may well imagine, I have had hundreds of communications from men and women throughout the country. Jews and Christians alike, the vast majority of whom are in sympathy with my viewpoint as expressed in my recent address. You so clearly understand the problem. You write with such fine penetration into the heart of the question that I need not make clear to you that what I said was gravely misunderstood and cruelly misrepresented. I feel deeply that I must show to Jews, particularly young Jews in America, that Jesus is not alien to us, that his faith and life are a part of the Jewish possessions and of the very fiber of our Jewish heritage. I do this not that they may go over to Christianity, but that they may remain loyal to Judaism. I would sooner cut off my hand than weaken the loyalty of any Jew to

the heritage of his faith and life. But I face the facts that owing
to the misunderstanding of the centuries, Christians deny Jesus
in fact and Jews deny him in name. I want to do what one man
can do to end that. Evidently you understood me and I am truly
grateful.

    . . . I cannot close without saying that I feel just as deeply as
you do about the sad, wretched conduct of this group of Orthodox rabbis. Surely, they cannot know what they are doing. Alas,
that Christianity had made everything associated with Jesus hate-
ful to the Jew. It will be a long, slow, painful process of education and Christians must help.

January 8, 1926

TO Richard W. Montague, Portland, Oregon

    The whole thing is over now. It was a sad, sad exhibit, and I
am sorry that I must confess to you, in the confidence of friendship, that there was some quasi-ecclesiastical politics that lay back
of the whole thing. The Orthodox, of course, don't like me, and
they have been trying to get me for twenty years. I never quite
gave them a good enough chance to decapitate me, but when I
seemed to have said that Jews must accept Jesus and embrace
Christianity, they felt my day had come. The fact is, I need
hardly point out to you, that I said nothing of the kind, that
basing my thought on the Klausner book, which you ought to
see, I urged that Jesus was a man not myth, human not God,
Jew not Christian, which, of course, is entirely commonplace,
save from the view point of the Agudath Harabbonim [Union of
Orthodox Rabbis of the United States and Canada]. Unfortunately, the newspaper accounts were twisted. The blessed
rabbis knew they were twisted and that I could not have said
the things attributed to me, and so they began their campaign
of abuse and vilification. I have never said a word against them,
not because I did not lose my temper, nor because I am fore-
bearing, which I "ain't," but because I did not want to add to
the disgrace of the whole exhibit. The vindication was really
quite splendid. . . .

January 29, 1926

TO Robert Moton, Tuskegee, Alabama

I cannot tell you how deeply I regret that I am again under the necessity of declining your very kind invitation to deliver the Founders' Day address at Tuskegee Institute, Sunday, April 11. Few things could give me greater pleasure than to see Tuskegee and to offer the tribute of my reverence to the memory of the founder of Tuskegee [Booker T. Washington], who was my dear friend. My inability to come to you arises out of the circumstance that I have been in uncertain health in the last months, and my physicians have made me promise that I am not to accept any new burdens for the coming year. This is a real disappointment to me. Perhaps, if you wish me to come, I can do so another year. I know I would like to do so, to see Tuskegee and you again.

March 10, 1926

TO Bertha Paret, American Legation, Riga, Latvia

. . . A few weeks ago the [textile] strike began in Passaic [N.J.]. As soon as it did Justine went over and spent a day investigating by the side, and under the protection, at my instance, of a glorious young Englishman, Basil Henriques, visiting us from London. Mrs. Wise also went over and organized a relief committee, and I think she has had several thousand dollars for the strikers by this time.

The day Justine went over, she met with the strikers and marched with them and Henriques told me, "Justine made such a speech to the strikers that you can retire, Rabbi." The New York papers were full of it and some of the picture [tabloid] papers, which I tried to send you, were very amusing. They pictured Justine as a most incendiary person with uplifted fist, smashing away in true Stephenesque fashion.

Justine has really been advisor-in-chief to me and I have done little more than closely to follow her counsel. She is a pretty wise child.

The first thing I tried to do, working at it for a week with

[Samuel] Gompers' successor [William Green] and [Thomas] MacMahon and the rest of that dreary and archaic crowd, was to drag the U.T.W. [United Textile Workers] into the strike and make them take over the burden of it, and, incidentally, remove the curse of communism which is charged against [Albert] Weisbord, a brilliant young New York Jew, Harvard Law School graduate (of Russian parentage, I presume), who performed the miraculous feat of getting out eight thousand strikers; and this is the seventh week.

I failed utterly with the U.T.W. They are hopelessly unseeing. They sit as tight and hopeless as a medieval guild.

Now I have tried to do something else. I have organized a committee including [John Lovejoy] Elliot, of the Ethical Culture Society, [Paul] Kellogg of the *Survey*, and Dr. [John Howard] Melish, rector of [Grace and Holy] Trinity [Episcopal] Church in Brooklyn. I had a bishop hooked, the Bishop of New Jersey, who escaped in time to save himself, if not Christendom. I could not help saying about him to some of his fellow-Christians, "Crucifixion is a most admirable thing, not to say holy, when suffered by a Jew, but the vicars of Christ don't particularly relish it for themselves."

But I am not going to burden you with all the details of it. I simply thought you would wish to know from me just what a wonderful part Justine has had in the strike, and how happy you will be to think that her possibility of service grew out of your life together in Passaic [where she and Rabbi Wise's daughter had worked in the textile mills the preceding year].

April 3, 1926

TO Mrs. J. N. Benson, Passaic, N.J.

I confess that I am a little disappointed in your letter, because I had taken it for granted, in the light of what Mrs. Norris said, that you would have a truer understanding of the situation in Passaic. I am quite aware that the woolen mills have had a poor season. Poor seasons come from time to time even to the most lucrative of industries, and surely the textile industry in Passaic had years of enormous and incredible profits.

With two matters that you discuss in your letter I must briefly deal. You make mention of outside agitators. It is shame enough to the mill owners of Passaic that it became necessary for outsiders to come to Passaic in order to organize the workers—the elementary right of organization having been denied to them for decades. Whencesoever the organizer of the strike may come and whatsoever his political views, he has done a fine thing in helping the men and women workers of Passaic to insist upon their elementary right, as Americans, to organize themselves in the face of the enormous and powerful organization of capital as represented in the Wool Council.

As for conditions in Passaic, I wonder whether you have been in the homes of the workers as I have. I wonder whether you understand how underpaid the workers have been. I wonder whether you know much about night work for women in New Jersey, which is continued by reason of the avarice and ruthlessness of those manufacturers who insist that women shall work at night. I wonder whether you know that it is necessary for two and three people in the family to earn a subsistence wage on the basis of the standards prescribed by our government.

I cannot for myself see the force of your reference to outsiders. No American is an outsider anywhere in America, and the manufacturers have made it necessary for outsiders to come to the relief of the workers, whom they have long and deeply wronged.

April 6, 1926

TO Richard Gottheil

For many years we have been looking with abhorrence upon the attitude of the Hebrew Union College toward Zionism and Zionists. Something more substantial than rumor hath it that no man could win a worthwhile prize . . . who is a professing Zionist, that the teachers who were Zionists were frowned upon, that no man was invited to the College to speak if his Zionistic views were well established. That intolerant attitude, as you know, is utterly unworthy of Jews.

The [Jewish] Institute [of Religion] was founded in some part, in order that there might be a place where every viewpoint in

Jewish life could secure a hearing. Is not this circumstance to be borne in mind? As Acting President of the Jewish Institute of Religion, I am a Zionist and, I suppose, in some sense, one of the heads of the movement. Ought I permit my Zionism, however much it means to me, to prevent me from inviting to the Institute the foremost living Jewish liberal [Claude G. Montefiore], because he happens to be a non-Zionist? If I fail so to invite him, then I deny my men an inspiration which may come to them from this man, who happens to be Montefiore, just because his views touching Zionism do not tally with my own. I cannot help feeling that it would be rather a fine exhibition of the larger tolerance for which the Institute stands, if we were to insist that a great Jew shall be heard whatever his views on Zionism may be.

April 9, 1926

TO Basil L. Q. Henriques, London

. . . I wish we might be at one with respect to Zionism. Some day I hope we shall be, but, in the meantime, our difference with respect to Zionism does not impair by one iota the value of your own message and the significance of your own contribution to Jewish life in our time. I am almost tempted to send you a copy of a letter which I have addressed to a distinguished Jewish gentleman [Professor Richard Gottheil], whom you met, his letter having urged me not to invite [Claude G.] Montefiore to deliver the commencement address, lest, like you, he attack Zionism. I made clear to him that one of the reasons that moved me to found the Institute was that I felt there ought to be one place where every Jewish viewpoint should be tolerated and even sympathetically heard. . . .

April 16, 1926

TO John Haynes Holmes

. . . The German Jews [in America] are stupid enough to think that, if it had not been for the coming of the latest immigrants, namely, the East European Jews, in the last thirty years, their own foreignism would go unnoticed and unchallenged, that they would have been able to get away with it as Simon Pure native Americans. They somehow felt that they were not the fellow-Jews of these more obviously Jewish aliens. We Jews have infinitely much to learn in the way of tolerance to one another, and until that time, I wonder whether we have the right to count upon the understanding of the world, which sees a minimum of difference between Jew and Jew and lumps us all together with very much more justice than we Jews separate ourselves from one another. I may say to you, and this letter, I presume, is not for publication, until long after both of us shall be dead, the finest Jews in the world are the Russian Jews. There is a savor of culture in the Portuguese Jew, such as [Benjamin] Cardozo. There are some fine outstanding Central European Jews, such as [Louis D.] Brandeis, [Julian] Mack, [Felix] Frankfurter and, of course, myself. But, after all, the distinguishing trait of the Jew, which is the capacity for sacrificial effort, is to be found chiefly in the Russian Jew. . .

April 16, 1926

TO William E. Borah, Washington

May I supplement my telegram of this morning by saying to you how glad I am to know that you are offering to intervene again in the matter of the Passaic strike? I had hoped that you would come to the rescue, for there are fundamental things involved. If the New Jersey police and sheriffs and courts are to be permitted to smash the strikers, because the strike is inconvenient or unprofitable, what becomes of law and our liberties? If the figure in the White House [Calvin Coolidge] did not rest on the pedestal of a broken strike [Boston police strike, 1919], I would appeal to him to speak out somehow, in any event, to listen to those who could tell him about the travesty upon justice which is being enacted from time to time in Passaic.

I beg to enclose a letter which came to me this day. As you

will see, it is a copy of a letter addressed to Governor Moore
of New Jersey by A[rthur] G[arfield] Hays of the [American]
Civil Liberties Union. Governor Moore told me in person that
as soon as the strike began, he was asked to send the state
police in, but refused—that was ten weeks ago. "I did not
want the state police to be used as strike breakers."

If you have followed things, as I am sure you have, you
must indeed know what precious things are at stake and that
the country will never forget a man in such high public office,
reinforced by his reputation for fearlessness and the respect
which goes out to him as a great jurist, who will have the
courage to speak up and make America listen, touching this
thing of awful moment.

April 16, 1926

To William A. Green, Washington

You remember, of course, that I came to you six weeks ago
and begged you to intervene in the matter of the Passaic
strike. At that time you turned me over to the United Textile
Workers in the hope that they would see their way to taking
over the leadership. It was not done. Personally I believe that
MacMahon and his associates made a very grave mistake.

It may even be too late to take over the leadership of the
strike. But surely you realize that the situation has become
critical and something must be done. Whatever is done in New
Jersey to these strikers will be attempted again to other workers
tomorrow under the aegis of the American Federation of Labor.
The police are being used to beat down and smash a strike,
although no violence whatever has been attempted by the
strikers. Can you not, will you not, as I believe you should,
speak out to the end that the American people may know that
your sympathies are with the strikers, whatever the political
views of their temporary leader? Disorder and lawlessness are
those of the state, not of the strikers. I believe that yours is
the opportunity, and that upon you lies the very solemn obligation as the titular and actual head of the largest group of

workers in America, to lift up your voice in solemn protest
against the intolerable abrogation of civil liberties, which is
being enacted from hour to hour in Passaic.

                                                    April 23, 1926

TO Basil L. Q. Henriques, London

   . . . Don't worry about the *Jewish Tribune*. It did not bother
me in the least [because of its editorial, criticizing Henriques'
anti-Zionist statements]. I would have replied to them to say
that there had not been a scintilla of violation of hospitality on
your part, of which you, as a gentleman, are quite incapable,
but I thought that it would dignify the thing too much if I
made reply to the editorial, which was meant to please my
enemies rather than to comfort me. I cannot even regret that you
said what you did about Zionism, even though some of my
Zionist friends have been unhappy about it and suspect me of
beng almost disloyal, because I had so vigorous an anti-Zionist
as a guest of the Synagogue and the Institute. But I am not
disturbed about that in the least. The important thing is that
there be utter freedom. I would be just as intolerant as some
of you, blessed intolerant anti-Zionists, if I did not welcome to
the Institute and to the Synagogue a message of beauty and
nobility, such as your own, just because you happened not to
agree with me with respect to Zionism. I am intolerant of intolerance and the way to meet intolerance is to be utterly tolerant
of those from whom one differs. I know that you are deeply in
earnest and utterly sincere in your opposition to Zionism. I also
believe that you are mistaken. I believe that you know me to be
equally sincere in my devotion to Zionism. You believe me to
be mistaken, and there you are; and all of that does not change
the fact that you brought something of the beauty of your service,
which means very, very much. And, someday, you will come
again, but when you do come, we will plan a circuit of the
country that you may be heard in many, many congregations. . . .
   In one matter with respect to Orthodoxy, I think we differ.
You have not quite seen or felt Orthodoxy at its highest. I have

seen something of it and I know more of it. Don't confound
Orthodoxy with the United Synagogue or with Joe Hertz [Chief
Rabbi Joseph Hertz of London] or with some poor creatures of
the East End of London who have lost the high grace of it. It
was beautiful. It may be beautiful. After all, the holiness and
even godliness of Jewish life have come out of it through the
centuries. I have yet to see Liberal Judaism do quite the same
thing, to help men and women to achieve the same things in
the realm of the spirit.

Mrs. Wise is pretty well. Justine is working very hard and
doing very well at Yale. . . .

The [Passaic] strike goes on [Henriques had been on the picket
line during his visit to America]. I must enclose a copy of an
address that I made before the strikers, who have been treated
dreadfully, sheriffs reading riot acts and then brutally dispersing
mobs, and now finally the injunction against the strikers, which
are not only mediaeval in their harshness but even archaic. And
so last Sunday night in a Russian Catholic church I met with the
strikers, fine patient, pacific creatures that they are. The thing
that most rejoiced my heart was their response when I spoke of
them as the friends of our dear daughter and hundreds of them
shouted her name [Justine had taken an active part in the
strike]. . . .

April 30, 1926

TO Jacob Billikopf, Philadelphia

Do let me tell you how much I appreciate the spirit of
your communication of April 28 [concerning James Waterman
Wise's decision not to be ordained to the rabbinate]. There is
much to be said, and I am sad at heart; but whatever my feeling
with respect to the loss to the ministry, I cannot help respecting
the boy's sincerity which, after all, is supremely important in a
man who thinks of the ministry.

May 8, 1926

TO John Haynes Holmes

. . . The situation in Passaic looks just a little more encouraging and I am to be in conference with the U.T.W. in the hope that something may yet be done. The whole strike could have been won at the very outset, if these people had followed my counsel and taken over the leadership of the strike. I wonder if you have ever come into close touch with Sidney Hillman and have found out for yourself how wise and statesmanlike a leader he is. I don't know of another quite his equal in American life today. . . .

May 10, 1926

TO Arthur Nash, Cincinnati

I want you to know how enormously I like your address on "Organized Church and Organized Labor." It is great in its simplicity, and I cannot help feeling that it is quite unanswerable. . . .

There is not much to report with regard to the [Passaic textile] strike, excepting that the mill owners absolutely refuse to enter into any manner of negotiation with the workers, even though [Albert] Weisbord [accused of being a Communist] has really eliminated himself. I am still trying to get the United Textile Workers to come into the situation, in which matter I am guided by your wise friend, [Sidney] Hillman. But I am afraid that nothing can be hoped for in that direction. I almost begin to wonder—I have not said it as yet to Hillman—whether the time is not ripe for the Amalgamated [Clothing Workers of America], under Hillman, who is far and above the most statesmanlike of the labor leaders, to go into the textile field and do there what he has done in the clothing industry.

June 29, 1926

TO Jacob Billikopf, Philadelphia

. . . We are off tomorrow. The doctors thought that my only real chance for a rest would be if I went abroad. There won't be very much rest in July, for there are to be five or six meetings, including the Liberal Religious Union, the Zionist Executive, the Hebrew University Board (which I hope to see meet with [Judah] Magnes), the Committee of Jewish Delegations, etc. But I must take a cure in August at Gastheim [a European spa] or somewhere.

I am very glad that you and [Julius] Fohs, of whom I know, are going to Russia. It is well that you should. The whole business of the past year [to promote Jewish colonization in the Crimea] has been a tragedy in the way of misunderstanding. It could have been averted if only [David] Brown had been wise and understanding, as he was not. He does not know and other people do not know what Palestine has come to mean, and that we dread, and will, of course, do battle against, anything which threatens its place in the program of the Jewish future. . . .

London, August 5, 1926

TO Richard Gottheil, Bad Wildungen

. . . You would have been distressed at the service today for [Israel] Zangwill. It was an utterly sorrowful occasion, very little mourning and very much rather vulgar curiosity-seeking. Mrs. Zangwill asked me to have part of the service and I paid such tribute as I could, there being no other address. It seems strange to have Zangwill gone. With all his faults he was a great person. And English Jewry so utterly unappreciative of him. . . .

Aboard the S.S. *President Roosevelt*
En Route to the U.S.A.
August, 1926

TO Claude G. Montefiore, London

Dear Montefiore, you are right. Zionism is not Judaism. But, I add, neither is anti-Zionism the equivalent of Judaism. It [anti-

Zionism] is not for you, but it is for not a few of those whose so-called "Liberal Judaism" is at one with yours only in that they are anti-Zionists. Frankly, I was loth to see a largely rationalist, anti-Zionist melange, calling itself "Reform Judaism," appropriating your name and annexing your influence [at a meeting of the International Liberal Jewish Conference in London].

I am a Liberal Jew, but have come to feel that I have little in common with a group which perpetuates the name of Reform Judaism, but after all is little more than a survival of mid-nineteenth century Reform, rationalist rather than religious—and rationalism and theology and its institutions are not incompatibles—without a breath of the spirit of the social passion, save for involuntary and largely imitative spasms, and, as it seems to me, chiefly a negative of that which is, and for nearly nineteen hundred years has been, the very breath of life to Israel. I cannot say it again, but the truth is that you and the American sponsors of the international Liberal Jewish movements are at one only, in any event, chiefly, in your and their anti-Zionism. But you have not substituted this for religion. If Judaism is not non-Christianity, neither is it anti-Zionism. Your anti-Zionism is for you an inevitable by-product of an *Anschauung* which is real, though, I believe, mistaken.

You do not think that great things, religiously, will come out of Jerusalem. I believe they will again come out of Jerusalem. You distrust Orthodoxy and you doubt the young upbuilding generation in Palestine. I must revert to an old thought which is not mine—what if that had been believed about the Babylonian resettlers of Palestine? What incalculable loss to humanity!

. . . I have regretted your failure to see the other, the nobler, side of Zionism and to share my hope that, in Palestine, Judaism might be liberalized and a new position taken with regard to the greatest of Jews [Jesus of Nazareth]. . . .

September 15, 1926

TO Alfred E. Smith, Executive Mansion, Albany

I had thought of writing to you ever since my return from Europe, but I put it off because I learned that you were ill. Now that you are better and getting back to work, I feel that I ought to take up with you frankly and fully a matter to which I have given a great deal of thought.

I know very well that you are considering the problem, because I know that you feel quite as I do about the extraordinary distinction of Judge [Benjamin N.] Cardozo. I need not say to you that I am not interested in Judge Cardozo because he is a Jew. He is one of the most eminent jurists in America. He is not only a great lawyer but a great person. If the President [Calvin Coolidge] had been half-wise, he would have named him in place of [Harlan Fiske] Stone for the Supreme Court, which his presence would have enriched. I know of no man in public life about whom there is such unanimity alike with respect to his attainment and his character. The feeling throughout the country among members of the Bar is that he is, outside of one or two members of the United States Supreme Court, the outstanding judge in American life.

And now the opportunity is come to promote him to the Chief Justiceship of the Court of Appeals. Do you realize that it would be a distinction to the Court to be presided over by him, that it is rendering a service to New York State to help place him there? I do not even bring up the question of his being on the ticket which I trust you will lead, but I assure you that many of your faithful friends, including myself, would be deeply disappointed and even grieved, if for any reason he should not appear as the candidate for the office of Chief Justice.

I know there are difficulties in the way and I know what they are. I know that the Democratic party does not wish to give up a judgeship for the sake of promoting Judge Cardozo, and I daresay that the Republican party will persist in its unreasonable demands. I also know that these considerations are of minor importance. Here is this very great man and judge, and the office of Chief Justice to be filled. No minor considerations must stand in the way of his nomination and election. After all, you are the leader of your party in this state, and yours is the responsibility. You are not being asked to "do something for somebody." You are being asked, as you ought to be asked by all your friends who seek your highest interests, to insist, as the head of the

Democratic party, that the State of New York shall enjoy the distinction of having one of the greatest of American jurists at the head of its chief court. I cannot bring myself to believe that you will make yourself responsible for any other course.

If you are to be in New York within the next few days, I should be very glad to see you.

January 10, 1927

TO Abraham Epstein, Harrisburg, Pa.

Your letter of some days ago is before me and I hasten to say that I am entirely ready to serve on the committee of the National Old Age Pension League. I would like you to add the name of my wife, Louise Waterman Wise, who is chairman of the Free Synagogue Child Adoption Committee and who is deeply interested in the work. Some time when you are in New York, I would like to talk the thing over with you. Perhaps we could have a meeting of the committee some time in the next weeks.

January 20, 1927

TO Justine Waterman Wise

Two things I must send you—Jim's letter that came this morning, and also a letter from [Richard Ward] Montague, which is so delightful that I want you to see it. . . . I suppose he is really the wisest and sanest friend I have.

I have some great news—not as great and good as it might be, but still significant. Norman Thomas just telephoned that [Thomas] MacMahon said to him yesterday at the meeting, which I could not attend, that he has the agreement with the F. & H. [Forstmann and Huffman] people in his pocket. The agreement does not install the union, but it authorizes the workers to return and to be free to organize a union. That might mean a great deal, Norman thinks, if the A.F. of L. [American Federation of Labor] were victoriously vital, rather than mournfully defeatist—the phrase, of course, is mine, not Norman's.

Norman hopes they will make a settlement, because they cannot possibly hold out any longer, the flow of relief having ceased, unless the A.F. of L. meeting now in Florida sends on $25,000 to $50,000, which it won't do. . . .

March 7, 1927

TO Charles H. Parkhurst, Lake Placid Club

. . . I wish I might run in and see you at Lake Placid, but, of course, as you know, the Club is not for me and mine.

I am glad you feel about Spinoza as you do [in response to Wise's tribute on 250th anniversary of Spinoza's death]. I have always thought that Novalis' tribute to him was most just and perfect—he was a God-intoxicated man. The more I read Spinoza, the loftier I come to feel is his genius. Yes, it was a thousand pities that his fellow-Jews drove him out, but, after all, he merely met the fate which is reserved for the heretics in all ages—and his persecutors had the added excuse of being fearful lest their new-found security be injured, if one among them came to be known as a heretic. . . .

March 16, 1928

TO Belle Moskowitz

Last Sunday I spoke on the theme, "The Religion of the President and the American Spirit." The address will probably be published in the near future. A great many letters have come to me, chiefly in criticism of my word that the inarticulate boycott against a non-Protestant as president must cease, and with it government by unwritten law, which is subversive to the Constitution of the United States. Of the letters that came to me, I send you two. I think the Governor would be amused by that from a lady with a name that leads one to suspect that she may have been born in the same land as the Governor's parents. The other letter is serious, and is being dealt with by me in a serious manner.

May 13, 1927

TO His Excellency, The Governor, State House, Boston

May I communicate to you the substance of a resolution adopted at the annual meeting of the Free Synagogue, which resolution was adopted upon the unanimous recommendation of the Executive Council of the Synagogue in pursuance of an address which I gave before my people upon a recent Sunday?

It is earnestly asked of you to institute a review of the case of Sacco and Vanzetti. We do not presume to ask you to do anything which may lie outside the jurisdiction of your office or the powers allotted to you under the constitution of your Commonwealth. We earnestly beg of you that you will institute such a review of the case as shall, whatever the outcome of that review may be, give assurance to the American people that there has been a full and unprejudiced examination of all the facts in the Sacco-Vanzetti case. . . .

June 2, 1927

TO Louis Bamberger, South Orange, N.J.

I presume you know of the plans looking to the Thomas Mott Osborne Memorial, some literature concerning which I herewith send you. The purpose is to memorialize the high achievements of Osborne in the field of human regeneration [prison reform and advocacy of self-government for inmates of penitentiaries]. A limited number of people who are interested in the causes which Osborne greatly served are being appealed to in behalf of this memorial. May I very earnestly ask that you be good enough to make a contribution that shall be expressive of your own personal appreciation of the great life ministry of Thomas Mott Osborne?

June 2, 1927

TO Richard W. Montague, Portland, Oregon

. . . I wish you could have been with us at the Synagogue dinner [20th anniversary of the founding of the Free Synagogue]. It was

a fine occasion, the big thing of the evening being the poem by
[John Haynes] Holmes, which, as I said, was a bit of self-portrai-
ture, rather than a characterization of me; a noble address by
Sir Wyndham Deedes, one of the few Christians I know, in
addition to you, worthy of the name; and finally a beautiful
word by Judge [Benjamin] Cardozo. By the way, I never told you
—some day I want to—the whole story. When I came home from
Europe in September, things were absolutely closed against
Cardozo; and [Governor Alfred E.] Smith, curiously enough, had
surrendered to the demand of [James] Wadsworth, his close
friend, that [Cuthbert W.] Pound, who was Cardozo's junior on
the [Court of Appeals] Bench, be named Chief Justice of the
Court of Appeals. I made a fiery written protest to Smith; and
then we had four hours together during which I hammered and
hammered and hammered, inspired, if I may say so, by what
I know was the rightness of my case, until Smith finally suc-
cumbed and named Cardozo. I don't know how you feel about
him, but most lawyers tell me he is one of the three or four
great jurists of America, that list including [Oliver Wendell]
Holmes, [Louis D.] Brandeis, Dean [Roscoe] Pound and
Cardozo. . . .

                                                June 20, 1927

TO Nathan Straus, Jr.

Now that the tumult and the shouting have died down, may
I discuss with you for a moment the matter to which I made a
brief allusion over the telephone a few days ago? I cannot help
saying to you that I feel, in connection with the [Charles A.]
Lindbergh affairs [to honor Lindbergh on his return to the
U.S.A. after successful solo flight to Europe], there has been an
almost obvious slighting of the vast and, I may say, significant
Jewish element of the population of New York. I single out two
typical functions, the [Clarence] Mackay dinner and the dinner
at the Biltmore Hotel, at which the Cardinal [Patrick Joseph
Hayes] and the Bishop [William T. Manning] were invited to

speak. It is true that there are perhaps ten times as many Jews as there are members of the Bishop's Church in New York, but it may be that Bishop Manning was chosen as the representative of Protestant Christians. One quarter of the population of New York City is Jewish. It would seem to me most fitting that some Jew—I care not who—should have been asked to speak, as were the Cardinal, or his representative, and the Bishop.

Again, there was the social function at Mr. Mackay's home. It cannot be said that this was a private function. All functions, which were bound up, particularly during the first days, with Lindbergh's visit, were more or less public and representative in character. As far as I know, only one Jew was present at the Mackay dinner, one of the many rich newspaper cronies of the Mayor. I think it is not too much to say that there are as many as half a dozen eminent Jews in New York, such as your father, one of the best loved and most honored citizens of America, Chief Justice [Benjamin] Cardozo, Colonel [Herbert] Lehman, former Ambassador [Abram] Elkus, former Ambassador [Henry] Morgenthau, Mr. Mortimer Schiff, Mr. Bernard Baruch, and I think I might make the list a little larger. Anyone of whom they chose to entertain would have been an honor to Mr. Mackay. There is a great deal to be said about the curious way in which those affairs have been arranged, and I believe that the manner of entertainment is a "hang over" from the [Mayor John] Hylan regime.

I did not wish to inject an unpleasant note into the situation. Otherwise, I would have made a public and, I believe, significant protest. If ever there should be a repetition of what I cannot help feeling was the studied slighting of the great Jewish population of New York in all affairs bound up with Lindbergh, I would make public protest, and such protest would do no more than voice the feeling of many, many Jews in New York, who feel exactly as I do. I forebore this time, not only because the general occasion was one of such jubilation that it should not have been marred by any complaint or protest, but also because I did not wish to hurt certain people, whom, however, I would not again find myself under the necessity of undertaking to spare.

January 13, 1928

TO Joel B. Hayden, Cleveland, Ohio

... I am not sure that I congratulate you upon the privilege of debating on February 11 [on the subject of "Companionate Marriage"] with my dear friend Ben[jamin Barr Lindsey].

Have you read the book [*The Companionate Marriage*] carefully? I have read it twice and so I know it pretty well. The thing that impresses me, or that depresses me most, is that there is no relation between the premises and the conclusion. The premises are that there should be birth control, which everyone outside of Rome grants, and that there should be fairly easy and uniform divorce, which likewise every person ought to grant. But what has that to do with the conclusion that he draws, namely that there be companionate marriage—companionate marriage meaning that two young people may live together in some sort of marriage; there is no economic liability upon either of them; they may part with a minimum of formality; all this provided that there be no child? As it seems to me, and I would like to have your judgment on it, he says to young people: "You may go through the form of marriage, and provided you have no child, you need not be fearful of the consequences." It invites temporariness; instead of making (as I ventured to put it in an address some weeks ago) the coming of a child the glory of marriage, it makes child-bearing a great terror to be avoided, and in the absence of which there comes a freedom to part whenever they choose to avail themselves of such freedom.

I confess I cannot see anything in it. I wish I could. I cannot see that it helps any situation whatever, and of course you do know that dear Ben deals practically altogether with the subnormal and the abnormal, and his deductions are from that type of life—the young people who come into his court.

What companionate marriage would really do would be to give a sort of legal sanction to temporary unions. Instead, you and I believe in the sanctity of the permanent marriage relation. Lindsey, with the best intention in the world, is willing to substitute or, to put it more fairly, to try the expedient of legal sanction for any relationship between men and women, however temporary. . . .

January 16, 1928

TO Mrs. Walter Rauschenbusch, Rochester, N.Y.

I cannot tell you how deeply I appreciate the receipt of this gift. It is a precious gift, because it comes out of the heart and in memory of Professor Rauschenbusch, one of the great spirits of our day. I have always felt, and I dare say you know I have said it from time to time, that he was one of the real prophets of the religious social awakening of our time. He was a beautiful spirit and I wish I might have seen very much more of him in recent years.

It may interest you to know—perhaps you do know—that often indeed I read *The Prayers of the Social Awakening*. I wish he might have augmented that collection. The spirit of the man is in these prayers. It is that which makes them so precious.

January 25, 1928

TO The Editors of *Unity*, Chicago

I learn with real satisfaction that on March 1, *Unity* will celebrate its 50th anniversary. I have been a reader of *Unity* for about two-thirds of that period. To me *Unity* is and always has been precious because of its editorship. Its first and long-time editor was my beloved friend, Jenkin Lloyd Jones, one of the prophets, if prophets there still be, of liberalism and unity in religious life in America. I cannot refrain from mentioning here that upon my invitation, Jenkin Lloyd Jones came to Portland, Oregon, during the period of my rabbinate there. He was one of the speakers at the Lewis and Clark celebration. No one came to us in Oregon who brought us a more vital, stimulating message. He seemed the very incarnation of the spirit of the unafraid in quest of truth. The liberals of our day know not how much they are indebted to Jenkin Lloyd Jones and *Unity*, the organ through which he communicated himself to the mind of America.

I shall say nothing about Jenkin Lloyd Jones' successor in the editorship of *Unity*. I love and honor him too much to speak of him with moderation. He is a true preacher of religion. He is a mighty prophet of righteousness and he is one of the most effective social forces of our generation. I often place the editor of *Unity*, John Haynes Holmes, by the side of Theodore Parker. It is no little thing to say of *Unity*'s present editor that he is equal to the traditions of Theodore Parker in his pulpit, and of Jenkin Lloyd Jones in the editorial columns of *Unity*.

March 2, 1928

TO James Weldon Johnson

. . . I never before had heard your and your brother's [J. Rosamond Johnson] anthem: "Lift Ev'ry Voice and Sing." I have never been more touched by a song. I presume that you wrote the text. It is a noble text. I cannot think at this moment of any national anthem that I like as well. There is a strong Old Testament turn to it. It is sturdy and bracing, and what a national anthem should be—a collective prayer; and the music is magnificent. I imagine, without knowing, that it derives from the treasury of the "spirituals." . . .

April 6, 1928

TO Mordecai Kaplan

I have just gotten the April 4 issue of the *S.A.J.* [Society for the Advancement of Judaism] *Review*, and I want to tell you how glad I am to note the first two editorials. I thank God that some one has the courage to speak out in the terms of decency about [Julius] Rosenwald's contribution [to colonization of Jews in the Crimea], which, despite all that may be said of it with respect to bigness, etc., is an affront to the Jewish people. It is a continuance of the attitude against which I protested in all earnestness, in Philadelphia, September 1925, namely the attitude of deciding for world Jewry by the power of one's money what ought to be done. The Rosenwald contribution, though Rosenwald personally is not of the Jewish Agency, is proof to me of the utter breakdown of the Jewish nation. Millions, including a very large sum from Warburg, are poured into Russia; Palestine gets investigations.

The second editorial, "Needed, a Sense of Self-Respect," is truer than you know. . . .

June 29, 1928

TO Belle Moskowitz

Next to my great rejoicing in Al[fred E. Smith] and our country [because of nomination by the Democratic party as candidate in November presidential election], I rejoice in the great triumph that has come to you. I know what you have been and have done for the cause—high wisdom and perfect self-effacement.

I am ready to help. But I want to talk things over with you and H.I.M. [Henry I. Moskowitz], so that certain things may be made clear. I have some suggestions to offer about the speech of acceptance which is going to be the platform. Like you, and Henry, I want the Governor to speak out in such a way at the notification ceremonies, as shall do most to make victory sure. We agree that "smart aleckness" will not help; and, happily, the Governor is in little danger of succumbing to the counsel of them that would substitute the expediency of cleverness for the reality of wisdom that is in him.

I have wired to the Governor; but if you *should* see him, tell him how happy I am to think that I was among the earliest of his non-political friends to believe in him, to hope for him, and to support him. . . .

July 11, 1928

TO Nahum Goldmann, Berlin-Charlottenburg

I had definitely resolved to attend the Zionist Actions Committee meeting [in Berlin], until the Pittsburgh Convention. The
Convention, its methods and its outcome alike, have made me
feel that I ought not go. . . . The Convention resolved itself into
nothing more than a battle between the Administration and the
so-called Opposition. . . . No problem in relation to Palestine was
ever touched—Palestine was barely mentioned throughout the
three days—until the closing hour of the Convention. . . .

. . . There was no discussion of Weizmann or the Weizmann
political policies in the Convention . . . Weizmannism was not
under review at the Convention, which was nothing more than
a vulgar and even scurrilous debate of personalities, out of which,
try as we could, the Convention could not be lifted.

. . . I could not go to Berlin and feel that in any critical
attitude to the [Jewish] Agency [on Palestine] report I had the
support of the organized Zionists of America. These believe they
can shift their burden at last, and that the [Louis] Marshall-
[Felix] Warburg group is ready to take it over. I dissent from
both views—we Zionists ought not to shift our burden, and the
Marshall-Warburg forces are not prepared and will not be prepared to take it over, excepting upon terms which will reduce
Palestine to a Near East counterpart of the Crimean provinces
of the [American Jewish] Joint Distribution Committee. It must
not be forgotten that ten millions in cash are being pledged
with a minimum of difficulty for Crimea, including half a million
from Warburg and a quarter of a million from Marshall. I find
no pledge or guaranty of help in the Agency report [of which
Louis Marshall and Felix Warburg were signators and designated
to be "non-Zionist members"]. There are pleasant and friendly
expressions of good-will, but inconvertible into the kind of help
which Palestine needs, and the forthcoming of which would
alone give a scintilla of excuse for having dragged non-Zionists
into an operation which is in danger of changing, if we permit
it, the character and heart of the Zionist movement.

September 29, 1928

TO J. Shulkin, Massena, N.Y.

I have your letter of September 25 and I have directed the secretary of the [American Jewish] Congress to telegraph to you immediately [as president of Congregation Adath Israel].

I cannot tell you how shocked and pained I am by the story that you write of even the faintest intimations of a rumor of ritual murder. I am writing by this same mail to [Police] Major [John] Warner, whom I know, that I may have a full report of the situation. I hold myself in readiness to see you at any moment. If necessary, some officer of the American Jewish Congress will go to Massena.

This thing must be cleared up and cleared up immediately and fully. The Jewish members of your community and we shall not rest content until there be the most ample and unequivocal apology. It is tragic enough that the term "ritual murder" should be used in European lands of darkness. I do not propose to let this matter rest until there be the fullest explanation on the part of those responsible for the rumor, to the end that apology may be made to the Jewish community which, in a sense, represents American Israel and has the honor of American Israel in its keeping.

September 29, 1928

TO The Mayor, Massena, N.Y.

There has come to me a most shocking story from your community, to the effect that as a result of the temporary loss of a child, a charge was brought against a Jewish resident of your city, with the implication that the child had disappeared as the result of a Jewish "ritual murder."

I am informed that the state trooper who originally made the charge stated that you had been consulted before calling the rabbi of the community to the police headquarters.

I trust that for your sake that story is not true and that you will find it possible to deny it. In any event, I need hardly point out to you what a hideous thing it is that this ancient and unspeakable libel should be resurrected in our country, with all the incalculable damage that it might do as a result of misunderstanding.

Taking it for granted, as I do, that you desire as far as possible to repair the hurt that has been done, I most earnestly suggest to you that you do whatever may be necessary not merely to contradict the base rumor of ritual murder, but point out in addition that no intelligent, decent person has ever given any credence to this charge which has been exposed whenever made, wherever made, and laid to rest time and again by the heads of the Christian Churches.

I should be very glad indeed to have a full statement from you covering the entire affair and also word with respect to the course that you intend to pursue.

September 29, 1928

TO John Warner, Albany, N.Y.

I find it necessary to bring a very painful and even humiliating matter to your attention [as commanding officer of the state police], upon which I must ask that action be taken without a moment's delay.

The enclosure contains a copy of a statement which comes from the president of the Jewish congregation in Massena, New York, telling the story of the disappearance of a child and of the charge made by a member of the state troopers under your command with the implication that Jews used human blood in connection with Holyday Services.

I dare say that you have heard that these hideous and ghastly rumors of "ritual murder" float about in East European lands in order that excuse may be found for wrong done to Jews. I know that you will feel as I do that the fullest amends must be made to the Jewish community of Massena and that nothing less than a most explicit apology will be satisfactory. You will note the statement in Mr. Shulkin's letter: "Now the rumor is being broadcast that after questioning the rabbi the guilty became frightened and gave up the child."

I take it for granted that you will send for the trooper, secure the fullest statement from him in the matter and see to it that such action follow as will make clear to the citizenship of Massena that this awful charge is completely and contritely withdrawn as far as the member of the state troopers is concerned.

October 8, 1928

TO George Gordon Battle

It is very good of you to write me as you do. I meant the first thing this morning to sit down and tell you of the deep appreciation which the American Jewish Congress instructed me to convey to you of the fine and generous service you rendered, not only to Congress, but the Jewish people, in the cause of better understanding between Jew and Christian, by taking so helpful a part at the hearing throughout the day of October 4, at Albany. I have long known you to be the friend of justice and of high causes. You proved it anew by the handsome way in which you identified yourself with our cause and then served it [by helping to secure complete withdrawal and repudiation of the false "ritual murder" charges, as well as an apology from the state trooper].

October 16, 1928

TO John Haynes Holmes

I am afraid I never wrote to thank you for your great address to my people [on issues of forthcoming presidential election]. I heard only five minutes but it was very, very fine. But don't you plume yourself upon being the only one who looks forward to being licked [in support of Norman Thomas]. I am just as sure as you are that my candidate is going to be. But if you knew what is happening in the South, where I was on Sunday, you'd go on the stump for Al [Alfred E. Smith] to stem the tide of hideous religious bigotry that is engulfing the nation. . . .

October 19, 1928

TO Henry I. Moskowitz

. . . Would not Saturday, November 3, at Madison Square
Garden, when I am to speak probably before the next President
appears, be the best time [to address himself to the matter of a
so-called "Jewish vote"]?

I mean to say among other things . . . after appealing to
Americans to vote as Americans, and not as Jews and Catholics
and Protestants, that I shall vote with equal satisfaction for
three men of three different Churches, without regard to the
Churches to which they belong—[Alfred E.] Smith [as president
of the U.S.], [Franklin Delano] Roosevelt [as governor of N.Y.
State] and [Herbert L.] Lehman [as lieutenant-governor], and
then make clear why Jews have no right to vote against a
superior candidate such as Franklin Roosevelt is, because against
him there has been nominated a man [Albert Ottinger] designed
to be a Jewish vote catcher, and not because of any real qualifi-
cation for that post.

I do think, however, that the strongest ground on which to
rest the case against Ottinger is that Ottinger thwarted Smith
as far as he could, and will undo his program. Roosevelt supports Smith, and will carry out the program. No other consideration ought to mean anything.

October 25, 1928

TO Julian W. Mack

Please notice this letter of [Harry Emerson] Fosdick (enclosed)
which appears in Christian papers all over the country, urging
visitors to go to the American Colony [Hostel in Jerusalem]. I
do not trust the American Colony. I don't know what your
experience with them has been. They have the mind and attitude
of [New York *Times* editor John] Finley and [former Ambassador
Henry] Morgenthau [Sr.]—nominally pro-British, in fact bitterly
anti-Zionistic; tremendously strong in their sympathy with
Chalukah Judaism [charitable dole from abroad for Orthodox

Jews in Palestine] but hostile to the nth degree to Chalutzim Jews [pioneering Zionist settlers].

Ought the W.Z.O. [World Zionist Organization] be urged to make its peace with them, with a view to their using Jewish guides, or ought we make a fight on them—Fosdick's letter, for example, to the *Christian Leader,* to be followed by one from me, saying that if people want to have no understanding of "the New Palestine" from the Jewish point of view, they should go to the American Colony, etc., etc.? It would be a savage thing to do, but heaven knows they deserve it. . . .

November 5, 1928

TO Julian W. Mack, San Francisco

Well, we are in for an awful licking [in the presidential election], and worst of all nothing will be settled. The religious issue is on and we have lost ground from every point of view. The only thing to do is for the Liberals to meet on Wednesday morning at breakfast and organize a real Liberal party. I don't believe we can work with and through the Democratic party any longer. It is gone. Its platform was wrong, it has gone back to a protective tariff, it is rotten on immigration, and there ain't no Liberalism in it!

November 7, 1928

TO Richard W. Montague, Portland, Oregon

I hope you are less unhappy than I am this post-election morning. I had no hope for the outcome [electoral college vote: Hoover, 444; Smith, 87], saying constantly that [Governor Alfred E.] Smith would have a maximum of a hundred electoral votes; but the character of the rout saddens me. I cannot help feeling that the debacle is really a thrust by the older Protestant folk of America against us inferior newcomers—Catholics and Jews, Irish, Italians, Russians and all the rest; and I am disheartened. Even at the risk of seeming unsportsmanlike I am going to cry out against the sin of compromise in American politics; and the Democratic party, which I think will be mine no longer, did compromise, with a cheap, rich, wet Republican like [John J.] Raskob at the head of the job and with Al [Smith] conceding everything with respect to the protective tariff, immigration, etc.

I am deep down in the dumps today and I felt that I just must write to you as a friend and brother sufferer. . . .

November 7, 1928

to Alfred E. Smith

You made a brave fight and a great fight. "Not failure but low aim is crime," and your aim was high; and you battled with the valor of a man.

With many more I had a little part in the contest, and I shall always remember with joy and pride that I stood at your side and fought under the banner of your leadership.

With affectionate greeting, and the hope that a happier day for American life may yet dawn. . . .

November 8, 1928

to Julian W. Mack, San Francisco

I suppose you don't feel very much happier than I do about what has taken place. . . . It [the election] is a saddening event, and it will take a long, long time to get people to be understanding and to put aside the matters of property and prejudice in dealing with national issues.

December 14, 1928

to John Haynes Holmes

I may not be able to reach you by telephone, so I must say "good-bye" in this way. Mrs. Wise and I are leaving for Berlin tonight. . . .

... I give you two letters to be sure that you have them when you get to Palestine. ...

December 14, 1928

TO Henrietta Szold, Hadassah Hospital, Jerusalem

Of course you know Dr. Holmes and something of what he is and means in American life. I write this line merely to say that I am hopeful for much from his visit to Palestine, but he must be enabled to see everything and all sides of things, and he must meet with and come to know, not only the glorifiers of the present regime but also those who venture to dissent from the "hallelujahs" of its praise.

He brings you the affectionate greeting of all the Wises. Send him back to us safe and well, because his visit to Palestine must prove a great help to the cause we love.

December 14, 1928

TO Judah L. Magnes, Jerusalem

Of course you have known Holmes for many years, and you know that he is coming to Palestine. He comes, as you know, as the personal representative of dear old Nathan Straus, and he is a very dear friend of [Julian] Mack and myself. I hope he will see all that may be seen and heard. I need not tell you that he is one of the noblest spirits in American life, an unafraid truth seeker and speaker. Help him to see whatever will give him the best understanding of all sides of the life of Palestine, and do by all means get him to speak to your men on some of the great themes which mean so much to him.

February 12, 1929

TO John D. Rockefeller, Jr.

I have just come in from the University of Chicago, where I preached a few days ago. I had looked forward to seeing the new chapel [given in memory of Laura Spelman Rockefeller], and had seen photographs of it. But it is more beautiful than I thought it possible for any new church to be. Though utterly new, the chapel has atmosphere and reverent beauty—by which I mean that its beauty does not suffer one to forget that one is standing at the altar of the living God.

The acoustics too are quite surprisingly good, and it seemed to me that the Dean [Charles W. Gilkey] is divinely appointed for his task.

What a rare memorial! . . .

April 29, 1929

TO Franklin Delano Roosevelt, Warm Springs, Ga.

It seems a wicked thing to break in upon your beautiful and sunny peace, but I believe you wished me to send you the statement which I am about to write with regard to names for possible inclusion within the make-up of the Old Age Security Commission.

My associates of the executive of the American Association for Old Age Security feel strongly that no better man could be chosen as head of the Commission than the Lieutenant-Governor [Herbert Lehman]. We assume that it will be possible, from the legal point of view, to make him a member of the Commission.

We feel that not less than one representative of the Old Age Security should be a member, and we have three names to offer:

Bishop [Francis J.] McConnell, who, I think you would find, would be acceptable to all groups in the community, though he himself is the Bishop of the New York area of the Methodist Episcopal Church;

Charles Burlingham, who would serve admirably;

Dr. I. M. Rubinow, author of *Social Insurance* and a distinguished authority in this field.

We have a suggestion to make to you which we trust you will not consider unseemly for us to make, because we think a woman ought to be a member of the Commission; and we strongly urge

upon upon Your Excellency the appointment of Mrs. Franklin
D. Roosevelt as a member of the Commission. It might be somewhat uncommon for a Governor to name his wife as a member
of a commission of this character; but we feel there would be
state-wide approval of, and rejoicing in, the appointment and in
the very delightful novelty of it, apart from its perfect fitness. . . .

July 2, 1929

TO George Alexander Kohut

I had a very cheering and happy note from Lady Rebekah
[Kohut], and I am very happy to think that she will not let you
work [due to illness]. Avoid Jewish students as you would a pest,
that is to say, unless they come from Pesth [Budapest], in which
case meet them, welcome them, love them and serve them.

If I am in a cheerful mood this afternoon while dictating this
letter, with the temperature somewhere between 100 and 200
and the humidity somewhere between 99 and 150, it is because I
am going up to New Haven to see the two little Stephens [Ste-
phen Andrews Wise and Stephen Wise Tulin], who are there
together—Jim [James Waterman Wise] being at the Zionist
Convention in the interest of Avukah [American Student Zionist
Federation].

I had an invitation from the [theological seminary in] Breslau
to send a rabbi to their 75th anniversary in November. Whom
shall we send? If one of our students were abroad we could send
him. We might deputize [Julian J.] Obermann to remain permanently in Europe and represent us at [the] *Feier* [ceremony].

We are to go off on the S.S. *Aquitania* Sunday night, at 11,
and just as soon as I get to Europe you will hear from me.

I wonder whether you remember our chauffeur, Ralph, who
had been with us for four years, a really devoted friend of the
family in every way? He left us Wednesday night apparently
perfectly well. He was only 29. He died of a cerebral hemorrhage
the following morning. I had the task of telling his lovely old
mother, and of being with them, together with Louise, at the

service in farewell. What a lot of sticks the Catholic priests are! They perform their offices but not a word or gesture of sympathy for the sorrowing. *In Vergleich sind wir noch Menschen* [In comparison, we are at least human]. . . .

July 7, 1929

TO Basil L. Q. Henriques, London

. . . How are you and how is Mrs. Basil, and how is the great C. G. M. [Claude G. Montefiore] in whose armor there still remains the single flaw of utter failure to understand the finer side of nationalism, although he, like you, is quite capable of understanding nationalism if it be English rather than Jewish?

We are a religious brotherhood, it is true, but "religious" qualifies "brotherhood." Religion is the chiefest achievement and the finest distinction of the people of Israel. As a gentleman from your country said, "Though all the world forget, we are a people yet."

But there is no use arguing with you. You are just as inhospitable to one of the great truths of Jewish history as is the otherwise impeccable Claude. I forgive you and love you both; but, oh, how I wish that you could see that Jews do feel that they are a people, and they must be given, as they shall yet take for themselves, the opportunity to develop a life of their own; and I believe that that life, when it comes, may be just as significant and enriching to humankind as were the earlier contributions of life and faith and men.

One thing I ought to add:—if I were an Englishman, I should be thoroughly ashamed of your government's conduct in recent years with respect to Palestine. I take it for granted that Great Britain will not formally repudiate the Balfour Declaration, nor annul the Mandate; but there are ways of avoidance of duty which are just as immoral as formal abrogation. England cannot afford, despite her great power, to fail to keep her pledge to the Jewish people. . . .

November 11, 1929

TO Jacob Billikopf, Philadelphia

. . . I read the manuscript of [John Haynes] Holmes' book
[*Palestine: Today and Tomorrow–A Gentile's Survey of Zionism*].
To two things I took exception. One of them was his reference
to Lord Balfour. He promised to tone it down as I strongly felt
he should. He is a curious anti-Britisher and has an unjust view
of Balfour. On the other hand, Holmes is so nearly right most
of the time that we must be patient with him if for once we
cannot wholly agree with him. A man like Holmes may occasionally lapse into a blunder; but what are minor blunders by the
side of the great power he has, and which, for the largest part,
he uses in a great way and for great ends? . . .

May 8, 1930

TO Robert Kesselman, Jerusalem

. . . There is a complete lull in things Zionistic in America.
The [Jewish] Agency [for Palestine] has not yet won the confidence of the Jewish masses; and, of course, England is doing
everything that it can in order to shake the faith of the Jewish
people. For the first time I begin to doubt the possibility of doing
anything in Palestine with and through England. It almost seems
to me that the future, whatever can be achieved, will come to
pass, not because [of] but, despite the British government. Governments seem to be pretty much alike, though the Labour government is a little more timid and tepid than the Liberal and
Conservative governments. The mere mention of [Harry] Luke
[the unsympathetic acting High Commissioner] in reference to
the Wailing Wall [Investigation] Commission is the deepest of
insults to the Jewish people, and now another civil service
official [Sir John Hope Simpson] is to be sent on a fishing expedi-
tion to Palestine [to prepare a report on land policies, immigration, and the possibilities for economic growth]!

We are pretty much disheartened over things in America. The
Zionist Organization is gone, though the corpse will make some

sort of noises in Cleveland [at the annual conference] ere it perishes. . . . I wonder whether we have not touched bottom and whether from this time forward there is not to be somehow some measure of gain.

I would be hopeless about the situation, I confess, if it were not for faith in the Yishub [Jewish community in Palestine], which I think in a very little time will take the Zionist movement, such as it is, into its hands and have done with London quibbling and New York playing with a great problem of national resurrection.

My pessimism is not of a moment. The British government's conduct for ten years by its Palestine administration, the incapacity or unwillingness of the Zionist leadership to deal vigorously with the problem, the Arab riots and the [Sir Walter Shaw] Report [of the Wailing Wall Commission], the equivocal utterances of the [British] government, plus the killing of Zionism as a democratic mass movement and placing it in the hands of millionaire-trusteeship [with the inclusion of non-Zionists in the newly formed Jewish Agency for Palestine], have robbed me of my faith. It will come to pass, I have no doubt, but only despite us of the Diaspora who have miserably trifled with a great situation.

July 3, 1930

TO George Foster Peabody, Saratoga Springs, N.Y.

. . . I . . . regret that a senatorial campaign should be fought around the liquor question. I had thought, when I favored the Prohibition Amendment, that we would have an end of drinking in this country and that men might begin to think of ethical and social problems seriously, with brains unbefuddled by alcohol. Far from that being true, we not only drink liquor now, but we think liquor; and I am afraid that Mr. [Dwight W.] Morrow may be right—that this issue has to be gotten out of the way before anything else . . . can be done in our political life. Personally, I believe in abstinence from the use of alcohol.

I believe the state has the right to prescribe that a poison such as alcohol shall not be purveyed, bought and sold.

I believe it a thousand pities that a fair trial of the 18th Amendment was not made through the spirit of lawfulness and cooperation. But in the light of all that I see and find about me, I am fearful, to my very great sorrow, that it is become necessary to face the fact that the 18th Amendment must be repealed. I consider repeal much less grave than non-enforcement.

December 26, 1930

TO Richard W. Montague, Portland, Oregon

What kind of friend are you, just to send me a perfunctory Christmas card and never to write a line while I was dying, and I was all but prepared to give you the privilege of preaching the funeral service, if you had not been a damned Nordic? Perhaps you did not hear that I was "right sick" the day after the Atonement Day, on which I most unwisely fasted and at the close of which I ate a most hearty dinner. I had an attack of acute indigestion that laid me low, and which I think got my doctors pretty well scared. On top of that came the Passfield White Paper [released in October] and then a hideous attack of vertigo, which knocked me out for hours. They put me in a hospital for complete rest for a few weeks. Since then I have been in Atlantic City, have not done a stitch of work worth mentioning, except to dictate a few letters. . . .

While I was sick, knowing that I could not "spout" for months, under the impact of the Passfield White Paper, which like most anti-Jewish proclamations is written by a Jew, Sidney Webb, I planned to write a book in answer to it. I drafted the thing, wrote the introduction, and then it became too much for me; and I had to call in [Jacob] de Haas to finish it. I have sent you a copy of the book [*The Great Betrayal*]. Its real value lies in the documents which I have brought together at the close [to indicate the direction of British policy, namely, to curtail Jewish aspirations in Palestine, assure doom of the idea of a national home, and tolerate Arab harassment of Jewish pioneers]. . . .

February 11, 1931

TO Moshe Menuhin

I was tempted a hundred times to go to you on Monday night [at the New York Philharmonic concert] and take your hand and join you in deep rejoicing over that God-given child. I just wrote to a friend that I never heard anyone whose playing touched me as deeply as did Yehudi's. He seemed to me to have reached the loftiest height of power, and he was not player; he was both interpreter and creator at one and the same time.

I suppose you have heard a thousand variations of the *berachah*. Blessed the parents who have begotten him! May you be blessed in him and in his expanding life and genius and in the loveliness of the younger children as well!

June 16, 1931

TO Walter S. Hilborn, Los Angeles

We are sailing tomorrow. I am to devote my time, by doctors' orders, to the quest of health—and, by my own desire, to work at the [World Zionist] Congress.

Things at the Synagogue and Institute have not gone so well because of the depression, but I suppose somehow we shall be able to weather it. . . . I must not fail to tell you of the magnificent Commencement Exercises. [Charles] Burlingham said they were the most impressive of any he had ever seen. [Benjamin] Cardozo's address ["Values"] was on the highest level. . . .

December 30, 1931

TO Julian W. Mack

I mean to act as quickly as I can in the matter of the Hitler papers about which F. F. [Felix Frankfurter] writes. I have two ideas under way, and we will discuss them when we meet—both in strictest confidence: (1) that one or two of us go to Germany and discuss the problem with leading Jews there to determine in advance what, if anything, is to be done in the event of Hitler's coming in; and (2) to get at the President [Herbert Hoover] and have him send a distinguished non-Jew to Germany to discuss the whole matter with [President Paul von] Hindenburg and [Chancellor Heinrich] Brüning.

TELEGRAM

January 16, 1932

TO Richard W. Montague, Portland, Oregon

TREMENDOUSLY GOOD CHANCE GETTING CARDOZO APPOINTED. NEEDS WESTERN AND MIDWESTERN SUPPORT TO INDICATE WEST PREPARED WAIVE GEOGRAPHICAL CONSIDERATIONS IN VIEW SUPREME AND UNIQUE FITNESS OF CARDOZO AS [OLIVER WENDELL] HOLMES SUCCESSOR. WIRING [OREGON GOVERNOR] JULIUS MEIER. PLEASE COMMUNICATE AND COOPERATE. IMMEDIATE ACTION NECESSARY. AFFECTIONATE GREETINGS.

January 20, 1932

TO Richard W. Montague, Portland, Oregon

A thousand thanks for the promptness with which you have acted. I hoped you would feel as I did about it. In fact, I was almost certain. . . .

. . . I know no lawyer in the country, even including [Charles Evans] Hughes, [John W.] Davis, [George W.] Wickersham and [Louis D.] Brandeis, about whom there seems to be such unanimity of approval as about Cardozo.

Confidentially, the glory of it will be, if the appointment come to him, that his father's name, because he came under the malign influence of [William Marcy ("Boss")] Tweed, made the name Cardozo synonymous with shame. In twenty years, [Benjamin N.] Cardozo has effaced the memory of his father and his name can nevermore be used save in terms of reverence and honor. What an achievement for a man!

. . . Even you cannot know, because I do not think you have met him, of the loftiness of the man's spirit and of the beauty of his private life.

February 17, 1932

TO Richard W. Montague, Portland, Oregon

I cannot let the day go by without sharing my joy with you in the appointment of Cardozo. Some day you will meet him, perhaps try a great case before him, and see for yourself why I feel about him as I do. He is one of the gentlest, rarest, and wisest of human beings.

I was terribly discouraged on Friday when Borah told me that the President had put Cardozo out of the running, not because he was a Jew or a Democrat or a New Yorker, but because he is a Liberal. Borah said, in confidence, of course, "The President seems to think the nation is tottering as a result of the onslaught of radicalism, so that Cardozo won't do." Sunday night Borah spent a long time with the President, and I think used his great strength to make the President see, what he told me he would say to the President, that the appointment of Cardozo would be as great a service to the nation as was the appointment of [John] Marshall by [President John] Adams.

I have no doubt whatever that Borah put the appointment over, and I am sure you will feel, as I do, that it is a very great service to the nation on Borah's part.

May 16, 1932

TO Emanuel Neumann, Jerusalem

. . . I wonder how you really feel about British cooperation, whether there is ever to be such a thing, or whether we must resign ourselves to the fact that we must go on and do our work with the hindering non-cooperation of a civilized government rather than the obstructiveness of the uncivilized government of Palestine [under Ottoman Turkey] prior to the War. . . .

I wish I might write you a cheerful letter, but it is not easy to be cheerful in America; in fact, it is not possible to be cheerful here just now. About the only cheering sign upon the horizon is the word that comes from Palestine that the lines are being firmly held and, irrespective of the British government, the Yishub [the Palestinian Jews] will stand and build.

June 13, 1932

TO Nahum Goldmann, Berlin-Charlottenburg

We are going forward with all plans [to convene a conference for the formal organization of a World Jewish Congress]. A meeting was held yesterday of representatives of organizations, city, state and national, which nominated delegates to the World Jewish Conference. The American Jewish Committee, as you know, has decided not to go along with us. They are governed solely by fear. We, on the other hand, are expected to join in their fears rather than insist upon our own faith that out of wise and united counsel something may come for the benefit of our people. Back of the opposition to the [World Jewish] Congress lies the spirit of the assimilationists, whether it be the liberal assimilationists of London or the conservative assimilationists of America.

Thanks, with all my heart, for all you are doing for the Congress!

August 1, 1932

TO Henry W. Allen, Wichita, Kansas

Will you not let me thank you for your kind note? One of the early memories of my life, and very precious, is a glimpse of Henry George when he was a candidate for mayor against [Abram Stevens] Hewitt and [Theodore] Roosevelt [in 1886]. . . . I need not explain to you, who understand, that my own support of [the Single Tax proposal of] Henry George is bound up with my assent to the supreme wisdom of the Mosaic

Law which instituted the periodical restoration of the land [to its original owners].

August 3, 1932

TO Louis D. Brandeis, Chatham, Mass.

I am to leave on Friday midnight for the World Jewish Conference at Geneva and to return immediately thereafter. . . . The Conference is an attempt to bring together Jews of different lands for common counsel and if need be for common action. It is a Conference, not a Congress, though out of the Conference a real World Jewish Congress may grow.

[Albert] Einstein has promised to be at the Conference and you and [Senator William] Borah are the only two men whom I have asked for messages. Borah has responded. I beg you will do this. . . . I know what a word from you would mean to all of us at Geneva.

August 4, 1932

TO Samuel Seabury

You have been doing one good job after another in the last year [investigating magistrate courts and city politics in New York], but you never did a better job in your rebuttal of the insolent and mendacious reply of Mayor [James J.] Walker. So few men dare to deal with that creature as he deserves to be dealt with. You have done it. You made made it impossible for Governor [Franklin Delano] Roosevelt to avert removal unless he [Roosevelt] is prepared to destroy himself morally. . . .

August 27, 1932

TO John Haynes Holmes, Kennebunk Beach, Maine

. . . On the boat [from Europe] I wrote an Introduction to your volume of sermons [*The Sensible Man's View of Religion*]. I cannot tell you how much I like them. I think it is going to be an extraordinarily fine book of addresses. . . .

. . . Your summary of the Walker-Roosevelt case fits into every-thing that I hear on all sides—that, as you put it, Walker is stripped naked, and that Roosevelt is handling the thing well and firmly. . . . [A week later Walker had resigned.]

November 7, 1932

TO Franklin Delano Roosevelt, Albany

We feel that we wish to tender you our congratulations and good wishes upon your triumphant election to the Presidency. We hope that the years will abundantly vindicate the judgment of the American electorate and that you may rise to the unique opportunity of service which that election affords you. We trust that, whatever have been the differences between us with regard to civic affairs, you may feel free to call upon us for whatever service it lies within the power of American citizens to render to their government and President.

(Co-Signatory: John Haynes Holmes)

November 9, 1932

TO Herbert H. Lehman

I rejoice more than I can say in your election [as governor of New York State]. Your triumph at the polls is a tribute to the character of your service during the past four years and an ex-pression of confidence in your capacity to deal with the tre-mendous problems which lie before the state. While the [Demo-cratic] party has been loyal to you, yours is more than a party triumph. Great numbers of people gave you their support irrre-spective of party lines because they believe in you, as I do. Mine is the fullest confidence that the next two years will mean much high service to the state and great honor to the Jewish people.

My first thought last night was of your dear father whom I re-member well and to the shrine of whose memory you are priv-ileged to bring the offering of a life of public service, honoringly acclaimed.

CHAPTER FOUR

THE LONELY AGONY
(1933-1939)

TO JULIAN W. MACK

I wonder whether many Jews realize that we are facing today, in 1933, a Jewish upheaval which parallels, if it does not surpass in significance, the upheaval of 1881 [large scale immigration of Russian and Rumanian Jews to the U.S.A.], which both of us remember, I rather dimly. In some ways this is graver than '81, for the frontiers of civilization have been crossed. . . . The trouble, Mack, is that none of us is quite alive to the fact that this may be the beginning of a world-wide movement against us, a world-wide conflagration, a world-wide undertaking against the Jews.

April 1933

March 1, 1933

TO Julian W. Mack, U.S. Circuit Court of Appeals,
San Francisco

. . . It seems a long time since I have heard from you but I
know how busy you are and I do not ask you to write. We are
terribly disturbed and fearful about what is happening and going
to happen in Germany. The news in the New York *Herald
Tribune* today is ghastly, with a St. Bartholomew's Eve Massacre
being planned on or before the election of Sunday. The awful
thing is to stand utterly impotent in the presence of impending
danger and disaster. The London *Times* speaks seriously of the
threat of danger to progressives in Prussia, including Jews. One
can only hope and pray that our people, and indeed all peoples,
may be spared the horror that threatens.

March 7, 1933

TO Walter S. Hilborn, Beverly Hills, Calif.

. . . Now that the banks are closed, I do not know what is going
to happen. We have all cut things down again. At a meeting last
night, at my instance, all salaries were cut down, all of us taking
a fourth cut in two years. We are assuming that the income of the
Free Synagogue from membership this year will be $30,000 in-

stead of $66,000, as in 1929. We are back now where we were
nearly twenty years ago. But what does that compare with the
suffering of millions who are without bread? . . .

March 8, 1933

TO Julian W. Mack, San Francisco

Day after day I have been trying to get off a real letter. . . . I
think all of us feel too excited or depressed to think or write
about anything.

The German situation is just rotten. I remember that a year
ago, Dr. Theodor Wolff of the *Berliner Tageblatt* spoke with
utmost assurance with respect to the future of the Jews in Germany. Today . . . he is in hiding. . . .

. . . Lewis Strauss tried last Friday to get [Herbert] Hoover and
[Franklin Delano] Roosevelt to send a joint message, but I understand that Roosevelt would not, but that Hoover did send some
word through to Ambassador [Frederick M.] Sackett. I also learn
that Cyrus Adler and Judge [Irving] Lehman are thinking of
going to Washington in the hope of getting Roosevelt interested
in the problem. We have forborne up to this time because, as I
have said, we hesitate to use up any of Roosevelt's limited time
and to add to his terrible cares. . . .

March 23, 1933

TO Louis D. Brandeis, Washington

My heartfelt thanks for your note. Our visit to you helped us
immensely. Of course we followed your advice. We found [Wil-
liam] Phillips, Under-Secretary of State, most helpful and understanding. He did exactly what we wished him to do and he did
one thing more that [Senator William E.] Borah suggested—he
promised to telephone to Norman Davis [chairman, U.S. delegation, Disarmament Conference, Geneva] to put the situation
before him and move him to urge the German government in
the name of sanity to end this awful business [persecution of

German Jews]. I telephoned to the White House and Colonel [Louis McHenry] Howe was most friendly but thought it would be a mistake for me to see the President at this time. I told him that we had followed your advice for weeks in not trying to gain access to F. D. R. He said that he would get the President to telephone Norman Davis to whom he was sure to speak before he left last Wednesday night.

The American Jewish Committee persists in its attacks upon me [for arranging a protest meeting at Madison Square Garden]. I think they have succeeded in keeping [Governor] Herbert Lehman and the distingushed Mayor of New York [John P. O'Brien] from participation in the meeting; but inasmuch as we have Governor [Alfred E.] Smith, Bishop [William T.] Manning, Bishop [Francis J.] McConnell, Senator [Robert] Wagner, Bernard Ritter, Editor of the *Staats-Zeitung,* and [U.S. District Attorney] Charles H. Tuttle, we think we have a fairly good group of speakers without the Governor and Mayor of New York. . . .

March 29, 1933

TO Julian W. Mack, San Francisco

. . . The Nazis, after thirteen years of teaching "Down with the Jews," set out inevitably to carry out the Nazi program and they did not dream that these "Jewish cockroaches" could either defend themselves or could bring about such world-wide protest as has gone up against them. They are amazed and indignant over the insolence of "those verminous Jews" rising up and moving a world to share their wrath.

I do not know whether you listened in on Monday night to the meeting, but you will note that we put only Christian speakers on the air. I gave up my time, but the N.B.C. [National Broadcasting Company] people extended the time of the broadcast and possibly you heard what was said. I tried to be as prudent and cautious as I could. The easiest thing in the world would have been to arouse that audience, that mighty meeting, the most wonderful meeting you have ever seen in your life, to murderous rage. If you will take the trouble to read in the New

York *Times* what I said, you will find that I spoke with absolute self-restraint.

... I am going through days and nights of hell, for I am mindful of our awful responsibility. But if you had seen the documents that we have seen, you would know that you would have had to choose between virtual silence—and silence is acquiescence—or supporting this tremendous protest. No matter what the Hitlerites do now, it will be nothing more than the overt commission of acts that would have been covertly performed, protest or no protest.

I do not give a penny for the counsel of the Berlin people [i.e. leaders in the Jewish community]. They have been saying for years there is no *Gefahr* [danger] of Hitler's coming to power. They have no judgment and certainly they can have no objective judgment now. The Rumanians said to me years ago in Zürich, "If we cable to you ten times not to take any steps, go ahead and do what you think is right. Your judgment will be better than ours."

April 3, 1933

TO John Haynes Holmes

Yours is the first personal letter I have written since the day of the [American Jewish] Congress meeting. I had your letter with me in my bag on Tuesday when I was in Boston and on Thursday and Friday when I was in Washington. It was a terrific job at Washington, but I must say that the State Department really tried to help. [William] Phillips practically lived on the Berlin telephone on Friday; and I can tell you, dear Holmes, if it had not been for the protest of the American people chiefly, and of other people secondarily, the boycott [in Germany against the Jewish merchants] which was inaugurated on Saturday would have continued indefinitely. I am not at all sure but that the boycott will be continued indefinitely in more subtle ways, but it is great to think that public opinion has triumphed and that the advocates of *Schrecklichkeit* have been moved to have regard to the consequences of world judgment. . . .

. . . I must smile at the generosity of your word about my own part in the meeting of last Monday night [at Madison Square Garden]. I was too sick and worn and miserable and worried to make an address that was equal to the occasion. You don't know the days of agony and the sleepless nights that I lived through before Monday with that hideous pressure brought to bear upon us from all over the world to call the meeting off, to which pressure I was at moments tempted to yield. . . .

. . . It warmed my heart to see how that great audience rose when you arose. It just showed, old man, that my people know you and love you. . . .

April 6, 1933

TO Ruth Mack Brunswick [daughter of Julian W. Mack], Vienna

. . . The situation, as far as Jews in Germany is concerned, is as grievous as it can be. We do not know what you hear from America, but of course the Germans are saying that we are spreading atrocity tales. That is not true.

. . . We have not organized a boycott, and we shall not organize one. A boycott would be the last and not the first weapon of the Jewish people; but there is no denying the fact that great multitudes of people, Christians as well as Jews, are not purchasing German goods, will not use German steamers and will keep out of Germany for a time.

. . . We had a great demonstration at Madison Square Garden, with twenty-two thousand people inside and fifty or sixty thousand in the street, at which not one bitter word was spoken against Germany. The term "boycott" or "reprisal" was never used. When the measure of provocation is borne in mind, the self-restraint of American Jews has been extraordinary and indeed most admirable.

April 8, 1933

TO Julian W. Mack, San Francisco

. . . I wish I could go on and on fighting, but for the first time in my life I feel that it will be good when the fight is over, seeing that one can do so little. If only one might be sure that the fight that we have tried to put up will be fought with unabated courage and without compromise! . . .

April 10, 1933

TO William Rosenau, Baltimore

I heard something yesterday which I must take up with you, for we have been friends for a long time. . . . I want a personal assurance from you that you never said directly or indirectly, explicitly or implicitly, that "Dr. Wise killed the Jews of Berlin," or "Dr. Wise is responsible for the killing of the Jews in Berlin."

April 15, 1933

TO Julian W. Mack, San Francisco

I have never felt so overwhelmed with work as I do at the moment. . . . I have practically given up all the work of the Synagogue and the Institute for the time being. . . . I have got to limit myself to this one thing. . . .

. . . The [American Jewish] Congress will have to do the very, very lamentable thing of crying out against the President who has not by a single word or act intimated the faintest interest in what is going on. . . . Only [Prime Minister Ramsay] MacDonald has been silent [in England]. [Winston S.] Churchill and Sir John Simon and [Stanley] Baldwin and many more have spoken out. No one in America has spoken out excepting [Senator Robert] Wagner who spoke for the two and a quarter million Jewish constituents in the State [of New York]. . . .

Roosevelt ought to know the story. Of course, F. F. [Felix Frankfurter] must have told Roosevelt much, but there is still much to be told. Very much, on the basis of the first hand stories of witnesses and participants that I see. . . . I imagine that F. F. brought it about, though it is only a guess, that no ambassador to Berlin is being appointed for the present. We are all horrified at the thought that Roosevelt will have to receive [the German Ambassador to the U.S., Hans] Luther in a few days and make a

speech about friendly relations, etc. He is acting with such independence of spirit and such extraordinary courage in many
ways that one cannot help feeling that he might in this case, too,
show something of the same spirit. . . .

*Due to the economic depression, Montague had been com-
pelled to cancel most of his annual contributions to social causes
but found himself "unable to write off the Free Synagogue" and
sent his gift with the message: ". . . I have no words to express
my wrath and indignation at the treatment of Jews in Germany,
and admire beyond measure your course, while I sympathize with
the burden it must lay on your generous soul."*

April 18, 1933

TO Richard W. Montague, Portland, Oregon

. . . I cannot tell you how touched I am by your letter. I know
how hard it is to keep things up and it must be hard for you to
send this generous gift for my work. If you cannot do it another
year, don't feel that you must just because we are friends. . . .

Yes, I am in the midst of a hideous job as far as the Jews of
Germany are concerned, with timid and fearful German-Jews
both in Germany and America at my heels to desist. I have reason to know in many ways that what I succeeded in doing
through the American Jewish Congress in channeling the protest of American Jewry and, above all, of non-Jewish America,
did much to make life livable for the Jews of Germany. It is a
war of extermination that Hitler is waging; and it is a deliberate
thing planned since the 25th of February, 1920, when the Hitler
program was first issued. . . .

April 19, 1933

TO William Rosenau, Baltimore

Your explanation is no explanation. . . . If you said, as you
admit you did (no matter what reservations may have been in
your own mind), "Dr. Wise will kill the Jews in Germany," you

have borne false witness against a man, a colleague, and a friend. I can nevermore have any word with you or see you again.

Men like you are responsible in part for what is happening in Germany. If counsels of expediency and timidity such as your own had not prevailed in Jewish life in Germany during the last ten years, this great disaster might have been averted. Alas, it seems impossible for you to have even a conception of what decent, courageous action is in the presence of a great menace such as Hitlerism is to German Jews and indeed to world Jewry.

. . . Your now private explanation . . . in no wise extenuates or even mitigates the enormity of your conduct: "It is needless for me to explain that I refer to an economic killing." Parenthetically I observe that "economic" is not used in connection with killing. One might speak of economic strangulation or economic degradation, but, as you well know, not killing. . . .

. . . If it were not for our friendship of a lifetime, I should feel nothing but contempt. Instead of that, mine is pity for one who could bring himself to utter these words.

April 26, 1933

TO George Alexander Kohut

I am not working too hard—I am not working hard enough. It is no exaggeration to say that as I see and hear the news [about the Nazis] from day to day, I am looking into the deeps of hell. Sometimes I feel as if I could hardly live through it and as if I hardly cared . . . as if release from it all would not be unwelcome —if death meant release.

I heard a man [James G. McDonald] who had seen Hitler within nine days say yesterday at a meeting of half a dozen Christian ministers and myself: "Only [John Haynes] Holmes is reacting like a man and a Christian [in protest]. Hitler will not rest until he has destroyed the Jewish people. His [Hitler's] word to me was, 'I will do the thing that the rest of the world would like to do. It doesn't know how to get rid of the Jews. I will show them!' "

God help us!

May 9, 1933

TO Albert Einstein, Coq-Sur-Mer, Belgium

I have not written to you all this time because I know how burdened you have been and continue to be. We are all very proud of the part you have played and, above all, the distinction which has been yours in being expelled from the [Nazified] Prussian Academy. Your expulsion or exclusion, whatever it was, is an everlasting stain upon the Prussian Academy.

We are doing everything we can with regard to the [German] situation. We do not feel like following the counsel of those who believe in silence and in what Justice Brandeis calls "super-caution." Our Madison Square Garden meeting was really a most solemn and impressive demonstration, and tomorrow we are to have our great protest march of which Justice Brandeis, our sagest head, said: "Let it go on by all means."

We here in America get not only the most terrible letters from individuals, lawyers, doctors, judges, who have escaped from Germany into surrounding countries, such as Belgium, but we have also heard from [James G.] McDonald, the secretary of the Foreign Policy Association, who declares that Hitler said to him, just three weeks ago:

> We will annihilate the Jews in every way. They do not belong to the White race and they will no longer be tolerated in Germany. We are going to destroy them and we are going to show the rest of the world how it can and should be done.

In America, I am sorry to say, there is *no* unity of opinion and action. Things are made infinitely more difficult for us by American Jews of German descent who believe that they owe it to their German past to disbelieve in the stories of Hitlerish barbarism and brutality. The serious thing is that these gentlemen have not insisted, as we of the American Jewish Congress have insisted, upon action by our Administration. The result is that, what with the London Economic Conference and the lack of pressure on the part of the rich German [-American] Jews, the Administration has found it simpler not to act, although I may say to you, in strictest confidence, that no ambassador has been appointed by the President to Germany because of Hitlerism. And you will be delighted to hear that Dr. [Hjalmar] Schacht has already said to a friend, after two days in America: "Is there nothing in America to talk about but the Jewish question? That's all I hear: Jews, Jews, Jews, and the Jewish question!" Several of us are to meet with him in a few days, including some of the most distinguished leaders in American finance. . . .

Please tell Madame Einstein that Mrs. Wise and I do not forget her, and that if sometime she has very, very special cases of need, she might be good enough to write just a line to Mrs. Wise. Mrs. Wise, within the limits of her modest resources, will always be happy and proud to cooperate with Madame Einstein. . . .

May 9, 1933

TO Zeta Beta Tau Fraternity

May I, as the first of the recipients of the Richard Gottheil Medal for the year 1925, be permitted to send my greetings to the meeting at which the award is to be made for 1932 to John Haynes Holmes, Minister of the Community Church.

Dr. Holmes needs no encomium from my lips. He is, as you well know, one of the outstanding figures in the life of our country. He is a great preacher and as mighty a power for righteousness as lives in America today.

Israel has many friends, some of them fair-weather friends, some of them occasional friends, some of them abiding friends. John Haynes Holmes is so much more than a friend of Israel. Out of the clarity of his vision and out of the richness of his generosity and out of his flaming passion for justice and the right, he has come, though an Aryan of the Aryans whatever that may mean, a Gentile and a Christian, to see eye to eye with the Jewish people touching many of the problems which they face. His majestic voice is not only lifted up at such a time as this which finds the Jews in Germany warred upon with relentless ferocity by the Hitler regime, in other words, in these days of Jewish fears and Jewish tears, but above all in the day of

Jewish hopes. For no non-Jew has had a finer, fuller understanding of or a deeper, truer sympathy with the Zionist movement than John Haynes Holmes. A great Jew, such as Nathan Straus was, held Holmes in affection. Justice Brandeis, Justice Cardozo, Judge Mack and Professor Frankfurter, surely our best and noblest, honor and reverence him.

I write merely to congratulate the Zeta Beta Tau Fraternity upon the distinction which comes to it from associating the name of John Haynes Holmes with the Richard Gottheil Medal. Will you not convey to my brother in aims and in arms, America's noblest preacher, America's loftiest spiritual leader, my most affectionate greetings?

June 1, 1933

TO John Haynes Holmes

... Things are about the same as far as the German situation is concerned. We had a good meeting in Washington, but we could get nothing public out of the President. He does speak privately. He tells friends that he spoke very vigorously to [Hjalmar] Schacht, and there is reason to believe that Schacht has repeated some of those things to Hitler. There may have been slight mitigation of the rigors of the decrees against the Jews of Germany, but their position is as bad as it can be. It could hardly be worse. The methods they have devised of torturing the Jews are just incredible. . . .

June 2, 1933

TO Henrietta Szold, Jerusalem

The bearer of this line is Miss Dorothy Kahn, a young journalist of real promise who resides in Atlantic City, New Jersey. . . .

May I present her to you? I would like her to write a real story about you and about your great work. Nothing in all Palestine is more interesting than your contribution to it. If she were very wise, she would make you talk and talk and talk, and then write out the story of one of the greatest and the noblest of Palestine's pioneers. That's exactly what Louise and I think of you, dear Lady.

I suppose you know that I have been rather busy dealing with the German-Jewish problems. The thing we are trying to do is to keep Palestine in the center of the whole picture, otherwise the whole thing will degenerate into nothing more than another inglorious Jewish *Schnorrerei* [begging].

June 7, 1933

TO Julian W. Mack, San Francisco

I had an illuminating talk with some men yesterday—Dr. [Emanuel] Libman, and Dr. [Leopold] Lichtwitz who, according to Libman, is one of the greatest metabolism men in Europe, and Dr. [Benjamin A.] Bernstein, friend of [Albert] Einstein and Morris Cohen, et al.—a mathematical statistician. I happened to say that we were nervous about doing a certain thing because of the possible hurt to German Jews. Both of them believe in this thesis—and restated it again and again—"You cannot hurt the Jews of Germany. They are finished. You may help them. You cannot hurt them."

I really felt, Mack, as though I had been struck a blow between the eyes to hear two distinguished German Jews, one of whom (Bernstein), is about as Jewish-looking as Hitler, speak in these terms. Again and again they said, "Nur heraus [only emigration]." I confess to you that when Brandeis said that two months ago, I could hardly believe my ears; and I could hardly believe that he was sane. A people to migrate! But again, as wisdom and prescience are made clear—if only that consummation could be effected!

June 21, 1933

TO John Haynes Holmes

. . . Things get worse and worse in Germany. Today I had a report which it will become necessary for me to verify—that

sixty-five Jews in Halle-on-the-Saale were taken to the local hospital and operations performed on them in order to sterilize
them. Four of them died, eleven are crippled, and all the rest
have been permanently and curelessly sterilized. . . .

London, July 14, 1933

TO Julian W. Mack

In the course of the week on the [SS] *Washington,* I had
half a dozen or more talks with W. E. D. [U.S. Ambassador to
Germany William E. Dodd]. He was most friendly and cordial,
and indeed confidential. He had seen Colonel [Edward] House
on Tuesday, who, I believe, bolstered up his own sympathetic
attitude and W. E. D. regretted that he could not have seen
L. D. B. [Brandeis] of whom he spoke in terms of affectionate
friendship.

The only disturbing note of the week was his statement in
dealing, as he did at some length, with problems of American
history:—"One cannot write the whole truth about Jefferson and
Washington—people are not ready and must be prepared for it."
If people must be prepared for the truth about Jefferson and
Washington, what will he do with the truth when he learns it
about Hitler, in view of his official post?!

. . . Whenever I suggested that the greatest service he could
render his own country and Germany would be to tell the truth
to the [Reich's] Chancellor, to make clear to him how public
opinion, including Christian opinion and political opinion, had
turned against Germany . . . he answered again and again: "I
cannot tell until I talk to Hitler: if I find I can do so, I will talk
very frankly to him and tell him everything."

Since coming to London, I have learned from [Nahum] Goldmann and others that the Chancellor has said again and again
that there are two subjects he will not discuss—the Jews and
Austria.

I gathered from all our talks that W. E. D. feels himself
deputized to cultivate American liberalism in Germany. Again
and again he said: "You do well to, indeed you must, tie up

your cause with the causes of liberalism and internationalism, all three of which are equally at stake."

The last thing he said to me as we parted was: "It will be pretty serious if I fail—serious for liberalism and all the things for which the President stands," and he added parenthetically: "for which I, too, stand."

I asked time and again that he do just two things: get the truth to Hitler about American feeling, and get the truth to F. D. R.

Prague, August 18, 1933

TO Julian W. Mack

. . . In the evening [at a meeting of the Actions Committee of the World Zionist Congress], after two hours of preliminaries on the part of the toothless but not speechless [Zionist leader Leo] Motzkin, [David] Ben-Gurion read a statement, citing acts of Palestinian terrorism and demanding that before the Congress assemble, a committee of the Actions Committee examine the proofs of acts of terrorism, with a view to recommending that the Congress name a tribunal for the fullest investigation of ter- rorism in Palestine. . . . Then came six hours of discussion. I myself urged that there be no investigation of terrorism until after the Congress, and that it be made the first act of the next Ac- tions Committee. . . . [The] Labor [party of the Zionist Congress] is implacable, though I asked them how they would have liked it if after the crime attributed to [Tom] Mooney all labor and socialist organizations had been accused of terrorism. . . . I am really fearful that we may have awful scenes at the Congress, and the tragedy is, even though Palestine must be purged of terrorism, that it comes at a time when we can least indulge in the luxury of strife and division.

August 20, 1933

Let me go on where I left off the other night to say I think I closed with the decision, though not the vote, on the question of setting up a commission to decide whether or not a tribunal should pass upon the problem of terrorism in Palestine. . . . The following morning there was a much better feeling and a compromise was reached, namely, not to have it appear that the committee is to be a tribunal, but merely to determine whether a tribunal is necessary, and the terms terrorism and Revisionism were omitted. . . .

Now I must tell you something still more important. . . . I met with three men, whose names I cannot give: one of them straight from Berlin, the other from Danzig, and the third from Marienbad, though a very distinguished lawyer in Berlin. I cannot even give initials—it would not be fair. We spent hours and hours together, going over the case. The ablest of the three men put it: "The moment I am out of Germany for a day, I feel I never want to go back. The moment I go back to Germany, I feel that I must never leave again, for there may be hope." He presented the case with clarity and adequacy. . . .

I had seen another group of Germans in the morning, who thundered against a proposal to pussyfoot re Germany on the part of the Zionist Congress. They say that Czechoslovakia and Poland will draw the conclusion that it is safe to smash the Jews as does Hitler, and Germany will feel, worst of all, that if the Congress refrains from open and adequate condemnation of Hitlerism, then the Reich government will assume that German Jews can control the thought and speech and action of the Jews of the world. . . .

September 18, 1933

TO John Haynes Holmes, Kennebunk Beach, Maine

. . . I am almost more worried about the spirit of Nazism than concerning the damage it is doing now in Germany. What that damage is even you do not know any more than I did, until after I had had the sorrowful opportunity to learn about things from hundreds and hundreds of refugees in London, Paris, Geneva and Prague. The world does not know, perhaps does not care to know. This is certain and perhaps most tragic of all—Hitler will talk the world into war again. He will wait, as Germany waited before in 1914 until ready to win, if he be permitted to wait; but I am afraid he will not be permitted to wait, and, shocking as my word may sound, I am not sure that he ought to be permitted to wait. I was told by eye-witnesses of boys of 12 and 13 who are being trained to throw hand-grenades. Germany is a military training institute, and the treatment of the Jews is one of the pre-products of the war spirit. I suppose the Germans feel, and rightly, that we Jews do not care for war, never knowing the *Gaudium Certaminis* [joy of battle], which is the breath of life to so many peoples. . . .

September 19, 1933

TO Louis D. Brandeis, Washington

Often and again throughout the summer I have remembered two words of yours. I remind you that eight days after the election of Hitler you said to me, on the day I visited the German Ambassador, "The Jews must leave Germany." I have met no one from Germany, including Germans who came expressly from Berlin to confer with me, who failed to agree with you. The Jews must leave Germany, apart from Germany's resolve that they shall. [Hermann] Goering's word to a friend, K. of Berlin, was "We will not consider *Regelung der Judenfrage* [settlement of the Jewish question] until two or three hundred thousand Jews are out."

. . . You urged me on the 26th of March, when I was hesitating and fearful, "Make the great protest meeting as good as you can." It was the almost unanimous testimony of hundreds of Germans whom I have seen in London, Paris, Geneva and Prague that our great protest in America had the largest part in saving German Jewry from the direst things.

Whether you know it or not, dear L. D. B., Thursday is the [Jewish] New Year. God give it that, for years and years, yours shall be unlessened strength and power of leading to the joy of us who love you and to the blessing of Israel and mankind.

The plight of the Jews in Germany impelled many to urge upon Wise the need for conversion by Jews to the Christian faith. This correspondent had heard Wise on the radio and disclosed her "prayer that you, a 'Saul,' may become a 'Paul' and . . . be the anointed of God to lead this poor old struggling world back to the God of Israel, thru Jesus Christ His son."

October 9, 1933

TO Mrs. Donald MacIntyre, Ellerbe, N.C.

. . . I cannot understand why you feel that I must come back, as you put it, to the God of Israel through Jesus Christ, His son. We do not believe that Jesus is in any unique sense the Son of God. He was a son of Israel, which fact Christendom for the most part has forgotten, and his was the immediacy of access to God which is the portion and privilege of all His children. . . .

October 18, 1933

TO Julian W. Mack

. . . Could not F. D. R. be moved to invite [Professor Albert] Einstein to visit him in the White House? We have had nothing but indifference and unconcern up to this time. Perhaps we can have something of help. Who would be the best person to suggest it? I do not know. What do you think? It would make such a fine impression if the President were, at the instance preferably of some Christian friend (I thought of [Charles] Burlingham), to invite Einstein to spend the night at the White House to talk to him.

Mack replied that Dr. Abraham Flexner, director of the Institute for Advanced Study at Princeton where Einstein was a recently installed professor, would probably oppose the move unless Einstein were spared publicity; otherwise his scientific work might be jeopardized.

October 19, 1933

TO John Haynes Holmes

Newton Baker has been the supreme disappointment of my life. He absolutely refuses to have any part in any protest, advises Jews against it, and would not attend the meeting at which I spoke in Cleveland last May. He wrote in a communication which I could get for you from [Barnett] Brickner, that other nations have troubles, too, and that the Jews must not merely think of themselves. [Everett] Clinchy is under his immediate and powerful influence without even knowing it, and the [Herbert] Lehmans and [Joseph] Proskauers fall right in with the Baker-Clinchy point of view. If we are undone in the end, it will not merely be because of the effectiveness of our foes but because of the timidity and cowardice of ourselves. You will never know how grateful I am for your voice that speaks as does none other! . . .

October 20, 1933

TO Julian W. Mack

I am sorry I must differ from the judgment of Abe Flexner [as anticipated by Mack]. I am not asking Einstein to make speeches. I am not asking him to do anything. I think I have the right, and I am availing myself of it today to suggest to Burlingham that he ask Roosevelt to invite Einstein to the White House. I think you ought to join me in the suggestion. We are not doing it for the sake of publicity. Einstein has nothing to gain. F. D. R. has not lifted a finger on behalf of the Jews of Germany and this would be little enough, and to have Einstein at the White House is at least as honoring to F. D. R. as to Einstein. I shall ask Burlingham to do it and if he will not offer the suggestion to the President, I will get at someone else who will. Of course, it must be a non-Jew who must make the suggestion to Roosevelt. We will not appear in the matter, and Flexner would not dare to have Einstein decline the invitation if it should be extended to him.

October 20, 1933

TO Charles Burlingham

May I, in strictest confidence, venture to offer a suggestion to you? [Albert] Einstein, as you know, is in this country preparing to teach at that new school at Princeton [Institute for Advanced Study]. It has occurred to me, and I rather think that [Julian] Mack will agree with me, that it would be most fitting if the President were to invite Einstein to visit him at the White House.

Without going into details, the President, as you know, has done nothing with regard to the German situation, though privately and to his intimate friends he has expressed himself with vigor; and what I have reason to believe he willed to do in the spring has not been put through by the State Department. . . .

Will you see the President soon and give him the hint? It would afford immense satisfaction to the Jews of America. It would mean a great deal for the Jews throughout the world. A gesture of hospitality to Einstein would be just the sort of thing that would in itself be technically unoffending and yet mean a great deal if the German government permitted it to be known through those government bulletins known as the newspapers.

If you are not to see the President soon, would you write him a line in your own best way, urging this thing if you feel, as I do, that it is a thing that F. D. R. can do and ought to do—frankly for his own sake as much as for Einstein and the sake of the Jewish people?

November 9, 1933

TO Louis D. Brandeis, Washington

A few of us among your friends and comrades in THE CAUSE rejoice in the coming birthday. We know that you would not have us send you gifts, but something has come into our possession which we offer you with renewed devotion to our friend and leader. It is, as you will see, a longhand letter of Theodor Herzl. We place it in the hand of him, worthiest of all living Jews on earth to have it in his possession. It goes, as it were, from the hand of Herzl, through us followers of Herzl and Brandeis, to him who in our hearts and in history will have his place by the side of Herzl.

February 9, 1934

TO Nahum Goldmann, Geneva

. . . I am just sick at heart over the whole business, which means not only that the World Jewish Congress is postponed and must be postponed, despite everything that is happening in Europe, but because it shows how the Zionist Organization has crumbled and how the Zionist spirit has deteriorated. There is no Zionism in America, because there is no Zionist leadership in America. There is just another Tammany Hall machine in New York calling itself Zionism, the supreme interest of which is to maintain its organization and to keep the jobs that go with the organization. . . .

The truth is that many of the so-called leaders are no longer Zionists—they are benevolent territorialists who rather like Palestine and who, I am afraid, will almost be ready to give up Palestine, excepting that the abandonment of Palestine might mean the destruction of their organization.

. . . [Judge Morris] Rothenberg had the insolence to say, "Is the house burning?" What can be said of a man or men who ask the question—whether the house is burning—as we read from hour to hour that Austrian Jewry is in greater peril even than German Jewry, and tomorrow may see Hitlerism triumphant over Austria!

May 11, 1934

TO Jacob Billikopf, Philadelphia

. . . One goes on working here and it is all so difficult. In the end, I suppose, the counsel of cowardice and silence that prevailed in Germany will prevail here. . . .

October 4, 1934

TO William H. Worrell, Ann Arbor, Michigan

. . . Jim's [James Waterman Wise] two books on the Nazi regime [*Swastika: The Nazi Terror* and *Nazism: An Assault on Civilization*] will be sent you and also another book, a symposium on *The Case of Civilization Against Hitlerism*. I hope you like all the books.

. . . A year ago, when I returned from Europe, I warned a group of some twenty Christian ministers in the home of Harry Emerson Fosdick that we Jews were being destroyed merely as an incident and that the real drive of Nazi Germany was against Christianity. My diagnosis has been confirmed. The real war of the Nazi is against Jesus and the prophets, and is almost frankly an attempt to reinstate Wotan and Odin.

November 6, 1934

TO Waldo Heinrichs, Middlebury, Vermont

I thank God for the spirit which is your own, but I sorrow over the lack of spirit which moved the International Committee of the "Y" to act as it did [in requesting Heinrichs' resignation from his position as General Secretary of the Young Men's Christian Association in Jerusalem]. Of course it is a great moral victory, and it is your own, to have removed the *Voelkische Beobachter* [official Nazi party newspaper] from the library of the "Y" at Jerusalem, but after all you made the fight and you ought to have been rejoicingly and proudly sustained. That is the sort of thing, dear Heinrichs, I must confess to you, which makes me so unhappy about much in present day Christianity. I do not find what you call the spirit of Christ, what I call the spirit of God, of brotherliness and understanding among the men who should be the first to have it and to reveal it.

. . . I wrote in order to reach out my hand to you and thank you for what you had the courage to be and do. . . .

November 12, 1934

TO Walter H. Meyer, Rochester, N.Y.

. . . Since I get my clothes from your establishment, I am considered the best dressed rabbi at 90th Street and Central Park West [home address]. But the suit is beginning to look rather shiny, so I think you had better send me two of them. I shall hardly need four pairs of trousers, three will do for the two suits, assuming as I do that I can always get an extra pair.

One thing more—the trousers, after being worn a year or two, get a little too radiant in the seat, when I should gleam at the other end of my anatomy. I like the material out of which you made the suit; but seriously, could the suit be made out of material very much like what you used, but with a little less disposition to become gleaming?

December 7, 1934

TO Fiorello La Guardia

I send you copy of a letter which the Rev. Dr. [John Howard] Melish of Trinity Church (Episcopal), your church, and one of the finest men in the ministry has just written to Dr. [John Haynes] Holmes. He speaks of the enthusiasm of the clergy of Brooklyn over a recent talk you gave to them in reviewing your first year as mayor. Dr. Holmes (though he does not know it) and the rest of us would be very happy if you could do something like that for us of the City Affairs Committee. . . . Under our auspices (and there could be none more fitting) you would give a report of your stewardship of the city administration during the first year—the address to be broadcast. . . .

Frankly, dear La Guardia, I really believe you owe it to the City Affairs Committee, which, after all, waged the great battle against one of your distinguished predecessors [James J. Walker], to choose it as the medium through which to offer New York the report of your first year in office. . . .

December 28, 1934

TO Mrs. Israel Zangwill, East Preston, England

It is so good to have your New Year's greeting and wishes which Louise and I reciprocate with all our heart. . . .

We are all very busy here. Louise has opened Congress House, a temporary refuge for German exiles as they land on our shore, and a social center for them once they have made a home for themselves.

I manage to keep fairly busy. I have really often thought what I. Z. would be writing, with what sombre beauty and power he would convey a sense of horror at the relapse of a once great nation to barbarism. I rather think I. Z. would modify some of the generous views he held concerning the Germany of 1914.

January 31, 1935

TO Mrs. Cyrus L. Sulzberger

. . . I do not believe that we Jews can be governed solely or even chiefly by our fear [that the founding of a World Jewish Congress might be misconstrued]. Need I remind you that the *Protocols of the Elders of Zion* were written before there was a Zionist Congress? What would you say if you read in history that the Christians of the first and second centuries, in order to escape the charge of the Romans that they were guilty of using human blood for ritual purposes, abandoned what they considered the holy communion? Are we Jews under the obligation of abandoning the Paschal Supper which, as you know, is bound up with the Last Supper of Jesus and the resultant holy communion, because of the cannibalistic charge that we use the blood of a Christian child for ritual purposes?

I cannot help saying to you, dear Mrs. Sulzberger, that all the things that are now dreaded in relation to a World Jewish Congress were uttered and dreadful nearly forty years ago, when you and Mr. Sulzberger and I were very young people. Herzl refused to be governed by the fears of the Jewish people, almost the most fearful among them being the German Jews and the German-

American Jews of that day. The tragic and yet blessed irony of history is that no one is in direr need of the Palestine which Herzl made possible than the German Jews who most bitterly scoffed at Herzlism and who made it impossible for the first Zionist Congress to be held at Munich.

I wonder how much we have gained by walking warily, by being afraid to be ourselves, by constantly looking over our shoulders to see what impression we make upon others. You know as well as I do that we cannot choose or indeed in any wise silence the mouth of slander. We have been "assailed by slander and the tongue of strife" even when we have been without guilt or blameworthiness. . . . We are a people and if we had a little more respect for ourselves jointly and a little more confidence in the not inaccessible good-will of the world, a well-organized and wisely ordered assembly of representatives of the Jewish people from all lands would do us good and not hurt. . . .

I know that I stand virtually alone among those who are supposed to be leaders of the Jewish people—it is you who use that honoring term, and I merely quote it. But as one grows older, one realizes how dear are the words of Herzl: "Mann muss es nur mit sich selbst Recht machen." ["One must be true only to oneself."] If I did not believe that the American Jewish Congress and the World Jewish Congress could and would bring great good to the Jewish people, I would today, without a moment's hesitation, refrain from giving my support to either and both. I am not afraid to change my mind. I have had to do so. I may do so again, but I am profoundly and unalterably convinced that what we Jews need today is to move forward upon the basis of what we believe to be right and not suffer our lives to be dominated by the judgment of others upon it.

May 1, 1935

TO John Collier, Washington

Some years ago when you were fighting from the outside [as executive secretary of the American Indian Defense Association] some of us came to Washington and did what we could to have a part in the fight [to protect the rights of the American Indian and to secure redress for past wrongs].

Is it really true that some Congressional idiots are now fighting you, as if you were [the dancer] Isadora Duncan? Is there anything that "we fellers" can do in New York—I mean those of us who know you, who know that in and out of the [Interior] Department you have come pretty near being the salvation of the Indians, even though you may not believe in that terribly ecclesiastical thing. . . .

May 7, 1935

TO Margaret Payne, Portland, Oregon

I can imagine what you must be suffering, for I know what pain your letter brings me. Father [Richard Ward Montague] never was strong, I mean he seemed wiry but never robust, sinewy but never very vigorous physically, and yet it comes as an overwhelming shock to read that Father has been ill. I had not heard about it at all, and he must have been gravely ill or you would not write that he has been quite helpless for the past six weeks. Has he suffered a shock? And if Dr. Jack feels that he is progressing, however slowly, is there hope that the thing will clear up? Would you say to Jack that I would be very grateful if he would dictate a line to me and tell me just what it is and how hopeful you may be?

I have always felt, dear Margaret, not quite as you do about your father; but I have never had a friend on earth for whom I had deeper affection and reverence. Our friendship dates back thirty-five years. We were both young men. He was kindness and graciousness itself. We stood together and we fought together. We have had much in common; and I have loved, and I love, him truly. I am writing a line to him; but of course it will be independent of this, and you can read it to him if it is not too burdensome for him to listen to letters, and say to him for me, as you know you may, "I am sure Dr. Wise sends this with all love to you, Daddy. You never knew what he has always felt about you. I do, for he has told me."

Is there anything Father would care about? Is he well enough to have books read to him? Is there anything else? How I would love to add a little to such comfort as is possible at this time!

June 17, 1935

TO Richard W. Montague, Portland, Oregon

. . . We shall be off in a few days for Palestine. We have not been there in thirteen years. In those thirteen years the Jewish population has trebled and quadrupled; and the Palestine, to the rebuilding of which I have given much of my life, is taking care of just ten times as many German exiles, actually, as England and America put together. So you see, Herzl and the rest of us were darn practical as well as idealistic. . . .

We shall have a few weeks of quiet in Switzerland; then the Zionist Congress. You will hear from me from time to time from Palestine, whence I shall send you an orthodox-Christian note, in the hope of regaining your soul from the vagaries of Unitarianism. . . .

June 24, 1935

TO Benjamin N. Cardozo, Rye, N.Y.

Of course we were disappointed not to see you Friday night [at dinner in Cardozo's home], but we were more grateful than we can say to Miss Tracy [the nurse] for complying with our request and frankly telling us that we were not to come.

Dear Cardozo, I write this line for Louise and myself to say good-bye for the summer. We shall leave for Palestine and Europe on Saturday. Above all, I write to ask you to spare yourself. I know the temptation to work and overwork, but you must not. You have important work to do for the nation and in your field, and your life is very, very precious to all of us. So, if one may be permitted such irreverence to one of the younger of the Nine Old Gentlemen [on the Supreme Court], do be a good boy and become well and strong again and delight our hearts upon our return with a hearty welcome.

Jerusalem, July 17, 1935

TO Joseph Levine, New York City

Here we are, settled in Palestine, and I must confess to you,
though it may seem quite unpatriotic, that I have never been so
thrilled in all my 60 years and more, as by these 48 hours of life
in Palestine. Everything is new excepting the beauty of the
country. It is a perfect summer resort. At night it is actually
cold—they call it warm—but, unless one walks in the sun which
is about 82 or 84, just perfect glorious weather.

These days we are visiting the Institutions, and being dined
and wined with the best of Palestine wines which are good indeed, night after night. Today, for example, I lunch at the
Government House with the High Commissioner, and the next
week we shall see the results of the Jewish genius for creativeness
in Palestine. Then we have another Shabbath in Jerusalem, and
the last five days visiting the Colonies north and south of Tel
Aviv. We are ending up at Haifa whence we are returning to
Europe.

Jerusalem, July 26, 1935

TO Joseph Levine, New York City

Merely a line in order to tell you of the wonderful days that
we have been having in Palestine, getting the sense of the development of the country and of its transformation by the devotion and sacrifice of the chalutzim, men and women alike, who
have pilgrimed to freedom from the bondage of Eastern and
Central Europe.

. . . I would be much happier than I am if it were not for the
awful news out of Germany, the worst of which I think is still
being withheld from us. . . .

Lucerne, August 15, 1935

TO Gertrude Hauser

Sorry about the family in Cologne. Germany is now gone
frankly barbarian. Worse things, in my judgment, are yet to
come.

Lucerne, August 19, 1935

TO Gertrude Wolf

. . . We had three wonderful but really indescribable weeks in Palestine. I do not know of such a miracle as our young fellow-Jews have wrought. I am more Zionist than ever I was. I have moved from 100 to 200%. We travelled everywhere, motoring every day and really seeing the land and the people, colonies, and settlements, the cities; Jerusalem's beauty is unspoilt and Tel Aviv did not prove to be the nightmare I so dreaded. . . .

September 19, 1935

TO Louis D. Brandeis, Washington

Of course you do not imagine that I have forgotten my promise to get in touch with you. There has been, however, ever since we touched Palestine, so much to see and so much to tell that I felt it wiser to wait until I returned, when we might have an hour or two together. At this moment, I can only say to you that Palestine has been worthy of everything that has been put into it by all of us and is today equal to every hope.

I have so much to tell you about it and about the Zionist Congress, which in the main was good. . . .

If I do not see you before the New Year, may I not wish for you a most joyous and blessed year? By the end of another year, one-third of the population of Palestine ought to be our own.

September 23, 1935

TO Albert Einstein, Old Lyme, Conn.

It was so good to be greeted by your word upon our return after a rather long absence. I think you will be satisfied with the outcome of the [Hebrew] University [board of governors] meeting. It retired [Judah] Magnes from the academic direction

of things and made him the President, which means that he
becomes a more or less decorative figure. The American university regime is to be ended, and the scholars of the University,
or *Wissenschaftler*, are to have charge of academic affairs, as
indeed they should. . . .

Things otherwise are very sad. The German delegates [at the
Zionist Congress] tried to be brave, but disaster stared them in
the face. Perhaps it is just as well to have the final proclamation
at Nuremberg [of the Nuremberg Laws depriving German Jews
of civil rights and prohibiting intermarriage between Jews and
non-Jews]. It reveals the utter hopelessness of the situation, touching which it may at least be possible to arouse America.

September 24, 1935

TO The Editor, New York *Herald Tribune*

Early this morning I picked up the *Herald Tribune* in order
to read the review of [the première of the play] "If This Be
Treason" by Dr. [John Haynes] Holmes and Mr. [Reginald]
Lawrence. Percy Hammond's review of the play is not criticism.
It is a savagely ill-tempered attack by one who ought to stick
to play-reviewing and not wander off into a pulpit of denuncia-
tion and incrimination. Mr. Hammond, as a critic of the theatre,
is, I presume, entitled to express himself with entire freedom,
but one remembers the great tradition of the dramatic columns
of the *Tribune,* and one is shocked and mortified to come upon
the vulgarity, which is the right name for the smartness of Mr.
Hammond's review.

I cannot help regretting, for the sake of the *Tribune,* the
mental and psychical processes of one who could see that noble
play, for nobleness pervades it from beginning to end, and speak
of it as "a greasy extravaganza, loud, boisterous and unreal."

I went to the Theatre Guild opening of "If This Be Treason"
with an open mind. If the play had been poor, or loud, or
boisterous or unreal, I would have been objective enough to
describe it. I think that, instead of having it said that "when the

Theatre Guild produced 'If This Be Treason,' there was a satirical tongue in its cheek," it might decently be said that the Theatre Guild has made yet another notable and enduring contribution to the theatre.

It may be a crime in the eyes of Mr. Hammond for the author of the play not to be a professional play-writer and to be wholly without Broadway background. Is one to be barred from writing for the theatre because in addition to having a sense of dramatic value, a power of fluent and sometimes thrilling utterance, one has committed the crime of being a teacher of religion—in the case of John Haynes Holmes, one of the two or three commanding figures in American religious life in our time?

January 13, 1936

TO Albert Einstein, Princeton

. . . I may say to you in strictest confidence that I saw the President yesterday for the first time in a long while (because of a serious difference which arose between us years ago [concerning the City Affairs Committee and the case of New York's Mayor James J. Walker]). Unfortunately, and I tell it to you with sorrow . . . his first word was "Max Warburg wrote to me lately that things were so bad in Germany . . . there was nothing that could be done."

You see how this bears out our theory that Max Warburg and his kind do not really desire to help. This is doing exactly what the Nazi government would wish him to do. The President threw up his hands as if to say, "Well, if Max thinks nothing can be done, then nothing can be done."

. . . When I saw Brandeis, he told me that the President would have acted in March, 1933, if it had not been for the Warburg family. You see, Professor Einstein, how these great philanthropists are our deadliest enemies and a fatal curse to the security and honor of the Jewish people!

January 28, 1936

TO Felix Frankfurter, Cambridge, Mass.

. . . You speak of your distress [after hearing the radio address by former Governor Alfred E. Smith in bitter opposition to the policies of President Franklin Delano Roosevelt]. I listened with nausea to Al on Saturday night. When he had finished, I turned to Louise and said, "Al Smith is dead." I felt as if I had been at a funeral and not a banquet, as if I had been looking for an hour upon a dying friend. Both of us believed in Al; trusted him and served him. I went through the country in 1928, at my own expense, on his behalf, when, as you know, it was not an easy thing to do. One does not expect much of the John W. Davises, the Newton D. Bakers, and the James Becks. But Al seemed different. Yet we now can see how lightly rooted was his philosophy of social justice, and that the moment it collides with those interests which have come to overwhelm him, it evaporates.

. . . I felt so sick and nauseous even on Monday that I was tempted to telephone you and invite such solace as you could offer. I want your judgment and counsel, too, on when to begin to speak [on behalf of the New Deal]. I think I ought to deal with the "Tories of 1936" in something like the way in which I dealt with them at the Ford Hall meeting [a few weeks earlier], including, of course, Al, about whom I do not wish to let myself forget that he did stand out bravely against the Nazis in 1933, when the whole American Jewish Committee crowd, including Joseph Proskauer (who, I understand, wrote a good part of Al's speech), were seeking to pull away.

. . . I cannot believe that Al's thoroughly dishonest sophistry is going to catch the masses in America with whom the verdict will rest. What a rotten thing to speak of Roosevelt as inciting the class warfare, when his sin consisted in nothing more than coming to the rescue, in the American way, of the masses made up of forty millions who would have been overwhelmed by the economic disaster of 1929 had not Roosevelt intervened on their behalf as against the Raskobs and the Du Ponts and Shouses [founders and backers of the Liberty League, formed to combat the New Deal].

. . . We will fight on. We may lose, but the battle must be fought; and I am going to put aside, as far as I can, all of September and October in order to make such contribution as it is possible for me to make [toward the re-election of Roosevelt]. . . .

London, July 3, 1936

TO Nahum Goldmann, Paris

. . . I think you should come to London without a moment's delay and have your part in the negotiations [with the Colonial Office concerning the Palestine Mandate] and actions here. [David] Ben-Gurion has left for Palestine to return either next Friday or a week from Monday. He goes primarily to bring to the members of the Executive [of the Jewish Agency for Palestine] the terrible news of what is happening. I cannot hide from myself that we face a most desperate situation. I sent for Felix [Frankfurter] yesterday that we might talk things over. [Chaim] Weizmann is not frightened, but is evidently fighting with his back to the wall, knowing just what the dangers are and prepared to meet them with amazing resourcefulness and unwearying strength. . . .

London, July 5, 1936

TO Julian W. Mack, SS *Ile De France,* Havre

This is the most critical hour for us since the Balfour Declaration. . . . I am to see [Colonial Secretary William] Ormsby-Gore on Wednesday morning. The thing that all of us most dread is an early announcement of a stoppage of immigration. As I have sadly written to L. D. B. [Brandeis], because one hates to be the bearer of evil tidings to that great heart, the question is whether it will be possible to hold the Yishub [Jewish Community in Palestine] in hand when the news breaks. B. G. [Ben-Gurion] thinks it can be done; he is an undismayed spirit, but the rest of us are more doubtful because we know the young men would be able if they chose, and if they felt that everything was against them, to reduce Arab Jaffa to ashes, and even Arab Jerusalem within a few hours.

London, July 7, 1936

TO Louis D. Brandeis, Chatham, Mass.

I hope I have your congratulations upon being unanimously chosen as the President of the Z.O.A. [Zionist Organization of America]. For me it means that my fellow-Zionists want an uncompromisingly vigorous Zionist, not non-Zionist nor near-Zionist, leadership. And they shall have it.

London, July 11, 1936

TO Gertrude Hauser

. . . Louise had a nasty tumble, but she is much better and has been making a beautiful copy of one of the greatest El Grecos in the National Art Gallery. . . . The situation has been very grave, graver than I have dared let my fellow-Zionists know. I do not think that Great Britain means to hurt us or delude us; but under the pressure of what has happened in Ethiopia, and what may happen out of Germany, Great Britain does not want to have any more troubles, and therefore feels, though wrongly, that she may have to "chuck" us Jews rather than get into further difficulty with the Arabs of Palestine who represent the great Arabic-speaking peoples of the world. . . .

London, July 21, 1936

TO Nahum Goldmann, Geneva

. . . The situation is far from good. For the first time C. W. [Chaim Weizmann] is really discouraged. He will recover again from his discouragement, but so it is for the present. B. G. [David Ben-Gurion] believes that the High Commissioner [General Sir Arthur Wauchope] is definitely against suspension [of immigration], but apparently someone in the Colonial Office is mightier than both O. G. [William Ormsby-Gore] and A. W. [Arthur Wauchope].

. . . I had an appealing telegram today from New York. The Treasury is empty. I must get money. A nice situation on the eve of the [World Jewish] Congress! We are paying the expenses of 10 or more delegates to Geneva.

London, July 21, 1936

TO Louis D. Brandeis, Chatham, Mass.

I know that in due course you will receive copy of the cable that came . . . today from Shertok [Moshe Sharett, Jewish Agency for Palestine, Jerusalem]. . . . The whole cablegram will show you how grave the situation is and how seriously and vigorously Shertok is handling things in Palestine. You will remember what President [Woodrow] Wilson said to me in Paris [1919] of a certain gentleman [Brandeis himself] whom you have met, with whom I trust you will continue to be on the best terms for the next 20 years or more—"I need him everywhere, but I must leave him somewhere." I feel about Shertok that we need him everywhere, but I suppose he must be left in Palestine. Nonetheless, I wish we had his wise judgment and his fine understanding of our problem here in London at this time, although I know perfectly well that cannot be. I really believe that B. G. [Ben-Gurion] is oversanguine in his confidence that suspension of immigration will not lead to some explicable and indeed defensible Jewish violations. Evidently Shertok is greatly concerned.

I thank you, dear L. D. B., for your good wishes about my assumption of the Presidency of the Z.O.A. I shall do the best I can to try to put aside as much [of his schedule of other responsibilities] as I can in order to make that possible.

London, July 24, 1936

TO Louis D. Brandeis, Chatham, Mass.

. . . It seems now as if nothing could avert suspension [of immigration of Jewish refugees to Palestine]; announcement may be postponed for a time but that is all.

... I am staying on here for another 48 hours and then leaving for the Continent. I know hardly what to say excepting this, the question will not be decided in London. Felix [Frankfurter] and I share your feeling. It will ultimately be decided in Palestine by world Jewry. If you had seen, as I saw, the unbroken courage of the incredibly poor Jews in Warsaw and the way in which some of the men of Prytzyz responded (note what I wrote about it for the August *Opinion*), you will see that no commissions and no decrees and no agitation will avail to avert a great Jewish National Home. It will be hard, but it will not be impossible; that is the glory of it.

P.S. I saw Jimmy Rosenberg last night and [Chaim] Weizmann, [David] Ben-Gurion, Felix [Frankfurter] and I agreed that he should send a message to [Felix] Warburg. He [Rosenberg] was more timid about it than if I had asked him to telegraph to His Majesty King Edward VIII. His comment was: "Warburg is such a skillful and astute negotiator, I do not dare to give him advice. All I can do is lay the situation before him. He will know what to do." It is against that sort of thing—the Park Avenue *Stadtlanut* ["Court Jew" role]—that the World Jewish Congress may yet prove to be an effective protest. I am even of the hope that the Congress, unless suspension shall have been decreed in the meantime, may intervene and express the feeling of the Jewish world with power.

London, August 3, 1936

TO John Haynes Holmes, Kennebunk Beach, Maine

I really have missed a letter from you. I have waited and waited, and hoped and hoped for one. I am not finding fault—heaven forbid—but just want you to know that I have missed some word, such as in other years I have had from you. Perhaps you have not written because you are as unhappy about the present world situation as I am. I spent five weeks in London, working with [Chaim] Weizmann and Felix Frankfurter, and trying to avert the worst in relation to Palestine.

Our real enemy, when all is said, is not the British government; our real enemies are Mussolini and Hitler. A member of the British government, whose name I shall give you when we meet, let the cat out of the bag; we have been humiliated by Italy and we are faced by Hitler—that is the truth of the matter. Two things are against us, the accursed Hitler-Mussolini conjunction; then the persistent perfidy of the underlings in the Colonial Office. Whether the High Commissioner represents the underlings or not, I don't quite know, although I don't trust him as Ben-Gurion does, as Weizmann did and in part does; but they are our underlying and most cunning foes, and more or less completely they control—certainly influence—every one of the colonial secretaries.

. . . I hear that [Winston S.] Churchill recently said . . . Europe is in the hands of two ruthless dictators. That seems to me to be true. . . .

To me the journey to Warsaw was the most dreary, most saddening, most tragic and the most inspiring thing I have ever done. I pity my fellow Jews more, but I also honor and revere them more because of what I saw. One cellar apartment, for example, in Warsaw had six families in as many rooms, and such rooms! With a total population in these six rooms of fifty-two people, and each of them paying $3 rent per month, or virtually one-third of their income for those quarters in which decent rats ought not to be placed! . . .

Monnetier, Switzerland, August 5, 1936

TO Rebekah Kohut, New York City

. . . We had a tough time in London—all of us. I am not as optimistic as Felix Frankfurter, who thinks there will be no suspension [of immigration]. I am afraid there will, and the awful thing is that the Arabs should be rewarded for their damnable conduct and our fine, doubly brave Jews punished for the heroism of their self-restraint. That is what it really amounts to. The leadership fought hard. [Chaim] Weizmann has tremendous endurance; [David] Ben-Gurion is a really great figure, one of the outstanding Jews of the world today; and Shertok

[Moshe Sharett] seems the very incarnation of sanity and wisdom.

We had just a week's rest here on the mountainside of Geneva, at Monnetier; and now we are at Geneva working at the [World Jewish] Congress, which will begin on Saturday night. I am almost happy over the outlook. We shall have thirty-two countries represented by not less than 200 delegates or more, of whom 70 or 80 are Americans. We have a fine and well-balanced program; and I think despite the American Jewish Committee, and it has acted filthily in the matter of the League of Nations re the Nuremberg laws, we shall have a dignified and impressive and perhaps even a noble assembly.

After that comes the Hebrew University meeting for a few days, with just four or five days intermission; and then the Executive of the Zionist Organization almost to the day of my home going, and I confess that for the first time in my life I shrink from what lies before me—U.P.A. [United Palestine Appeal], Z.O.A. [Zionist Organization of America], [American Jewish] Congress, [Free] Synagogue, [Jewish] Institute [of Religion].

September 9, 1936

TO B. A. Hoover, Young Men's Christian Association, Springfield, Mass.

I have your letter and am deeply interested in what you write. With one sentence in your letter I must deal at once: "I certainly do not wish to think of you as taking the stump because of any financial remuneration that may be coming to you." Seeing that you have written to me, you ought to know me well enough to assume that I have never taken a penny from any political party, nor accepted any favor, nor been in any relation to any political organization, excepting to use it in the interest of public service. So much for that, and the rather grave misunderstanding which is implicit in that not pleasant sentence.

As for the other matter, I believe there are great issues involved in the present campaign—issues which go to the heart of American life and which involve the future of our American democracy. Against Roosevelt, in very large part, are those forces which I consider to be inimical to the highest interests of democratic life. I shall give the fullest measure of my support to the Roosevelt campaign because I believe that President Roosevelt's election is not only essential to the well-being of America, but to the highest interests of the human race. Against him, whether they are prepared to admit it or not, are arrayed the forces of that type of capital which damns Roosevelt because he dared to act on behalf of all the people when forty millions of Americans would have been without food and clothing had he not dared bravely and effectively to intervene.

The candidacy of [Alfred Mossman] Landon has one fatal demerit. He is endorsed, as in truth he was nominated, by [William Randolph] Hearst. Anyone whom Mr. Hearst nominates is sure to be imperiling to American ideals, and, if victorious, perhaps fatal to our American democracy.

I forgive you for presuming to suggest that I would accept financial remuneration for such service as I mean to render my country through the support of President Roosevelt. In return, I would ask you carefully to reconsider the issues that are at stake and whether you, as an American and religionist, do not owe it to your country and your fellow-Americans to re-elect to the Presidency a man who has merely served all the American people and against whom nothing graver can be said than that he has dared to use American resources in order to serve all the American people.

October 12, 1936

TO Harry Friedenwald, Baltimore

It was really providential that I returned [from the London meetings] because, as Judge Mack may have told you—I do not wish to put it all on paper—with [Postmaster General James J.] Farley's help, the Administration, including F. D. R. and the Secretary of State [Cordell Hull], proved decisively helpful the day before suspension [of immigration to Palestine] was to be declared. As a result of seeing the President at Hyde Park a few days ago, I now know that his intervention saved the situation, at least temporarily.

October 13, 1936

TO Emanuel Neumann, Tel Aviv

I am delighted to have your letter of September 22. I do not quite know how you heard about the intervention. Evidently you did. I wish you were here to vote for the Great Man [President Roosevelt]. If I could tell the whole truth about what was done, even the well-to-do Jews in America, who seem unanimously against him, would support him. He intervened, and the head of the State Department [Cordell Hull] intervened instantly, vigorously and effectively [with the British Colonial Office].

I went to Hyde Park last Monday, and the Country Gentleman, who lives there, told me that he had word from one of the two leading members of the [British] cabinet that suspension [of immigration to Palestine] had been dropped because of Hyde Park's and America's wish. . . .

November 18, 1936

TO Irma Lindheim, Haifa

Firstly, I must tell you we are very, very happy over Roosevelt's re-election. He is not going to be a Messiah to America; but his defeat would have been a disaster of the first magnitude. It would have given heart and hope to all the anti-Semitic and all the Fascist and all the Hearstian elements of American life. We have in him a warm and understanding friend. He and I have made up: and I spent October practically going through the country in his behalf though we know he needed the help of only one man, namely himself. He affectionately reveres L. D. B. [Brandeis], to whom he always alludes, in the innermost circle, as Isaiah. Of course he is tremendously fond of Felix [Frankfurter], and likes and respects [Julian] Mack, as everyone must.

I am working terribly hard as President of the Zionist Organization of America, and Chairman of the United Palestine Appeal. . . .

. . . I will write again as soon as I find time. Be patient with a very tired and a very busy old gentleman.

December 18, 1936

TO Julian W. Mack

. . . Do you get the [*Juedische*] *Rundschau?* This is a very good
article on Brandeis except for that curious opinion that Brandeis'
withdrawal from the Zionist movement was bound up with
Wilsonism, etc. Of course, the truth will not be known until a
long time hence, and then it will not matter—that Brandeis'
withdrawal was due to his lack of respect for the "Great Chaim"
[Weizmann]. . . .

We must have a smile after all this deadly serious business.
Louise [Waterman Wise] had a note today from a family asking
for a child [from the Free Synagogue Child Adoption Service],
and concluding: "We have tried four times to have children of
our own, but have always been unsuccessful in carrying this
through."—What an impatient lady!

January 18, 1937

TO Edmund I. Kaufmann, Hollywood, Florida

. . . What you write about your visit to L. D. B. [Brandeis] is
exactly what I feel about him when I see him. You are right—he
is truly a great man and would have made a great President. Did
you know that both [William Jennings] Bryan and President
[Charles William] Eliot of Harvard said that at different times;
that he ought to be President of the United States? And I have
no doubt that he would have been but for the fact he is not
an Aryan. . . .

March 19, 1937

TO Julian W. Mack, Hollywood, Florida

. . . I am most unhappy about [Secretary of State Cordell]
Hull's reference to what he calls "row" and "vituperation." He
interprets Hitler's war upon civilization and our non-violent
resistance as a "row," and that is very sad! In the interest of
Palestine, we are going to do what we can to let that pass from

the scene. We cannot press the Hitler button and the British-and-Palestine button at one and the same time!

April 9, 1937

TO J. L. Zlotnik, Vancouver, British Columbia

. . . I consider it very honoring that you should feel that I might have given my life to scholarly work. I did two things in the field of Jewish learning—one, the [Solomon ibn-] Gabirol volume [*The Improvement of the Moral Qualities*]; and the other, the translation of the Book of Judges, on which I worked for a year with the Jewish Publication Society. Then Zionism came and all the multifarious claims of Jewish life, as a result particularly of the fact that, out in the Northwest from 1900 to 1906, I was the only rabbi who was thoroughly active in Jewish life, especially in Zionism.

You will never know how I envy those men who, like yourself, manage to steal some time for *"Wissenschaft"* [learning]. . . . I have patience enough to be a scholar; but, alas, fate and Jewish history and Herzl and Hitler have decreed a different fate for me. I would have loved nothing better than to have been a student all my days; but I am afraid that such gifts as I have for propaganda and administration have forever taken me away from the possibility of being a scholar.

I have done one thing by way of self-compensation, namely, created an institution of Jewish learning [Jewish Institute of Religion]. There, at least, I vicariously serve Jewish learning and help our great faculty, including such men as [Shalom] Spiegel and [Chaim] Tchernowitz, to do the things that I would fain do, and give to our young men an appreciation of the dignity of Jewish learning and its supreme importance to the maintenance of the Jewish tradition. . . .

June 18, 1937

TO Chaim Weizmann, London

. . . I can well understand, dear Weizmann, how heavy and wearying must be the burden that rests upon you, for I, who am

far from the scene, feel almost crushed by the responsibilities
that are ours on this side of the Atlantic. May you bear up under
the strain, and be enabled to bring about happier things than
are promised in this hour. . . .

P.S. This letter is meant for Ben-Gurion as well as for you.

June 23, 1937

TO Emanuel Neumann, Tel Aviv

I do want you to know for your comfort—whether it will avail
to help us or not—that in the District of Columbia we have a
great, good Friend. He is thinking about us and for us. He is
planning for us. We are in his mind and on his heart. Thank
God for that little *"refuah"* [balm or healing] in a time of
endless *"makkot"* [beatings or plagues]!

Zürich, August 3, 1937

TO Julian W. Mack

. . . One word about yesterday. Practically the whole day was
spent at the meeting of the A.C. [Actions Committee of the
World Zionist Congress]. . . .

. . . A really excellent address was made by [Abba Hillel]
Silver. He only spoke for 15 or 20 minutes, but it was a powerful, passionate protest against partition [of Palestine as recom-
mended by the Peel Commission]. . . . Then came adjournment,
which was a very unpleasant scene for me, because I had to listen
to a lot of angry and envious Americans, namely Solomon Goldman, [Barnett] Brickner, [Elihu] Stone, and [Jacob] Fishman,
protest that no one had been called upon to speak and that
there was no general discussion. . . . I have not spoken at all.
I am waiting for the Congress. Silver was the only one who
insisted upon having a chance to say a word and he was very,
very fine; but still I am sorry to say, particularly about my
precious colleagues, that they are bitterly and lamentably envious

of Silver and his very great power of public utterance. There is
no doubt about that whatever.

TELEGRAM

Lake Placid, N. Y., September 9, 1937

TO The President, Hyde Park, N.Y.

DEAR MR. PRESIDENT: I HAVE BEEN SICK AT HEART SINCE RETURNING
FROM EUROPE OVER STATE DEPARTMENT'S SENDING ENVOY TO NUREM-
BERG NAZI PARTY FESTIVAL DESPITE AMBASSADOR DODD'S PROTEST.

NOW AS AN AMERICAN CITIZEN AND YOUR SUPPORTER I CAN NO
LONGER REFRAIN FROM CALLING YOUR ATTENTION TO SPEECH YES-
TERDAY BY ALFRED ROSENBERG, NAZI CULTURAL LEADER, UPON RE-
CEIVING FIRST NAZI PRIZE AT NUREMBERG. QUOTING ASSOCIATED
PRESS: "HE RELENTLESSLY ATTACKED DEMOCRACY, CHURCH AND LIBER-
ALISM, PREDICTED THE DESTRUCTION OF ALL DEMOCRATIC STATES,
RIDICULED THE HEADS OF DEMOCRATIC STATES FOR THEIR DEFENSE
OF LIBERAL PRINCIPLES."

CAN YOU, THE GREAT LIBERAL LEADER OF THE GREATEST OF DEMOC-
RACIES, PERMIT THIS OFFICIAL INSULT TO DEMOCRACY AND LIBERAL-
ISM TO GO UNREBUKED? IT CANNOT BE TOO LATE TO ORDER THE
RECALL OF OUR AMERICAN REPRESENTATIVE TO NUREMBERG. THE
SUPREME OPPORTUNITY IS YOURS NOW TO REAFFIRM THE INVIOLABLE.

November 7, 1937

TO Julian W. Mack

Had two interesting days in Chicago, with only four addresses,
one at the University in the morning, one at Northwestern, . . .
I spoke [at the Temple in Cleveland, Ohio] for [Abba Hillel]
Silver at a symposium with [Reinhold] Niebuhr, and heard an
address by Niebuhr which was a tour de force. There is not
another man in America who could have done it, excepting
Felix [Frankfurter]. Felix would have been more insinuatingly
persuasive, but this man hammered and pounded himself into

our heads. I felt like a fat old dray horse coming after Maud S
[celebrated trotting mare of Saratoga Springs, N.Y. in 1880s].

November 10, 1937

TO Julian W. Mack

I write to you in order to get your judgment on something
which I consider of possibly great importance. I need not tell
you what the Jewish situation throughout the world is. We try
to do a lot of little things, but I do not know that we have
reached the heart of the situation. Perhaps nothing can be done,
though that would be a heart-breaking admission to be forced
to make.

I have thought of a plan—I'd like to have your mind on it—
namely, that [Cyrus] Adler, and [Morris] Cohen, possibly Sol
Stroock and I, and you with us, I hope, bring together the Jewish
members of [the United States] Congress, most of whom, alas, are
uninformed and nearly all of whom are little concerned. But it is
our business to get at their souls. My idea is that we tell the
whole story of what is happening in Germany, Austria, Hungary,
and above all, Poland and Rumania, to these gentlemen, eight
or ten in all, with a view to their going as Jews, or together with
a group of non-Jewish members of both Houses of Congress, to
the President, putting the Jewish question before him and asking
him whether something cannot be done to bring to European
lands a sense of American horror, though, alas, it must be added
parenthetically that there is not too much of such American
horror.

I am not sure that I know what the President could do. He
could, of course, send for the ambassadors of the different countries and tell them that public opinion in this country is revolting
against the hideousness of the Jewish situation in European
lands. I do not mean any public protest. The Jewish Congressmen might name two or three men of their own and they might
or might not be accompanied by us, representing larger Jewish
organizations.

The thing is not clear in my own mind, excepting for this:

you remember, though you were not present at the time, when Chatham [Justice Louis D. Brandeis] and B. N. C. [Benjamin N. Cardozo] and Felix [Frankfurter] met with a number of Congressmen and the rest of us in May or June of 1933, to discuss the Nazi situation. The world Jewish situation is infinitely graver today than it was then. I know the President is worried and harried, but I do not know that anyone has made a real effort to bring home to him, burdened as he is, the evil of the present world Jewish situation.

Please think it over and call me up or write to me about it. I have not written to Felix or to anyone else. I know Felix feels that the "Skipper" [President Roosevelt] ought to be spared. Have we the right to omit to do anything which holds out the faintest promise of relief for our people? The Central and East European situation is catastrophic. . . . . I lie awake at nights. I have ceased to be able to sleep. I cannot shake off the awful responsibility. Perhaps the thing could be tied up with Palestine in some way. I do not know. Give me your judgment.

January 31, 1938

TO Joseph Rauh, Jr., Washington

Your letter is really heartening. I know we dare not be too hopeful at present, but the faintest gleam of light in the darkness is so welcome that my wife and I, with countless others, rejoice in it. The President [Franklin Delano Roosevelt] was so happy over my last Saturday morning's report of some gain, that if things continue to go well you [as private secretary to Justice Cardozo] might write a line to him and let him have the happiness of knowing that things are a little better.

Even the hurried glimpse of B. N. C. showed that even in sickness and pain the majesty of his being had not left him. Let us hope on and pray that he may yet be spared and, if it be the Divine Will, that he may be restored to that vigor of mind which has blessed our country.

February 8, 1938

TO Emanuel Neumann, Tel Aviv

. . . I am so miserable about the Jewish situation (what with damnable Rumania and Poland, to say nothing of Germany) that I am almost prepared to swim over [to Palestine] and live in a hut with my fellow Jews; and the deepest tragedy for me is that, excepting for Jews in Eastern and Central Europe, I have a minimum of sympathy with my fellow-Jews in America, who today are wasting more money in two winter months in Florida than they have put into Palestine in twenty-five years. This generation is not worth saving. What we do must be for generations unborn, and, therefore, without sin and guilt, unlike our present generation in its shameful unconcern and tragic indifference to our dangers and our hopes. . . .

London, March 6, 1938

TO Felix Frankfurter, Cambridge, Mass.

. . . You may be amused by . . . my meeting with [newly appointed U.S. ambassador to the Court of St. James] Joe Kennedy. As his friend you will be glad to hear that he has already made an impression on the country. I don't know whether the American papers reported that when he was asked why he didn't bring his wife and nine children along, he answered, "Because of the housing situation. I mean to bring them over in installments."

Best of all, he gave me what seemed like a genuine report of his interview with [Lord] Halifax. Fancy anyone on earth presuming to say to this saintly gentleman . . . "The Irish Americans have always considered you Englishmen s.o.b.s, and now $4\frac{1}{2}$ million Jews are going to say the same thing, etc., etc." . . .

I may have mentioned in my earlier letter that [Harold] Laski . . . was unbelievably rude, having the distinction of being the only person I have ever called upon, who not only failed to rise to greet me, but did not even do me the honor of uncrossing his legs on the desk. His first word upon *not* arising was, "Who are

you? And what do you want?"—something that I would not say
to the humblest German refugee. But I must add at once that
everything was made good by his enquiry, "How is your adorable
daughter?" I should have told him in advance that I am the
grandson of a Hungarian Baron. Had he known, he might have
uncrossed his legs! Who knows?

April 1, 1938

TO Ludwig Lewisohn, New Rochelle, N.Y.

. . . I am not hopeful at all that there is such a thing as a
Christian conscience to be aroused. That prostitute [Austrian
Cardinal Theodor] Innitzer selling himself into the arms of
Hitler, and [the Archbishop of] Canterbury thanking God for
the "peaceable invasion of Vienna"—two hundred thousand sol-
diers, hundreds of tanks and bombing planes. This is what our
Christian brothers mean by the glory of non-resistance.

But on the other hand, we Jews are still worse. We do not
care. We give one tenth of one hundredth of one per cent of
our possessions and we think we have done our duty. I confess
an almost fiendish glee in the thought that all of them will yet
have to yield up 92½%, as do the German Jews today whom I
saw on the homecoming ship. I almost despair of doing anything
for our people because our people simply wish to go on, to live
from day to day, and from hand to mouth without feeling, without sacrificing. In that way no people can live.

May 13, 1938

TO Philip Slomowitz, Detroit

I am delighted to have your fine review [in the Detroit *Jewish
News*] of the book of [John Haynes] Holmes [*Through Gentile
Eyes*]. Please send him a copy. He is the dearest, finest human
being in the world. I think it is precious and I share your feeling
that tens of thousands of copies should be in the hands of
Christians, as well as American Jews. The latter need a stiffening
of the spine at least as much as do non-Jews.

May 28, 1938

TO Rosemary Krensky, Chicago

I have your letter; and you, Milton and I can discuss things fully when I get to Chicago. For the present let me say that unity is not what they desire who talk about unity. It is dominance. They resent the introduction of democracy into Jewish life, and there we part, and part hopelessly and forever. While I live I will not tolerate the oligarchic method of control which repudiates democracy. Democracy means that all people shall have a share in the management of their affairs. This the older generation of German Jews is determined to deny the masses. This I am resolved to assure them. Everything else could be settled, but there is no compromise here.

We had a meeting for three hours yesterday—[Louis] Lipsky, Professor [Jerome] Michael and Professor [Horace] Kallen and myself with representatives of the B'nai B'rith and the American Jewish Committee and the [Jewish] Labor Council. What can you do with people who frankly say to you that they are afraid of the unfortunate impression which will be made upon the non-Jewish world by the appearance of Jewish solidarity? It is hopeless. The fight is on. Win or lose, we shall go through with it.

June 9, 1938

TO Julian W. Mack

. . . I begin today X-ray treatment which, it is hoped, will reduce this hideous spleen of mine and thus relieve other pressures. I am terribly anxious to see you. I will come in just as soon as I can. Today, for example, after having been absent since Monday night, I have three days' accumulated mail (personal, Institute, Synagogue, U.P.A. [United Palestine Appeal], Z.O.A. [Zionist Organization of America], A.J.C. [American Jewish Congress]); X-ray treatment; A.J.C. and U.P.A. meetings; and an address in Newark at nine!

June 27, 1938

TO L. Bakstansky, London

. . . I am devoutly of the hope that Dr. Weizmann will go to
Evian [Conference of Intergovernmental Committee on Refugees
at Evian-les-Bains]. As a member of the President's Committee
on Political Refugees I have so shaped things that I am sure
he will have, as is becoming, a most gracious welcome. And
there is no one who can present the Jewish case as he can. I am
cabling to him at some length so that he may understand. It
becomes the more necessary to do this because Jonah Wise will
be there on behalf of the Joint Distribution Committee, and he
is one of the profoundest of our enemies.

I have been tempted to go to Evian, but the members of the
President's Committee—[Paul] Baerwald and I—felt that it would
be wisest for Jewish members of the Committee not to go. In
fact no member of the Committee is going to Evian excepting
Dr. [James G.] McDonald as our representative. Things may
safely be left in his hands. He has not been in Palestine, but he
is one of its warmest non-Jewish friends and advocates.

I may say to you in confidence that another reason for my not
going to Evian—though a lesser one—is that I ought to be in
Detroit on the 3rd and 4th of July, when I retire from the Presidency [of the Zionist Organization of America]. And finally—
what is absolutely confidential—I have been far from well. In
the last few weeks, even in the terrible excitement of the American Jewish Congress elections, I have been under X-ray treatment, and until that X-ray treatment is over and the doctors
declare that I may be released—pending my return to X-ray
treatment in the fall—I may not go to Europe. . . .

June 28, 1938

TO Rosemary Krensky, Chicago

. . . There is too much soft-soaping in American Jewish life.
No one speaks the truth, excepting secretly and clandestinely the
bitterest lies, spoken by those who disagree with us. . . . I shall

not change my method of frank and direct speech. If I have any influence in American life, it is for two reasons—because American Jews know I am not afraid, and because they know I speak the truth as I see it. Sometimes I speak it roughly and brusquely, but I shall continue so to speak it.

August 8, 1938

TO Joseph Rauh, Jr., Washington

I thank you more than I can say for your note. My wife and I are sad because of what you write, that you are breaking up the dear Judge's home [Benjamin Cardozo died July 9, 1938]. It is very good of Miss Tracy [the nurse] to wish us to have the Judge's tea table, which both Nellie and Elizabeth [Cardozo] loved, and to send me the Judge's favorite walking stick, which I shall prize as long as I live. . . .

September 13, 1938

TO Emanuel Neumann, Tel Aviv

It was a great delight to hear from you in July. I would be ashamed to admit it was so long ago; but, as you may have heard, I was in very bad shape in June and July—spleen trouble, from which I have suffered for years, ever since the Lucerne [Zionist] Congress, having come to a head and requiring continuous X-ray treatment. I feel better, but it seems as if this would be a constantly recurring thing, and I shall need X-ray treatment from time to time. My one hope is that I may be well enough to render service to our cause.

If we had talked about it before, you would have understood —while I was delighted to hear from you about C.S.R. [Czechoslovak Republic]—there is never any need for appealing to me to do everything possible for the Masaryk Republic. It will interest and almost amuse you to learn that the first address of the Free Synagogue during the Succoth week of 1907 was given by [Thomas] Masaryk himself, then the little-known Prague ex-professor. [Theodor] Herzl spoke to me about him as early as 1898 when he [Masaryk] was magnificently defending [Leopold] Huelsner [a Jew accused of "ritual murder" in 1899 at Polna, Bohemia], Angelo Goldstein and the C.S. [Czechoslovak] people here understand there is nothing I would not do for them. I even suggested a certain course to them, which they have not followed: to invite great American journalists such as William Allen White [of the Emporia, Kan. *Gazette*] to go there and report on the true state of affairs with regard to the Sudetens, etc.

I am still under the impact of the raucous, revolting, rabble-rousing speech of Hitler yesterday. Though one hate war as little else in the world, one wonders whether the world will again be completely united against the Nazis as it has been in the last few days. Will he not wait until disaffection arises between England and France, or between London and ourselves, before embarking on the C.S. invasion?

. . . To talk about conditions in Palestine would take an eternity. We cannot quite make things out here. It is too much for us . . . . I feel . . . that, bad as indecision may be, it is better than decision at this time. This is no time for a decision, because if war should come, the Arabs will take their place with the Fascists and Nazis, where their leaders, if not their people, belong. War, on the other hand, may be immensely helpful to Britain, and that would mean that Palestine would be ours. It would be a low ground on which to reward us; but, after all, England would have the opportunity to test its friends and learn who were its foes. . . .

September 23, 1938

то Milton Krensky, Chicago

. . . I had known for some time that the chief pressure against F. F. [Felix Frankfurter] is being wielded by Jews. These unspeakable cowards are afraid that another Jew on the Supreme

Court bench may bring us hurt. I think I shall mention the thing in my Holy Day services. . . .

September 30, 1938

TO Rosemary Krensky

I . . . regard yesterday as one of the dismalest days of world history, because it means the destruction of Czechoslovakia, that great bulwark of democracy, by collusion between the so-called democratic powers, England and France, and the ruthless dictators of Germany and Italy.

TELEGRAM

October 6, 1938

TO The President, Hyde Park, N.Y.

DEAR MR. PRESIDENT: I HAVE EVERY REASON TO BELIEVE, FROM CABLES I HAVE RECEIVED FROM DR. WEIZMANN OF LONDON WHICH ILLUMINATE THE NEWS DESPATCH IN THE MORNING'S PAPER, THAT THE LIQUIDATION OF THE DECLARED POLICY OF THE BRITISH GOVERNMENT, IN FAVOR OF A JEWISH NATIONAL HOME IN PALESTINE, IS IMMINENTLY THREATENED. BEFORE DOWNING STREET MAKES SO GRAVE AND IRREVOCABLE A COMMITMENT, I BESEECH YOU TO PUT IN YOUR WORD.

MAY I RECALL HOW EFFECTIVE WAS YOUR WORD OF TWO YEARS AGO WHEN TEMPORARY STOPPAGE OF IMMIGRATION WAS THREATENED? YOU ALONE AVERTED IT THROUGH A PERSONAL APPEAL TO NEVILLE CHAMBERLAIN.

ALTHOUGH I DISLIKE TO BREAK IN UPON YOUR REST AT HYDE PARK, THE THREATENED ACTION OF THE BRITISH GOVERNMENT IS SO GRAVE A MENACE TO EXISTING AS WELL AS FUTURE JEWISH SETTLEMENT IN PALESTINE THAT I SHOULD WELCOME THE OPPORTUNITY OF DISCUSSING IT WITH YOU AT HYDE PARK THIS FRIDAY OR SATURDAY BEFORE WE ARE PRESENTED WITH A FAIT ACCOMPLI. . . .

December 15, 1938

TO Mrs. G. S. Best, Warsaw, North Carolina

Many letters come to me such as your own. I cannot as a rule answer them because I am too busy. But your own letter is conceived and framed in such an understanding way that I feel I must say a word to you. I have no doubt that you believe exactly what you say, that Jews ought to accept Jesus as the redeeming Son of God. You will understand me when I say to you that Jews cannot accept Jesus or anyone else as the one redeeming, atoning Son of God. We believe we have access to God without intermediary. Such is the teaching, implicit and explicit, of Israel. I have no quarrel with you because you believe honestly what you believe. But you must have no quarrel with me because I am as loyal to my faith as you are to yours.

I cannot, however, but ask you whether you really believe that God will deliver Jews from their persecutions only if we turn to Him and repent and ask Him to help us to accept His son. I cannot believe that. Whether we are persecuted or not, I believe that what is suffered by the Jews today at the hands of so-called Christians is regarded by them as a trial to be endured. I will not bargain with God through Jesus or in any way whatsoever. We may want for a time and endure again, as indeed we do. But He is still our shepherd, our refuge, our redeemer. . . .

January 19, 1939

TO A. B. Horwitz, Duluth

I have your letter and I hasten to answer it. . . . I pause long enough to deal with one sentence . . . you quote, namely, "I do not consider myself an American Jew, but a Jew in America." In the course of an address before the American Jewish Congress in June 1938, I was dealing with a self-contemptuous statement of the American Jewish Committee, in which they spoke of themselves as Americans who were Jews. I answered, "I could not speak of myself as an American who is a Jew. I am an American Jew. I have been a Jew for four thousand years. I have been an American for sixty-four years. I am of the Jewish race and people. I am of the American nation, and an American citizen; and there is no conflict between my Jewish race and faith and my American citizenship, of which I am most proud."

On behalf of refugees stranded abroad, Stephen Wise signed countless affidavits, assuming financial responsibility for them when they arrived in the United States or borrowing from his own limited resources to ransom them and send them to some other land. No effort, no expense, was too great for him if he could rescue the persecuted and bring Jewish refugees either to Palestine or the United States. Their problems and their plight were now his, too.

London, February 25, 1939

TO William Stricker, New York City

Your letter has come and I need hardly say that I share your hopes over your father's complete release. I did try my best and moved in the highest quarters, of which I shall tell you, to effect his release, but now, as you know, Dr. [Nahum] Goldmann has succeeded in seeing to it in a certain way, and I was happy to bear my share of the rather large expense in effectuating what all of us desire. I am sorry to think you and I will not be able to see your father before he leaves for Palestine, but the important thing is that he is free. . . . When I get home as I shall within a fortnight, I will write to him, assuming that at that time you will know his address in Palestine, and he will have left, as Nahum Goldmann says he will be permitted to leave, after a month or two in Vienna. I earnestly trust this is so, for his sake and for the sake of all who love him. . . .

May 17, 1939

TO The President, The White House, Washington

In this hour of sorrow over the betrayal of Jewish faith and hope by the Chamberlain government [in its White Paper on

Palestine, reducing immigration to 15,000 annually for five years and stopping it completely in 1944], we feel impelled to say to you that we are mindful of all that you have sought to do on behalf of our cause in recent years.

On several occasions it was your understanding and your intervention in London that averted disaster. Today, alas, your earnest and devoted effort has not availed; and the British government has, at one and the same time, the melancholy satisfaction of violating its pledged word by Balfour, and of refusing to answer your own great vision and your desire to see justice done to our people.

World Jewry and particularly the Jews of Palestine will not, dear Mr. President, forget all that you have done or sought to do on our behalf. We shall remember and be grateful always.

May 26, 1939

TO Rosemary Krensky

. . . What with the tragic Palestine situation and the really rising tide of anti-Semitism everywhere, I do not know what to do! . . . Last night, after Carnegie Hall was refused to the so-called Christian Front, made up of Coughlinites, they marched up and down 57th Street, shouting, "Hang Rabbi Wise to a flagpole! Lynch Rabbi Wise!"—Thousands of them and the police didn't even interfere. . . .

July 21, 1939

TO S. Ralph Harlow, London

. . . We are all so hurt by the White Paper. It is such a hideous repudiation by [Prime Minister Neville] Chamberlain of England at its best in the authorship of the Balfour Declaration. And now comes the still worse report that [Colonial Secretary Malcolm] MacDonald has, three or four months in advance, cancelled the October schedule, which is really shutting the door of hope to my people throughout Central and Eastern

Europe—indeed throughout the world. This is not the England that I have known and loved. It was [Arthur James] Balfour and [William] Gladstone—and my father, who never set foot on English soil—who made me love and revere England. Chamberlain and [Samuel] Hoare and Sir John Simon have done their best or worst to exorcise my longtime loving reverence for everything English. . . .

August 31, 1939

TO Julian W. Mack

. . . One can hardly write about anything, excepting the deepening shadows that overhang. Will Hitler be mad enough to choose war? One does not know which horror is deeper, the horror of murderous war, or the horrors of surrender in the name of peace!

September 1, 1939

TO Fanny Mayer Korn, Sharon Springs, N.Y.

We are in town for the day, having vacated the premises at Lake Placid because of eviction at the hands of our children, who have a house full of guests we are not hospitable enough to enjoy. We shall look about for the next day or two, hoping to find a place within forty or fifty miles of New York which we can test out for another summer, with a view to deciding whether we can have a sort of little week-end place instead of motoring all day to the Adirondacks.

How trivial it seems to speak of these things, in the light of the great and overwhelmingly tragic reality! Hitler has chosen war, and, oh, the horror of Stalin going with him! That ends our hope that Communism might arrest the power of Fascism. Evidently, they are one, and they are both equally the enemies of democracy. . . .

September 5, 1939

TO Julian W. Mack

. . . We were looking and looking for a little [vacation] place
for September and next summer, but have given up the quest.
House hunting seems a little too trivial an occupation in these
awful days. One is heart-broken over the war; but it would
have been still more heart-breaking if Hitler should have gotten
away with this, as he did with all the other crimes since 1933.

September 7, 1939

TO A Bereaved Family

Needless to tell you, who are suffering so much, how shocked
I was when I learned of the catastrophe that had befallen all
of you, and most especially your dear boy. It seems incredible
and inexplicable. I sorrow for M.'s parents and for R., on the
eve of his facing the great happiness that was to have been his
own, and that of all of you who loved her. How the beautiful
romance has lapsed into ruin and desolation!

I wish I knew what to say to you and to her parents, and
to R. It is one of the unexplainable mysteries of life, and,
alas, there are so many! All one can do is try to keep one's
faith, if one have it, or to achieve it, if one have it not. Even
though the children did not have their life together, as they
had dreamed and hoped, still, they had at least a gleam of the
high rapture which was to have been their own. But I remember the word of Lowell,

> For all the preaching since Adam
> Has not made Death other than Death.

How low one is to utter the word "Death" in connection
with a young and beautiful life! I confess I am at a loss for
words. I wish I were near enough to all of you to press your
hands and tell you that if sympathy can help those who are
in sorrow and who have suffered awful loss, you would feel
some slight measure of comfort in your unutterable loss. . . .

September 16, 1939

TO The Bereaved Family (a week later)

I know what these hours must be to you—how grievous to
you . . . and how torturing to R., for tomorrow should have
been their wedding day. If it had been humanly possible, I
would have gone [the 170 mile distance] to spend the day with
you. But it is not. . . .

All this merely by way of explanation of my failure to come
to the help and solace of cherished friends—if there can be any
help and solace for you, other than that which comes from
within, strengthened by the fortitude that dwells within your
own souls.

I am afraid I have not any message for the boy. He must
battle his way through, alone. In the last analysis, it is only
when, as I tried to say in my New Year's sermon, excerpts of
which I enclose, one stands alone with the Alone that one can
find some sense of strength. No life is livable on any other
hypothesis.

But I do not mean to philosophize; merely to offer my hand
to you . . . who suffer, but who, I pray, suffer not without
hope that, with time, the boy will become stronger and stronger
and think back upon the disaster that has befallen him with
gratitude for all that he had rather than with rebellion against
that which robbed him of his treasure.

November 1, 1939

TO Julian W. Mack

They [the officials and staff members] had a beautiful farewell
dinner at the Palestine Pavilion [of the New York World's Fair],
and I was presented, in a gem of a speech by [Louis] Lipsky,
with the [Jacob] Epstein bust, which looks as though I were a
man of 87 with a running nose.

CHAPTER FIVE

IF I FORGET THEE, O JERUSALEM
(1940-1949)

TO JOHN POLACHEK

> . . . In connection with my 70th birthday . . . there is nothing personal whatsoever which I could accept for myself, whether as pension, or annuity, or capital fund. I will not accept any personal gift, whether it be an umbrella or a million dollars. I will be most grateful for anything that you and other friends will do for the causes [the Free Synagogue, the Jewish Institute of Religion, the American and World Jewish Congresses, the Zionist movement, etc.] which mean much more to me than my personal affairs.
>
> *December 27, 1943*

January 15, 1940

TO Chaim Weizmann

I send you a copy of a letter which I have just addressed to
Dr. [James G.] McDonald. I hope you will agree that it would
be worth your while accepting an invitation from the President's
Advisory Committee for Political Refugees, in order that you
may present the case of Palestine. You and I have done it with
Myron Taylor, and, of course, with McDonald in earlier years;
but in view of the ceaseless persistence of the J.D.C. [Joint
Distribution Committee] people, [Paul] Baerwald, [James] Rosenberg and the rest, in urging such *fata morgana* [mirages] as
[Jewish colonies in] Santo Domingo, British Guiana, and Min-
danao, it would be exceedingly important for these people at
first hand to hear the story of Palestine from you.

February 6, 1940

TO Walter S. Hilborn, Los Angeles

. . . Whether we like Dr. Weizmann's leadership or not, he
does represent the Zionist government or control, and those of
us who wish to help Palestine must work with him. He has
his limitations; he has his faults, but in many ways he is statesmanlike; and there is no living Jew except Brandeis who im-
pacts as he does upon non-Jews. It is little less than miraculous.
He is a man of undoubted eminence and power.

February 29, 1940

TO Julian W. Mack

. . . The luncheon [at the Jewish Institute of Religion] after the degree [of Doctor of Humane Letters] was conferred upon [Chaim] Weizmann was very enjoyable, excepting for your comment on my citation. Did it ever occur to you that you cannot confer an honorary degree upon a man and at the same time call him an "s.o.b."? Your answer will be: But you do not have to laud him to the skies. An honorary degree is just that—*cum laude!*

May 18, 1940

TO Edmund I. Kaufmann, Washington

Thank you with all my heart for your kind invitation to join in the Springtime Frolic of 1940 [fund-raising event of the Jewish community]. Even if I could find time to go, dear Ed, and I have four or five engagements in and out of New York between the 21st and 25th of June, I would still feel—and you will forgive me for being perfectly frank about it—that this is no time for frolics, whether Spring or Autumn. This is a time for solemn and prayerful meditation on the part of Jews on how Jews are going to live in the future, and what they must give of their substance and of their lives in order that they may live. What I say may sound pontifical and much too solemn, but I mean exactly what I say.

When, for example, I heard in your city the other night that one of the so-called "big shots" there satisfied his conscience, if he have any, by giving $400 to the United Jewish Appeal, including three great urgent causes [American Jewish Joint Distribution Committee, Jewish Agency for Palestine, and United Service for New Americans], and that the same man, I am told, flips a coin for a thousand dollars a throw on the Springtime Frolic, it moves me to feel that, as an educational institution, the Springtime Frolic up to 1940 leaves much to be desired.

August 30, 1940

TO The Bereaved Family (one year later)

... Monday will be the anniversary of that dear child's passing. What awful days Sunday and Monday will be for you, and, of course, above all, for R., who loved her. It is inexplicable, just as many, many things are. How can one keep one's faith, men ask. My answer, inadequate and unsatisfying though it be, is— how can one live without faith? Without faith everything in the world is reduced to chaos or malignity. Chaos almost rules the day; still, there is wisdom and tenderness, and there are memories of these things, which are hardly the concomitants of chaos. As for malignity ruling the world, that, of course, is an impossible hypothesis, for it is much more difficult to reconcile the evils of the world with providence, than beauty and love with either chaos or malignity. Remember the line of the great German poet—

> Entsagen muss der Mensch, entsagen!
> [Human beings must renounce!]

Of course it is hard, and life's hardest task, and bitterest! And one would not choose the hardest and bitterest and cruellest renunciation. But if one cannot voluntarily renounce, one must yet, in time, be resigned. It is the only way, though I am not unmindful of the infinite loss and sorrow which your dear boy suffers! ...

September 17, 1940

TO Otto Nathan, Cambridge, Mass.

Your letter has been before me for some days. I held it chiefly because I had hoped that I might send you some cheerful word. Alas, I cannot! I tried to do what could be done in the matter of Leon Blum, appealing through Felix [Frankfurter] and Archie [Archibald MacLeish] to the highest quarters. As late as September 14, Archie wrote to Felix: "I am assured this morning that Blum is in no danger, that there is some hope of arranging Blum's departure from France, and that everything that could be done seems to have been done." The following day he was taken into custody [by the Nazis].

With respect to the other matter of which you write, it is a long, long story and I cannot deal with it adequately in this way. There are certain things that we get done, other things cannot be done at all. One of the things that could be done could only be done because Eleanor R[oosevelt] and Marshall Field appealed to the Skipper [President Franklin D. Roosevelt] for the liberation of the refugees on the *Quanza*. All of them were released. They were denied admission to Mexico, although every one of them had paid $100 for a transit visa; and many of them, if not all, had paid $200 apiece for visas to Venezuela, etc., etc. They were shipped back; but after infinite effort on our part, both the President's Committee and the J.D.C. [American Jewish Joint Distribution Committee], and [Cecilia] Razovsky and others, we were able to get them landed, and now they are ashore. But of course it could not have been done unless the Skipper had taken the needful step.

With regard to the political refugees, we are in the midst of the most difficult situation, an almost unmanageable quandary. On the one hand, the State Department makes all sorts of promises, and takes all our lists; and then we hear that the consuls do nothing. A few people slip through, but we are afraid—this in strictest confidence—that the consuls have private instructions from the [State] Department to do nothing, which would be infamous beyond words. What I am afraid lies back of the whole thing is the fear of the Skipper's friends in the State Department that any large admission of radicals to the United States might be used effectively against him in the campaign. Cruel as I may seem, as I have said to you before, his re-election is much more important for everything that is worthwhile and that counts than the admission of a few people, however imminent be their peril.

September 17, 1940

TO Eliezer Kaplan, Jerusalem

. . . Why should we expect Jews to give in generous measure
for Palestine, when those Jews in America, who have large and
even great fortunes, have not the intelligence to see that if—
heaven forfend—Britain were defeated, Jews could no longer
live in Europe; and even Palestine might become Jewishly un-
tenable? If the Jews of power in America had any intelligence
or even an elementary desire to save themselves, they would do
all on behalf of Britain. I think I am almost more discouraged
over my own people than I am over the threat of Hitlerism.
Whether the British government meets all our wishes or not,
we Jews can hardly live with any degree of security and self-
respect in a world in which Hitler becomes military dictator. . . .

February 12, 1941

TO Louis S. Posner

. . . Personally, I have no objection to [the religious revival
of] "Buchmanism" as a fad, but as a substitute for the solid im-
peratives of a great ethical and spiritual faith such as our own,
it is little more than Dutch-Pennsylvania bunk. It may be that
I cannot think straight with regard to Buchmanism because of
the humbuggery of its assumption of the title, the Oxford
[Group] movement, which was the name, exactly one hundred
years ago, of the Pusey-Newman movement at Oxford, and
second, because [Frank] Buchman [founder of the movement in
1916] frankly gave his full and extenuating support to Hitler
two or three years ago [1937]. I remember to have written the
stiffest kind of editorial in *Opinion* about a damnable statement
by him which was entirely characteristic of the Pollyannaism of
the so-called Oxford [Group] movement plus its damnable unconcern with respect to the fate of peoples.

February 25, 1941

TO Willard Uphaus, New Haven, Conn.

I regret I cannot be at the meeting [of the Executive Committee of the National Religion and Labor Foundation] next
week. But I must register my protest against the Religion and
Labor Foundation adopting a resolution against the Lease-Lend
Bill. I do not see any relation between the Religion and Labor
Foundation and the Lease-Lend Bill, excepting this—that support of it may help to destroy the forces which have virtually
annulled both free religion and organized labor. It is beyond
my understanding that they who have united in the Religion
and Labor Foundation should be ready in the remotest way
to withhold aid from the democracy [Great Britain] which
heroically battles on in resistance to the fascist forces that
would destroy religion, labor, civilization, democracy.

August 7, 1941

TO Fanny Mayer Korn, Sharon Springs, N.Y.

. . . You will be interested to know that I really came down
in order to raise hell at the President's [Advisory] Committee
[on Political Refugees]. I am really sick over what is happening
to the refugees, the utter denial to them of the right to come
in. I shall urge vigorous action of the President. . . .

September 13, 1941

TO Mrs. Solomon M. Stroock

I can imagine what your overwhelming sense of loss and
grief must be, knowing as I do how bereft I feel by Sol's
passing. . . . I drove home [from the memorial service] yesterday with some of Sol's closest friends. . . . I told them proudly
and even gladly that, in the fifty-two years of our friendship,
not one unpleasant word had ever passed between us. We did
not see eye to eye on certain problems of Jewish life, but noth-

ing touched or marred our friendship. That remained unbroken and, indeed, unbreakable. Whenever we met, and even when we did not, the old, deep-rooted affection was a part of our lives. . . .

It seemed to me that he could hardly have gone on unless . . . you had been at his side to give him strength. . . .

. . . I cannot but add a word to Alan, whose being with Sol must have been a source of deepest joy. There can be no higher satisfaction in life than to have a son at one's side, sympathetic, understanding, loving, revering, who shares one's life and purposes, and Alan shares—and I trust may for many decades share —Sol's innermost purposes and program of life.

And I want you to know something else of which Sol may never have told you—my dear father passed when Sol and I were twenty-two. It was, as Sol may have told you, a very great and overwhelming shock to me. I could not have gone through that awful time without Sol's help. He was with me day and night. He really nursed me through the bitterest hours of my life, for I was not old or strong enough to bear up under the blow as I should have done. I can never, never forget what Sol was to me and all that he did to make that affliction endurable without breaking under it. That was only one of a great number of kindnesses which he showed to mine and to me throughout his days. . . .

March 6, 1942

TO Chaim Weizmann, London

I need not tell you how we have all felt about the possibility of hurt to your dear boy. It is a blow to all of us to think that this may have happened. For myself, as well as for you, I have reason to feel that if Michael [in the Royal Air Force] descended in France, he may have exercised his best judgment and thrown away his passport in order that the name he bears should not bring additional hurt to him in German-occupied French territory. I somehow believe the miracle of his restoration to you and his mother will yet come to pass. I pray with all my heart

it may be so, and I press your hand in the prayerfulness of one
who wishes for you that the light of Michael's life may gleam
again to the benediction of all who love him. [The body of
Michael Weizmann was never found.]

With all love, dear Chaim. . . .

TELEGRAM

March 30, 1942

TO John Young, State Department, Washington

I KNOW YOU ARE DOING EVERYTHING TO FACILITATE DR. WEIZ-
MANN'S COMING BY EARLIEST POSSIBLE PLANE. I CAN ONLY ADD THAT
THERE ARE PERSONAL REASONS, WHICH ARE BOUND UP WITH RECENT
LOSS OF HIS SON IN R.A.F., WHICH MAKE YOUR INTERVENTION DOUBLY
IMPERATIVE. MY DEEPEST THANKS IN ADVANCE.

In February 1942 a ship named STRUMA *steamed into the Istanbul harbor, seeking a dock for 769 refugees, 250 of whom were
women and children, so that they might migrate by land to
refuge in Palestine. The Turkish government refused to let the*
STRUMA *land because the passengers had no permits for entry
into Palestine. In Jerusalem the Zionist Executive sought permits from the British Mandatory for the passengers on the*
STRUMA, *but to no avail; even the children were denied permits.
The authorities in Istanbul ordered the hulk of 200 tons to
leave the harbor. Already in sinking condition, the* STRUMA *de-
parted; but while only a short distance from shore, the ship
sank. All, save one, perished.*

April 1, 1942

TO Eleanor Roosevelt, The White House, Washington

Justine felt that, inasmuch as she had spoken to you upon my
suggestion with respect to the *Struma* disaster, I might continue
the correspondence, which included the two items that you
were good enough to send her—both of which I herewith re-

turn. It is very good of you to have intervened in this way with Mr. [Undersecretary of State Sumner] Welles, and I am grateful to you for permitting Justine and her father to see the letters which Mr. Welles had written.

May I offer a few words of comment upon Mr. Welles' letter? If Palestine is to be ruled out, the situation of the unhappy refugees indeed becomes hopeless. Assuming that Mr. Welles is right in saying that refuge cannot be found for these people in South American countries or in Africa, is not the obvious answer that they should be admitted to the one country which they can call home, to which they could go—in the words of Mr. Churchill—"not on sufferance, but of right"? I need not remind you that Palestine has been recognized as the Jewish Homeland not only by Britain and fifty-two other nations of the world, but by unanimous resolution of the United States Congress.

As for the fear that German agents might have been included in the passenger list of that ship, that fear is hardly convincing. The Nazis have no need for such precarious method of transportation as was the *Struma,* in order to introduce into Turkey additional Nazi agents; and through Turkey across the land borders into Syria and Palestine the way is not really hard. Moreover I beg to remind you that it would have been possible for the Palestine government, having permitted the refugees to land, to intern them until their *bona fides* could be established with our help. This has been done in other cases, and today, instead of building roads as slave laborers for Hitler, hundreds of these former internees are fighting soldiers in the armies of the United Nations; or they are busy on the land or in the factories of Palestine producing for our war effort and their own. On grounds of sheer expediency no less than on moral grounds, the attitude of the British administration in Palestine seems inexcusable.

A word about the repercussions that Britain fears among the Arabs. Is it too much to say that the sacrifice of friends in the interest of appeasing the unfriendly has repeatedly been proven to be vain? The rebellion in Iraq, the presence of the Mufti in Berlin and Rome, the failure of Egypt to live up to her treaty of alliance (thousands of Palestinian Jews, but no Arab-Egyptian soldiers, have been defending Egyptian soil against invasion), indicate that this policy has failed in the Near East, as it has failed everywhere else.

I cannot help saying to you, dear Mrs. Roosevelt, that the Palestine [Mandate] government's policy in regard to these refugees is as shortsighted as it is cruel. It does damage to the cause of free men everywhere, and it accords ill with those great ends of justice which the United Nations have set themselves.

May 21, 1942

TO Felix Frankfurter, Washington

... I think he [Chaim Weizmann] is acting with truest wisdom in remembering a Jewish war must not be against England, but against Hitler. It is very easy for some of the grand Zionist statesmen to urge us to smash England, and I think Emanuel Neumann errs a little on that side. But if England goes, everything is lost; if England wins, we still have a chance re Palestine and a Jewish future. . . . Weizmann's attitude has not been feeble or cowardly, as is alleged, but wise in its comprehension of the immediate issue.

You must know that I am personally very fond of both [David] Ben-Gurion and [Nahum] Goldmann, but I cannot help feeling that in this hour Weizmann's course, unlike their own, is one of higher statesmanship.

September 4, 1942

TO Felix Frankfurter, New Milford, Conn.

My heart is so full that I just must write to you. You may not be able to help any more, alas, than I can, but I want you to share the knowledge of this horror. You may think of something that could be done.

There came to me the other day a cablegram, through [Sidney] Silverman of the House of Commons, whose name you may recall. It came from one who is an unperturbably and really conservative representative of the World Jewish Congress at Geneva, Dr. [Gerhardt] Riegner. I took this cable up with Welles. Welles tried to be reassuring. He seems to think that the real purpose of the Nazi government is to use Jews in connection with war work both in Nazi Germany and in Nazi Poland and Russia. A moment ago another message came from Berne, saying that in the past days one hundred thousand Jews have been killed in Warsaw, and that their corpses are being used to make soap. I enclose this copy of both cablegrams.

I was tempted to call up Henry [Morgenthau], Jr., and ask him to put it before the Chief [President Roosevelt], just that he might know about it, even though, alas, he prove to be unable to avert the horror. . . . Perhaps you will feel that in the face of this circumstantially confirming message from Berne, coming two or three days after the earlier message from Silverman, the Chief ought to know about it. Perhaps he will not be able to avert the thing, but one somehow feels that the foremost and finest figure in the political world today should not be without knowledge of this unutterable disaster which threatens and may now be in process of execution.

I wish I had more joyous tidings to send you. Alas, that I must share this with you.

At the 40th Anniversary Dinner of the founding of the Free Synagogue, April 20, 1947, Henry Morgenthau, Jr., said: "I will never forget the day in '42 as long as I live when Dr. Wise and his son James came to call on me in the Treasury and read me that unbelievable cable telling about the crematoriums in Europe. I think that day changed my life. I will never recover from it. . . ."

September 9, 1942

TO Fanny Mayer Korn

. . . I have been so overwhelmed with work that I have hardly had time to think about the Holy Day preaching. I should, these few days before Rosh Hashana, be writing at my desk. Instead of that I am meeting all day with committees, and at midnight I must go to Washington to see what, if anything—and I wonder whether it will be anything—can be done for our poor fellow-Jews, threatened with extermination.

Did I write you that we had a cable from Berne saying that 100,000 Jews had been massacred in Warsaw, and their corpses have been converted into soap and fertilizers by the Nazis? It is too foul to think about. I haven't been able to sleep since that earlier cable to me telling me that the plan is to kill all the Jews in Hitler Germany, and prussic acid was mentioned as the method. It is all too unspeakable.

Meeting today with Myron Taylor and the President's Committee on Political Refugees, I shall urge that Taylor try to get the Pope to intervene. But the further difficulties are these: Roosevelt cannot intervene, because Hitler will rightfully do nothing for him. Hitler would have won the war if it had not been for our President and America. Why should he comply with any request of Roosevelt? And as for the Pope, he is just an enshrined prisoner—little more—without real influence or authority. He could, of course, use the mighty ban of his Church. His predecessor [Pius XI] might conceivably have done so. Pius XII is a politician first and a churchman second. . . .

September 16, 1942

TO Felix Frankfurter, New Milford, Conn.

. . . I have been in Washington twice this week. [Sumner] Welles was gone, but I felt I had to see someone in the [U.S. State] Department on the question of feeding the Jews in Poland. There is a great deal of complaint over the fact that Greeks are fed, but Jews in Poland remain unfed. I don't know whether I am getting to be a *Hofjude* [a court Jew, interceding on behalf of his people], but I find that a good part of my work is to explain to my fellow Jews why our government cannot do all the things asked or expected of it. . . .

I saw [Vice-President Henry] Wallace, who had Milo Perkins at his side. They seem to think that [Assistant Secretary of State Dean] Acheson was the best man to deal with the problem, but

we ought also to see whether [Ambassador-at-Large] Norman
Davis would undertake to lead off in the thing with the International Red Cross. Both to Acheson and Wallace I showed the
two awful cablegrams. Have you noted that I have kept the thing
out of the press up to this time, thus accepting a great responsibility if the threat should be executed? . . .

. . . In all my discussions, I got this one impression—that Hitler
might ultimately destroy his Jewish subjects, but that for the
present, as put by the Polish Ambassador through underground
information, the hundred thousand Jews in the Warsaw Ghetto
were not killed but were sent to the new Russo-Polish frontier to
build fortifications. . . .

September 29, 1942

TO Lavey Bakstansky, London

. . . Yes, it was a great Madison Square Garden demonstration
[to protest Nazi persecutions], but alas, the news continues to be
as bad as ever; and somehow, alas, in time of war it is very difficult to get people excited, generally speaking, about atrocities. All
of war is basically such an atrocity that it is difficult to move people with respect to special atrocities, even though they are special
and, in the case of the atrocities practiced against us, unbelievable. . . .

I am very grateful, dear Bakstansky, for what you say about my
having part in the [fund-raising] effort of February or March; but
I am almost certain I cannot make it. My physicians will not let
me fly. It is absolutely forbidden. I am far from being well and
have a chronic ailment [polycythemia, an enlarged spleen, and
an inoperable double hernia], which necessitates X-ray treatment
rather frequently. I do not like to talk about this, because I seem
to go on with my work normally; but as for flying, it is forbidden,
and there is no other way of getting to your country at present.
I am more unhappy than you believe about this. I would love to
go to England. I would love to have part in the great work; but,
alas, it is denied me. . . .

P.S. I had meant to write you about C. W. [Chaim Weizmann]

and B. G. [David Ben-Gurion]. C. W. is not well. I think that the probable—though I hope not certain—passing of Michael hit him very hard. He has had some recurrence, including a hemorrhage, of a youthful pulmonary trouble. Not too much is to be said about this, of course. He is now in the Catskill Mountains trying to regain health and strength.

B. G. has made things rather hard for him, having gotten it into his head that C. W. is dangerous to Zionism and that everything would be lost if he remained the political leader of the movement. I hope he isn't going to be unwise enough to take it up with the Executive of the Agency. He will find himself in a very small minority. The Actions Committee, even if it had the power to deal with the situation, would overwhelmingly say that C. W. must stay, as you and I know he must, as he is the only person of adequate stature in the movement.

I think we should train other men—for example, [Lord] Melchett in your country if he be well, and [Abba Hillel] Silver in our country, who is a very, very able man. But if, heaven forbid, C. W. had to give up today, I do not at this moment think of anyone who could adequately take his place. I suppose that such a condition always exists, just as [David] Wolffsohn was unequal to taking the place of the immortal Herzl.

October 14, 1942

TO Felix Frankfurter, Washington

... I really am inclined to [believe] ... that there is a cabal in the State Department deliberately and, I am afraid, effectively working against those Palestine interests, which are precious to some of us.

November 30, 1942

TO Philip Guedalla, Dunmow, England

... I do not share the unlimited confidence of some of my friends in Mr. Gandhi. I know, for example, how he has trafficked with the Moslems of India and how ready he is to have the Jews denied Palestine, in order that a more helpful adjustment be made with the Moslems in India. I believe that India should be a self-governing Dominion. I also believe that England wishes it to be that and that it will be a self-governing Dominion after the war, unless there are to be two dominions, including a Moslem Dominion. . . .

December 2, 1942

TO The President, The White House, Washington

I do not wish to add an atom to the awful burden which you are bearing with magic and, as I believe, heaven-inspired strength at this time. But do you know that the most overwhelming disaster of Jewish history has befallen Jews in the form of the Hitler mass-massacres? Hitler's decision was to exterminate the Jewish people in all Hitler-ruled lands, and it is indisputable that as many as two million civilian Jews have been slain.

I have had cables and underground advices for some months, telling of these things. I succeeded, together with the heads of other Jewish organizations, in keeping these out of the press and have been in constant communication with the State Department, particularly Under-Secretary Welles. The State Department has now received what it believes to be confirmation of these unspeakable horrors and has approved of my giving the facts to the press. The organizations, banded together in the Conference of which I am Chairman [Joint Emergency Committee for European Jewish Affairs], feel that they wish to present to you a memorandum on this situation, so terrible that this day is being observed as a day of mourning and fasting throughout the Jewish world. We hope above all that you will speak a word which may bring solace and hope to millions of Jews who mourn, and be an expression of the conscience of the American people.

I had gathered from the State Department that you were prepared to receive a small delegation, which would include representatives of the American Jewish Committee, the American Jewish Congress, and the B'nai B'rith. It would be gravely misunderstood if, despite your overwhelming preoccupation, you did not make it possible to receive our delegation and to utter what I am sure will be your heartening and consoling reply. . . .

(Undated—probably late December, 1942)

то Charles Clayton Morrison, Chicago

In *The Christian Century* of December 9 I read an editorial statement, presumably from your pen, under the title, "Horror Stories from Poland." It would appear that you are more interested in seeking to prove that the figures which I gave out in the name of five important Jewish organizations of America [American Jewish Congress, American Jewish Committee, B'nai B'rith, Jewish Labor Committee and the Synagogue Council of America] are inaccurate in respect to Jewish mass massacres in the Hitler-occupied countries than you are in making clear to American Christians how unspeakable has been the conduct of Hitlerism against the Jewish people.

You make what I would regard as a false charge against me if it were true, as it is false, which charge moreover is of a piece with a number of your references to the writer in recent years. *The Christian Century* writes: "Although Rabbi Wise went out of his way to place the responsibility for the charges on the State Department, that branch of the government has conspicuously refrained from issuing any confirmation." Had you taken the trouble to inquire, you would have learned that the State Department not only authorized the publication of the statement I made, but for months had been seeking with our help to make sure of the accuracy of the statements with respect to Jewish mass slaughter.

I assume that you may have read the declaration in the House of Commons a few days ago by the Minister for Foreign Affairs, Mr. [Anthony] Eden, which declaration spoke for the United Nations, including our own country, the governments in exile and Free France, and has made a permanent record of the Hitler infamy.

I am not interested in having an apology from you for your insinuation with respect to the lack of veracity which you chose to impute to me. What interests me profoundly as a Jew, as an American, as a reverent comrade of many Christian ministers and laymen throughout our country, is the knowledge that *The Christian Century* almost uniformly takes a frankly or disguisedly anti-Jewish attitude whenever it deals with Jewish subjects. Whether this is merely the reflection of a personal Judeophobia on the part of the editor, or whether it conveys the considered attitude of the editorial board of *The Christian Century*, it is not for me to say. Christian ministers with whom I have discussed the problem have felt that your article reflected the subconscious desire not so much to express compassion for the victims of Hitlerism as to shield Hitler from the consequences of his crime. I confess that I cannot quite understand that you should seem to be spiritually unconcerned about the tragic fate of the people whose gift to the world you purport to revere and worship. . . .

In the January 13, 1943, issue of THE CHRISTIAN CENTURY, *containing this letter from Stephen Wise to Charles Clayton Morrison, "The Editors" appended a paragraph:*

"*On the day Rabbi Wise's statement was published charging Hitler with paying for Jewish corpses to be rendered into fats and ordering that all Jews in German-occupied Europe should be killed by the end of last year,* THE CHRISTIAN CENTURY *inquired of the State Department concerning the authorization by that agency of the government which Rabbi Wise again claims in this letter. The State Department promptly replied through an accredited officer. Unfortunately, it specified that its reply was 'Not for publication.' We have that reply in our files; it does not support Dr. Wise's contentions. Our editorial comment on his charges was written in the light of the State Department's reply to our question.*"

January 18, 1943

TO *Time* Magazine

I do not care to enter into any further controversy with *The Christian Century* [in response to a request from a correspondent of *Time* for an interview].

If I had to make a statement, I would say that I took exception to the statement of *The Christian Century* because it set out not to deal with the guilt of Hitler in perpetrating crimes, but with my own sin of exaggeration. I have no hesitation in saying that this indictment of me for reporting, rather than of Hitler for committing, the most awful crime in history is of a piece with the distorted and thwarted mind of Dr. [Charles Clayton] Morrison touching every Jewish question that is brought up for discussion in the pages of *The Christian Century*. Unless the editor's associates take a hand in the matter, *The Christian Century* will come to take over the task left unfinished by the Rev. Mr. [Father Charles] Coughlin.

February 10, 1943

TO Chaim Weizmann

I am very sorry indeed that I cannot join you at dinner tonight when Dr. [Abba Hillel] Silver and others are to be with you.

I assume that you will make clear to Dr. Silver how glad all of us would be if he were to take over the too onerous duties of the chairmanship of the Emergency Committee [American Zionist Emergency Council]. He could do the work and do it exceedingly well, as all of us know. The work should come into the hands of a younger and stronger man—and he is the man. I would most cordially welcome him and be prepared in every way to cooperate with him as a member of the Emergency Committee, which I presume I would continue to be. I earnestly hope that Dr. Silver will find it possible to accept a responsibility, the meeting of which will mean much to our cause.

February 16, 1943

TO James Waterman Wise, Hollywood, California

. . . I want to tell you . . . we had a meeting last night at [Chaim] Weizmann's [hotel]. I called him in on the matter of doing something for the Hitler victims. Someone of the B'nai

B'rith; [Herman] Shulman, [Nahum] Goldmann, and myself of the [American and World Jewish] Congresses; Meyer Weisgal as *shamus* [assistant] for Weizmann; [Joseph] Proskauer and [Morris] Waldman for the American Jewish Committee; two rabbis for the Agudah [Union of Orthodox Rabbis] and [Adolph] Held for the Laborites [Jewish Labor Committee].

The two big things that Proskauer proposed were that he and I should speak with [Myron] Taylor, [James G.] McDonald, and Dr. [Paul van] Zeeland, and see whether we could get them to move on the several plans we have for rescue and relief, and then he added pontifically: "I alone will go to see [Undersecretary of State Sumner] Welles. He will talk to me and I will get his judgment on what you call 'action,' even though you resolve to go ahead March 1 [with a protest meeting under the auspices of the American Jewish Congress, Church Peace Union. Free World Association, American Federation of Labor, Congress of Industrial Organizations, *et al.*] and we face a *fait accompli*." . . .

Then Weizmann spoke. I have never heard a man speak with more earnestness and power than he did. It was a prophetic word. He said to Proskauer that American Jews stand today as the German Jews did in '32. Personally, I think '29 or '30 would have been truer. "I warn you that you may not be able to save yourselves, but at least you can save your dignity and honor. Don't let others speak for you, excepting as they supplement what you say. My son [Michael] did not die in order that you might become second class citizens of your country." It was really majestic! No man who has not greatness in him could have spoken as he did. . . .

We are going ahead with the [protest] meeting of the 1st [of March]. We yielded the 2nd to Madame Chiang Kai-shek [for the use of Madison Square Garden]. Ben Hecht [of the Emergency Committee to Rescue the Jews of Europe] would like us to merge our meeting with theirs on the 9th [of March]. But we have decided against it.

That is all there is to tell, excepting that Justine and Shad had dinner with the Roosevelts on Saturday, including the President, who, Justine said, sent his affectionate regards to me. If only he would do something for my people!

The American Jewish Congress, represented by Stephen Wise as president, joined with four other organizations and their presidents (American Jewish Committee, Joseph M. Proskauer; B'nai B'rith, Henry Monsky; Jewish Labor Committee, Adolph Held; and the Synagogue Council of America, Israel Goldstein) in a Joint Emergency Committee for European Jewish Affairs to submit to the U.S. State Department a program of rescue to be undertaken for the Jews of Nazi-occupied Europe.

April 14, 1943

TO Sumner Welles, Washington

. . . These memoranda set forth the principal projects representing, in our considered judgment, basic action to be undertaken immediately by the United Nations if the remnants of European Jewry are to be saved from destruction. Among these are:

(1) Negotiations with the Axis Powers through neutral governments to permit the exit of Jews from Axis-occupied countries;

(2) The creation of temporary and permanent sanctuaries for them by the United Nations;

(3) In view of the fact that planned starvation is one of the methods of accomplishing the extermination of the Jewish populace of Europe, the feeding of those sections of the Jewish population in occupied Europe who will not be permitted to leave.

We would be less than frank if we did not convey to you the anguish of the Jewish community of this country over the failure of the United Nations to act until now to rescue the Jews of Europe. For many months it has been authenticated that the Nazis have marked the Jewish population of Europe for total extermination and that it is estimated that almost three million Jews have been done to death, while a similar fate awaits those who remain. World civilization has been stirred to its depths by these horrors. Every section of public opinion throughout the world, and more particularly in England and in the United States, has spoken out in the demand that the United Nations act before it is too late to save those who can still be saved. Six months have elapsed, however, and no action has as yet been taken. In the meantime it is reported that thousands of Jews continue to be murdered daily.

When first the Conference, which is now to open in Bermuda, was announced, it was our hope that at last effective action would be immediately forthcoming on the part of the United Nations. These hopes are seriously disturbed by three developments:

(1) Both our State Department and the Foreign Minister of Great Britain have announced that the Bermuda Conference is to be primarily exploratory.

(2) At this writing neither the United States nor Great Britain has seen fit to call into consultation the representative organizations of the Jewish communities of their respective countries. Nor has either government seen fit to invite delegations representing the organized Jewish communities of these two countries to participate in the deliberations to be held in Bermuda.

(3) There are the doubts aroused by the isolation of the Conference in a place completely inaccessible to the influences of public opinion or public personalities, except by government permission.

. . . . The time for exploration has long since passed, and the time for action is long past due. Unless action is undertaken immediately, there may soon be no Jews left alive in Europe.

In communicating these views to you it is our purpose at this time also formally to place before you the request that a delegation representing the Joint Emergency Committee for European Jewish Affairs be invited to the Bermuda Conference to present our views on the program of rescue to be undertaken for the Jews of Europe.

It is our sincere hope that you, who have long had an intimate and, I believe, sympathetic knowledge of this problem, will lend your influence to insure that the Bermuda Conference may serve as the instrument of humanity in rescuing a defenseless people who are otherwise doomed to complete annihilation.

The request for a representative delegation's being invited to the Bermuda Conference was not granted.

May 18, 1943

TO Lord Halifax, British Embassy, Washington

I learn with regret that you have been disturbed by reports which reached you with reference to an address I gave on May 3 at Constitution Hall, Washington, on behalf of the United Jewish War Effort. Whoever brought the report to you should have made clear to you—what it ought not be necessary for me to say—that among American Jews since September 1914 I believe, without immodesty, I have stood out as a warmly admiring friend and supporter of Britain. I do not need to speak of the sacrifices I made, when, beginning in 1914, I gave my undivided support to Britain and thereby alienated not a few of the leading supporters of my congregation who were German-born and of unchanged German sympathies. Together with Justice Brandeis and the then Professor Frankfurter, I believe I did most to bring about among American Jews the relationship of understanding and friendship between the Zionist cause and the British government. There is no need for me to make clear even to you, Lord Halifax, that the last thirty years I have felt—and even more after the Balfour Declaration in 1917—that there was a unique relationship between your country and my people in respect to our hope for the Jewish resettlement of Palestine.

Having said this, I must add that I have, time and again throughout the years, expressed myself with frankness and even sharpness with respect to what have seemed to me to be mistakes on the part of the Mandatory Power in Palestine. I deeply feel that, much as the British government has done, it might have done—indeed, it ought to have done—much more than it did in furthering and facilitating the Jewish resettlement of Palestine. The Mandatory Power certainly failed to do its duty in the matter of fostering rightful relations between Arabs and Jews. I have not hesitated to make clear that I considered the White Paper of 1939 [limiting Jewish immigration to 15,000 certificates per year for five years and stopping it completely in 1944] a lamentable and inexcusable error of policy on the part of your government. It is explicable only in the light of the policies of your government, which ended with the Nazi invasion of Poland,

and the breakdown of the policy of conciliation of groups powerful for evil, such as the Nazis, and other groups impotent for
good, such as the Mufti [of Jerusalem, Haj Amin el Husseini]
and his followers in Palestine. My condemnation no more implied
or connoted hatred or dislike of England than it implied such
things in the no less strong condemnation made at the time by the
man who is now Prime Minister [Winston S. Churchill]. On the
contrary, it is precisely because of my feeling for Britain that I
feel so strongly when she falls short of what I expect from her. . . .

I should deeply regret it if anything were said or done that
would affect the, to me, pleasant relations between you, as the
British Ambassador—whom I hold in deepest personal respect
and admiration—and myself, as one of the leaders of the Zionist
movement. But you will understand there are times when personal relationships and even impersonal relationships must yield
to the imperious necessity of truth-speaking on the part of one
who feels a personal responsibility because of his calling, and an
impersonal responsibility as one of the heads of a great cause.

I believe it was suggested . . . that I had spoken as if I were
one of those Americans who desire to weaken the alliance between your country and mine. That is utterly false. To do that
would be completely foreign to my spirit and one of the major
purposes of my life and its ministry. I believe that nothing could
be more conducive to the peace and security of civilization and its
finest values than the strengthening of the bonds which in this
hour of stress link your country and my own. Without desiring—
any more than you can desire—an Anglo-Saxon hegemony over
the world of civilization, I yet believe that England and the
United States are together capable of rendering the highest service to the cause of human freedom and human peace. It is impossible for me to think—let alone to speak—or do aught which
would tend to shake the faith of the American people in the (I
had almost said "sacredness of the") bond between our countries.

. . . I made as strong an allusion as one could to our common
devotion to the cause of human freedom.

*Lord Halifax thanked Wise for his reassurances about their
common cause and desired objectives, reaffirmed Wise's right to*

criticize British policy in Palestine or any other subject he might
think desirable, but reminded him that Zionist protests at that
time were capable of poisoning American minds against Great
Britain rather than effecting changes in British policy toward
Palestine.

May 19, 1943

TO William Beveridge

You do not know the writer, but may I, by way of self-identification, state that I presided over the Mass Meeting at Madison Square Garden on March 1, to which you were gracious enough to address your fine broadcast.

I write to you now on behalf of the American Association for Social Security, the guiding spirit of which, since its founding and up to his lamented death a year ago, was Dr. Abraham Epstein. I take it you are familiar with his work in the field of Social Security. May I say to you, on behalf of Bishop Francis J. McConnell, who is the Chairman of the Association, and my associates, that we have had and continue to have great difficulty in finding a successor to Dr. Epstein; and his death has raised other questions which have not yet been solved.

My purpose in writing to you is to ask whether you will permit us to have the privilege and pleasure of arranging a luncheon or dinner at your convenience, at which you would meet with and address a group of worthwhile men. Such meeting would in part have the effect of reviving interest in the work of our Association which, under the leadership of men like Dr. Epstein and Bishop McConnell, Mrs. [Mary] Simkhovitch, and other people of their significance in American life, has pioneered in the field of social security. Awaiting your early reply, and looking forward, if we may, to your acceptance of our invitation to our meeting, to be arranged at a time convenient to you. . . .

July 23, 1943

TO The President, The White House, Washington

It gave me deep satisfaction to find while with you yesterday that out of the depth of your understanding sympathy with Hitler's victims you welcome the proposal which is now before the State and Treasury departments to permit funds to be forwarded to Switzerland by Jewish organizations of our country. These funds are, of course, to be held in escrow by our government representatives or such people as they may designate, and would not be handed over to officials (as may survive) of the satellite powers until after the war. These officials with whom the arrangements will be undertaken, will create such conditions within the Hitler territories as shall enable many Jews in those countries to survive, to escape deportation and ultimately to come out of those countries, continued residence in which would mean torture and death. The whole arrangement is to provide especially for the saving of many little children. We feel that these funds may make possible the salvation of thousands of otherwise doomed beings, especially in Rumania, Slovakia and France, without, I repeat, one penny falling into the hands of enemy representatives for the duration.

I am happier than I can say to think that this proposal, which deals in a feasible and concrete way with an unspeakable situation, commends itself to you, and that you will be good enough to discuss it with the Secretary of the Treasury, whose subordinates are dealing with the problem.

I cannot make clear enough what it would mean to us, and indeed to all civilized people, if you once again, and for the last time, uttered a solemn warning to the representatives of the Nazi regimes in the Hitler conquered territories with respect to the crimes committed against civilians, especially Jews, marked out, as you know, for slaughter as no other people. Is not the recent announcement of the Commission on the Crimes in the Fascist Countries a suitable occasion for such warning as is likely to have a deterrent effect, especially upon Nazi officials within the satellite states?

In the early autumn Secretary of State Cordell Hull, for reasons not divulged, requested the resignation of Sumner Welles as Undersecretary of State.

October 3, 1943

TO Sumner Welles, Oxon Hill, Md.

. . . The nation understands, as does the writer, how distinguished and far-reaching has been your service in and through the State Department. Throughout these hideous Hitler years, you have been an oasis of refreshment in a desert of arid unconcern, a fount of healing to my deeply sorrowing soul. For you have spoken and acted as an American gentleman and statesman in seeking to lift burdens unjustly laid upon others.

Your vision and your wisdom, your courage and effectiveness cannot long be lost to the American people, which cherishes your service, as my fellow Jews in all free lands will, when the whole story can be told, bless your name.

December 27, 1943

TO John Polachek

I feel I ought to say a word to you as one to whom you have been a friend and to whom you wish to act in the most friendly way. I have heard that your feeling is that, in connection with my 70th birthday, something personal should be done for me. I know what is in the back of your mind and do not imagine I am without appreciation thereof.

But I must make clear to you, as I did a year ago, when we undertook the plans for the Institute, which have, in part, materialized, that there is nothing personal whatsoever which I could accept for myself, whether as pension, or annuity, or capital fund, which term has been used. I shall not mar the record of a lifetime by becoming a dependent or pensioner now, at this late date in my life. If my friends desire to do something for me, there are things they can do, but not for me personally. They can help so to increase the funds of the Synagogue as to insure the building of it the moment the war is ended. They can increase the support of the Institute. They can help support the American and World Jewish Congresses and the Zionist movement. These are all causes dear to my heart, and any help to them is the one type of gift that I could accept for my birthday, *no other*.

I cannot put this too strongly to you. I want my birthday to be marked in an absolutely impersonal way. It was done on my 50th birthday, when $50,000 was given to me, including a gift of $5,000 from Julius Rosenwald, every penny of which I turned over to the Institute. It was done on my 60th birthday. I trust it may be done at this time. If you have moved the Committee to accept your view, I must ask you to discuss the matter further with the Committee and to let them know that this is my final and absolute judgment in the matter.

May 4, 1944

TO Anna Clare, Albany, N.Y.

I have your letter and it pains me, not to repentance but to sorrow that you [a Roman Catholic nun at the College of St. Rose] should not see that I do honor to your great Church, and to the late Pope [Pius XI] and the late Cardinal of England [Arthur Hinsley], by speaking with reverent admiration of them, as contrasted with the lamentable un-Catholic and un-Christian things said and done by Father [Charles] Coughlin [the anti-Semitic "radio priest" of Royal Oak, Michigan]. Surely you can but share my sorrow that a priest of your Church should use the Church and its altar in such a way as to bring about bitterness and strife. His is the sin of crucifixion of the people of Christ; and far from regretting what I have written, you should thank me, for it is doing honor to your Church and Communion.

I am, with much respect, dear and reverend Sister. . . .

July 31, 1944

TO Serge Koussevitsky, Boston

So you have caught up with me and with all the seventy-year-old folk! I think with lamentation of the difference between us —you have brought music and beauty and harmony to the world; and I am afraid I have had to bring dissonance and discord into a world in the midst of which fairness and decency and justice have to be fought for.

My heartfelt congratulations to you. . . .

November 15, 1944

TO Abba Hillel Silver, Cleveland

. . . I do not find it my duty to retract anything of what I said. I considered, as I believe you do, the conduct of [Rabbi William] Fineschriber and [Rabbi Louis] Wolsey [two of the founders of the anti-Zionist American Council for Judaism] to be treasonable to every high Jewish interest, and therefore I consider both men utterly unworthy to occupy the places of their great predecessors, including most especially [Rabbi Emil] Hirsch.

December 13, 1944

TO David Matas, Brooklyn

In regard to your question concerning the Jewish celebration of Christmas, I must answer, as I have a thousand times, that Christmas is the very beautiful festival of Christians and that Jews, as Jews, should not, in loyalty to our own faith, celebrate the religious festival of a sister religion. I do not say that Jews are not to attend Christmas functions to which their non-Jewish friends invite them; but I do insist that Hanukkah is so full of meaning for us . . . that we should celebrate it, particularly at this time, with all the fervor that characterized our fathers. The Menorah and the kindling of the lights are a vital part of Jewish tradition and are symbols at least as beautiful as the Christmas tree.

December 18, 1944

TO Julius Livingston, Tulsa, Okla.

. . . I am miserably unhappy over the development of things. It would take me ten or twenty pages to write the whole story. It must suffice for the present if I tell you that Dr. [Abba Hillel] Silver has acted in grossest violation of decisions of the [American Zionist] Emergency Council. He was with Dr. [Nahum] Goldmann and myself when we said to Secretary [of State Edward] Stettinius: "We will not proceed with the resolution unless we get a green light from the President." The answer of the President through Secretary Stettinius—uttered, I have every reason to believe, in good faith and with the best of goodwill—was: "Say to Stephen that the thing is to be left in my hands a little longer. I shall soon see certain people." Meaning, of course, Churchill and Stalin. In defiance of that, Dr. Silver did go ahead, overrode the objections both of Congressman [Sol] Bloom and Senator [Robert] Wagner and invited defeat in the Senate Committee, which is nothing less than, in any event, a temporary disaster.

I have nothing more to say about it excepting that I will not remain one of the heads of the Emergency Council if Dr. Silver is continued in office. More than that, I feel it would be infinitely better to break up the Emergency Council by having Z.O.A. [Zionist Organization of America] do its own political work in conjunction with the Jewish Agency than expose ourselves further to the danger which inheres in the present situation of Dr. Silver's continued defiance of and attacks upon the President. . . .

When Felix Frankfurter asked him for information concerning the reported rescue of persecuted European Jews by Christians, Wise assured him that, while the quest for data might take a long time, Frankfurter would have all the information the World Jewish Congress could compile; soon he would have "the figures and facts. . . ."

March 19, 1945

TO Felix Frankfurter, Washington

... As you know, they are very honoring not only to the priests but to bishops and to lay Catholics. Did you recall that when, in Vichy, France, Jews were compelled to wear the Shield of David, not a few Catholic priests did the same thing? It is a wonderful story, including the tale of that Polish priest who would not let the Gestapo into his church cellar to seize Jewish children. They had to kill him first. I have written to the Papal Nuncio to ascertain the name and the full story so that perhaps we might make a very special note of his sacrificial deed. ...

April 23, 1945

TO Mrs. Nathan G. Schuman, Alexandria, Va.

I am delighted to have your letter, in which you tell me that my mother is to be the subject of comment at the Mother's Day program at Temple Beth El.

Even though I, her son, say it, I believe that my mother was one of the most remarkable women I have known. Her full name was Sabine de Fischer. She was the daughter of Baron Maurice de Fischer Farkashazy, founder of the porcelain industry of Hungary, having been ennobled by Emperor Franz Joseph in 1866. My mother had many brothers and one sister, but she was much the ablest of all the children of the family.

She and my dear father, Dr. Aaron Wise, who, in 1875 became rabbi of Temple Rodeph Sholom in New York, were married in the late '6os, I think it was. My mother was a woman of fine understanding, of goodly sympathies, and of great courage. All of her children—and there were seven of us—were always agreed that she was much abler than all the rest of us put together! She was capable of great industry, of deep understanding, and altogether was a true Mother in Israel. ...

... I owe much to my mother—more than I could make public. She was widowed in 1896 and, happily for her children, lived until 1917. I am grateful to you for thinking of her who was and remains my blessed mother.

October 31, 1945

TO Sumner Welles, Oxon Hill, Md.

I cannot deny myself the privilege and pleasure of saying to you how grateful we are, many, many of us, for your illuminating and constructive piece in this morning's [N.Y. *Herald*] *Tribune* on Palestine. I presume you know that President Roosevelt brought that very plan to my attention when last I saw him in March and urged that just that be done, namely, the settlement of the problem be transferred from England as Mandatory to the United Nations Organization.

Once again, my deepfelt thanks!

January 15, 1946

TO Reinhold Niebuhr

I cannot tell you how grateful I am, indeed all of us are, for your contribution to the [Anglo-American Commission of] Inquiry. Mr. [Abraham] Tulin, who was the leading lawyer in the case [on behalf of the Zionists], told me over the telephone a moment ago: "Professor Niebuhr made the finest presentation of the Zionist case I have ever heard and all the members of the Committee were tremendously interested. He showed why the Jewish State in Palestine was a necessity not only for the Displaced Jews of Europe but for all Jews, including Jews in America and Britain. He lifted the question completely out of the realm of refugee-ism and revealed the philosophy of Zionism and its need."

We cannot thank you enough for your great help. When I asked you to go, I took it for granted that Professor [William Ernest] Hocking and Dr. [Henry Sloane] Coffin were to appear [with anti-Zionist testimony], which made your appearance all the more necessary. Though they failed to appear, you still were needed; and I am ineffably grateful for your going and participating. Mr. Tulin seems to think that your closing of the case made all the difference in the world and may fundamentally affect the decision.

January 18, 1946

TO Lorna Wingate, London, England

. . . I may never see your young Orde Jonathan, for he is very young and I am very old. But some day, when he is old enough to understand and without trying to influence him unduly— and that you will best understand—tell him enough of the writer to make him understand that he (I) was infinitely grateful to Orde Jonathan's father [Orde Wingate, British soldier and military hero], for the great things that he did for my people and my people's land [in training men for the Haganah in Palestine], and that I shall never cease to pray, here and hereafter, that he may be equal to the matchless heritage, which is his own, from his distinguished father—a truly great man—and his fine mother. Who knows but that it may be given to him to complete the work at which his father toiled; and, even if it seemed to be completed, out of the richness of high memories he may add not a little to the storehouse of Jewish dreams and Jewish gifts to the world. . . .

January 28, 1946

TO Scott Nearing

I have read with interest your reaction to my Ford Hall address on Zionism and am amazed by your attitude. You take issue with my reference to "my people" who, numerically, constitute only a small segment of "humanity." Is one required to forget one's family to become a servant of one world? Can one not serve one's people and, in addition, all who are oppressed? I cannot quite grasp your use of the abstract term "humanity." It seems to me to be the easiest thing in the world to be devoted to mankind in general and to be oblivious of the suffering of men in particular. It is not hard to lecture throughout the country in behalf of a new social and economic order, forgetting the urgency of people suffering now. Six million of "my people" have been slaughtered and millions of others are in chains. Would I be a greater humanitarian to forget them, that I might speak vaguely of Kingdom Come? It would be easy for me to list the non-Jewish causes to which I have given my devotion; you must know them. I have been a better servant of "humanity" because I have dedicated myself to "my people."

I wonder whether you see the logical consequence of your thought? You point, incidentally, at the Jews, as only a tiny segment. Do numbers matter, when justice is at stake? Shall we refuse to support the striking steel workers, because the majority of American workers are not unionized? Was I wrong in supporting the Gary steel strikers, starving Armenians, the suffering Chinese, the underprivileged Negro? Or am I wrong only when I defend Jews?

May 6, 1946

TO Stephen Wise Tulin, Oberlin, Ohio

I have been too excited in the last two weeks to write or to do anything very much but cuss the British government. We got a fairly good report, as you may have read, from the Joint Anglo-American Palestine Committee [Anglo-American Committee of Inquiry]. That report was made with the definite understanding with the British government that they would accept it as a directive and act accordingly. Instead of that, [Prime Minister Clement] Attlee says he will accept the report, but names two intolerable conditions: (1) that we as a nation join in the military arrangements in regard to Palestine, and (2) that the Haganah, our volunteer defense body, be dissolved. America will not and ought not meet the first condition. The Jews of Palestine will never assent to the second. We will not be left helpless in the hands of the British, whom we have no reason to trust. It is a nasty mess. I have seen [James G.] McDonald and [Bartley] Crum, two of the American members, who came to me at once to report on the work of the Committee.

I am afraid that our Zionist Congress in Palestine will go aglimmering, in which case I will have to endure a month in Lake Placid without your presence; and it will be pretty lonesome without you and Cousin Stephen, although I am not wholly indifferent, as you may have suspected, to Jonny [Polier], who, I suppose, will join Bobbie and Shad [mother and father] for their month's vacation.

How are things going in Oberlin? It must be a great experience. You are the first one outside of Shad among all of us in three generations to have gone to a small college. I have a sneaking notion that you are going to like it, and I am not quite sure that you will be ready to go to a great university even when you are free to do so. Ama [Grandmother] joins me in much love; and I wish, dear Steve, that you would write me and tell me what you would like in the way of food or cash. What's a grandpa for, save to be bled and fleeced by his grandson?

May 17, 1946

TO Stephen Wise Tulin, Oberlin, Ohio

You are right—the Palestine business is a mess. I agree with you, excepting that I would have said not "sure a mess," but "surely a mess." You will forgive the subtle suggestion.

I shall be in Washington on Monday, through Dave Niles [administrative assistant to President Truman]. If he is to be trusted entirely, we get rather hopeful reports that "Missouri" [President Harry Truman] will insist upon Britain's action and that he is ready to order the [United States] War Department to move and transport the hundred thousand [displaced persons in detention centers in Europe to Palestine]. He will be crazy if he fails to do so.

Need I tell you how happy Ama [Grandmother] and I are over your plans for the summer [to attend summer school at Columbia University]? You speak of my old Alma Mater. But I am speaking today under the inspiration or impact or compulsion of Shad [Polier] at the City Council in order to compel a decision upon the petition (which I signed, and Shad and his legal gangsters wrote) urging that Columbia be denied taxation exemption on the ground that it is not, in the true sense of the term, an educational institution [due to racial and religious quotas]. . . .

I wish you could have heard Bobbie [Justine Wise Polier] speak the other day over the air. Eddie Warburg said that his mother had said to him (she had been at the luncheon at which Bobbie spoke) that she never heard a finer or more beautiful address upon the social subject than was your mamma's. Shad is working like a Trojan in and for the [American Jewish] Congress. We have our convention next week. He has prepared the major material for Mrs. [Eleanor] Roosevelt's speech. . . .

June 18, 1946

TO David Niles, The White House, Washington

Professor [Reinhold] Niebuhr feels very strongly that my editorial which appeared in *Opinion* should be widely used at this time, especially in the light of the Revisionists' telegram to all the members of Congress against the loan [by the United States to England of $3,750,000,000].

I remember you said you would put it in the *Congressional Record*. Professor Niebuhr feels that it should be done without delay. We should proceed to counteract the [Abba Hillel] Silver mischief.

I am not prepared to hurt the interests of the American and British people alike involved in this loan to spite a man [British Foreign Secretary Ernest Bevin], however nasty his speech and however lamentable his conduct against Zionism.

July 10, 1946

TO Lady Eva Reading, London

. . . There is the deepest dissatisfaction among American Jews with the policy of Messrs. [Prime Minister Clement] Attlee and [Foreign Minister Ernest] Bevin since the fall of 1945. [Bartley] Crum and [James G.] McDonald assured us that Mr. Bevin said to all of the twelve members of the [Anglo-American] Committee [of Inquiry on Palestine]—and I believe that is borne out by Mr. [Richard H. S.] Crossman—that any unanimous recommendation, that might be presented by the Committee, would be implemented. You will be interested to learn, if I could tell you, as I cannot, how deeply the highest circles of America feel about the British government's policy of delay and evasion, initiated by Messrs. Bevin and Attlee, plus the rather infelicitous remarks of Mr. Bevin, etc. ["They want to get to the head of the queue. You have the danger of another anti-Semitic reaction through it all."] Over and above all, there came the abhorrent incidents in Palestine. Dr. Weizmann put it well when he said: "The Mufti, the murderer, in an Egyptian palace; the Jews behind barbed wire in Palestine." It is intolerable, and we cannot change the views of the Jewish masses in America with regard to this.

I need hardly prove to you how unwise your government can be. I made up my mind to go to Palestine at once, though I must go, alas, by boat because my physician will not permit me to fly. I applied for a visa to Palestine last Friday; and within one hour was told that the British government would not at this time give me a passport to Palestine. . . . In the meantime, however— even though Zionistically I took my life in my hands—I did make a strong statement in favor of the British Loan, which Dr. [Abba Hillel] Silver and many of the so-called leading Zionists have vigorously opposed. . . . Yesterday, two or three days after being refused a visa to Palestine, I made the statement on the British Loan. . . .

October 31, 1946

TO David Niles, The White House, Washington

I have an extraordinary request to make of you: I want some Democratic patronage, and it is the first time I have ever asked for it. And the patronage I yearn to have is something very important, indeed momentous—two tickets for the Notre Dame-Army game, either for Jim's Stephen, who is at Harvard and who has a little sister of six weeks, Deborah; or for Steve, now eighteen, who is at Oberlin. If you don't send those two tickets, I warn you I shall join [Abba Hillel] Silver, fight all Administration candidates and join the entourage of Bob T. [Senator Robert A.

Taft, Republican of Ohio] or Tom D. [Governor Thomas E. Dewey, Republican of New York]. That is the kind of a boy I am, who rests in the hope that his request may not be wholly ignored; and, reminding you that President [Woodrow] Wilson offered me an embassy, perhaps you will feel that I have risen to two football tickets for one or both of my grandsons.

January 8, 1947

TO Nahum Goldmann, London

Your letter of December 31 [concerning the conclusion of the Basle Congress] is before me. It does not make me very happy. You write that you were reluctant until the last moment to go into the Executive [of the Jewish Agency for Palestine] but that you did it for two reasons. I cannot help feeling that you might have stipulated that you would not be a member of the Executive, but that you would be prepared to represent it in London if there were a Conference. I think you are needed at the Conference, if it takes place, and I believe it will take place, although, if it takes place, [Abba Hillel] Silver and B. G. [David Ben-Gurion] will run it, not you, even though [Foreign Secretary Ernest] Bevin knows you and has confidence in you. I am confident that, in the light of all that you write, you will not be able to remain in the Executive unless you have a greater capacity for digestion of the indigestible than it has ever occurred to me to attribute to you.

I take it for granted the Executive will go to London. The dishonest thing is that that decision could and should have been made at Basle [at the World Zionist Conference]; but, in that event, [Chaim] Weizmann could not have been ruled out. That is the terrible thing. No, as far as Basle is concerned, no clearcut decision—trickery and treachery everywhere.

I learned something of the Actions Committee and the proposal that I serve as President; moreover, that everybody would have accepted but that Silver prevented it. You say it was 4 in the morning and it was "impossible to make a row." Was it really impossible? Should not the row have been made, not for my sake but to avert the *Diktatur* of Silver? As for being Senior Vice-

President of the Actions Committee, of course I shall decline it when I am formally notified. I would not dream of accepting the post, which is offered me by way of appeasement after the Actions Committee permitted Silver to dictate that I should not be named as President thereof.

. . . As for the Latin American Conference, at the end of March, it has become very doubtful. My doctors think I am not equal to a pilgrimage of six weeks and more. . . .

Incidentally, with due appreciation of your kind thought, I do not have to go to South America to know how the Jewish masses feel about me. I do not require any solace or sustainment. Silver can keep me out of the Executive and out of the chairmanship of the Actions Committee, but he cannot erase certain facts in Jewish history; nor affect my place in the life of America; nor yet my place in world Jewry.

January 21, 1947

TO Fanny Mayer Korn

. . . I am not interested in [Rev. Martin] Niemoeller or the Federal Council [of Churches of Christ in America]. I am interested in the total, complete indifference of the Christian world to the fate of the Jews, even when that fate becomes as tragic as that involved in the slaughter by Niemoeller's Hitler, to whom he offered his services as a warrior, of more than six million people. . . .

January 24, 1947

TO Samuel McCrea Cavert

I have watched the rise and development of the Federal Council [of Churches of Christ in America] since its founding. I have not forgotten the incident of Edward Everett Hale's protest over his exclusion from the Council because he was a Unitarian Christian. Such exclusion has now become history.

I am deeply concerned about the current inclusion within the

now more inclusive Federal Council of the Rev. Martin Niemoeller. The Council has of course the right to invite to this
country for the widest hearing any personage whom on certain
grounds it deems worthy of hearing. I trust it will not be regarded
as unduly intrusive to set forth the reasons which have moved us
of the American Jewish Congress to deplore the opportunity
granted by the Council to Mr. Niemoeller of being heard by great
numbers of American people.

The record is such that not only as president of the American
Jewish Congress but as an American minister of religion, I am
bound to declare that Niemoeller has not so borne himself
throughout the unspeakable Hitler years as to merit the respect
or confidence of Christian peoples in America. When Hitler
launched the movement destined to be most disastrous in human
history, Rev. Mr. Niemoeller became his enthusiastic supporter.
He went to the unbelievable length of hailing Nazism as "an
instrument approved by God." From 1933 to 1937, while Hitler
was laying and solidifying the foundations of the Nazi Reich,
Niemoeller was neutral and silent. Not until 1937 did he find
his tongue and then only with respect to the threatened regimentation of the Christian Church or Churches of Germany. He
paid the penalty of his opposition to church regimentation by
being sent to concentration camps where he suffered no more
than other victims and far less than thousands of Jewish residents
of concentration camps who, unlike Niemoeller, never emerged
alive.

I must frankly state we hold him unworthy of attention of the
Council or indeed any group of American Christians. In 1939 he
volunteered his services to, and in, Hitler's navy which had
shelled the free and neutral city of Danzig. Thus he offered to
serve under the banner of Hitler who had, in 1937 and 1938 alike,
raped Protestant Czechoslovakia with its glorious memories of the
martyred Zwingli [sic—but Wise must mean not Zwingli, the
Swiss, but John Huss—ed. note] and had ruthlessly violated the
little Catholic country of Austria in defense of which a true
Christian prelate, Cardinal [Michael von] Faulhaber [of Munich],
had lifted his fearless voice. It is not fitting for us to point out
that whatever may now be, in spite of the belated confession of

the collective guilt of the German people with regard to the Hitler treatment of Jews, the record is that neither before nor during his incarceration in concentration camps did Niemoeller speak one word of protest against one of the foulest crimes in history.

It may be well, from a certain Christian point of view, to welcome Niemoeller's admission of guilt with regard to the slaughter of more than six million Jews by the hand of Hitler. But the truth is that it appears never to have occurred to Niemoeller from 1933 to 1939 to have spoken as a Christian minister against the infinite hurt done by Hitler, to them, whom the German people must have regarded as "merely Jews," but whom Niemoeller, Christian minister, should have viewed and defended as brother Jews of Jesus of Nazareth—alike, the children of One God.

What my associates of the American Jewish Congress and I are most deeply concerned about, is the indirect effect of Niemoeller's words and utterances in our own country. No one can study, as we have studied, the Niemoeller utterances without recognizing that subtly perhaps, but nonetheless unmistakably, Niemoeller is seeking to move the American people to deal "softly" with the German nation. We do not dream of urging punitive or vindictive action against the partially misled German millions; but we are concerned profoundly lest the "soft" treatment of the up-to-this-time unregenerate, anti-democratic and, alas, invincibly anti-Semitic German people bring it to pass that Germany will come to regard itself not merely as forgiven but as approved and commended in its fanatically anti-democratic courses by the American peoples.

I assume that the business of the Federal Council of the Churches of Christ is to take no step which may weaken those democratic forces in the life of the world, of which our country is the outstanding exponent. To bring the Rev. Niemoeller here with his lamentable past of unequivocal support of Hitler until his Church was hurt, and with his obvious appeals for the German nation, irrespective of its present political trends, is to render a very great disservice to our own country and that democratic idealism which is its conviction and distinction.

February 3, 1947

TO Stephen Wise Tulin, Oberlin, Ohio

I cannot tell you how happy I was to get your telegram. How did you know of my concern with the Niemoeller matter? I felt that I must protest; and I wonder whether your mother told you that Mrs. [Eleanor] Roosevelt was the first person to protest against the Federal Council [of Churches of Christ in America], and that she has never had as many letters in protest in turn as she had after writing as she did.

. . . I have stated the facts despite the Federal Council. Niemoeller never protested against anything short of regimentation of his own Church. Minister of Christianity though he is, he never spoke one word in behalf of the Jews. He let them perish miserably without one word of protest or appeal. . . .

February 18, 1947

TO Samuel McCrea Cavert

I am very sorry to think that you found it in your heart to write to me as you did under date of February 12. There is no parity between the coming of Cardinal [Martin] von Preysing to this country and the coming of Pastor Niemoeller. As far as I know, Cardinal von Preysing will not be "toured" through the country as Pastor Niemoeller was toured through the country by the Federal Council.

I have not answered your earlier letter, nor that of Henry [Smith] Leiper. I consider both letters unfair. When I find time, I shall explain to you and Henry why I do.

I wonder whether you and Henry are serious in urging that Niemoeller volunteered to serve under Hitler after September 2, 1939, because he did not know whether Poland invaded Germany or Germany invaded Poland. That is really too much to swallow. The people in the [concentration] camps knew what was happening through the underground. Niemoeller surely knew. As for the plea that that was his way of undermining the Nazi strength,

I am afraid that my skepticism will not permit me to give the slightest credence to that notice.

Perhaps I rest my case on too high a ground. Whatever may be said of Christians, I take Christianity seriously. For me it involves obligations not only upon Christians, but most especially upon men who, like Niemoeller, are teachers of Christianity. I may say to you I deeply feel that Christendom almost uniformly failed from '33 to '39, and that is almost equally true of the Christian ministry as it is true of the Christian laity. Germany was a Christian country—roughly two-thirds Protestant and one-third Catholic. How many Christian leaders stood out and took the risk of defending and seeking to save the fellow-Jews of Jesus? . . . Perhaps it will be just as well to end the correspondence; you, defending Niemoeller and I, charging a Christless attitude toward the people of Christ. It may be that you do not consider that a grievous sin. I do.

April 5, 1947

TO Chaim Weizmann, Rehovoth, Palestine

It was such a joy to have your letter and to know, for one thing, that your work proceeds and that you may move so far by December as to be able to think of getting the new library in working order in March. Oh, how I yearn to attend the dedication ceremonies. I have never been in Palestine with you. I want to be. Perhaps that blessing may yet be granted me. . . . Thanks a thousand times for your generous greeting for the fortieth anniversary [of the founding of the Free Synagogue]. Nominally, I have retired. Actually, I work as hard as ever, though for a number of weeks I was in very poor shape, and enjoyed—if that be the term—the new experience of not finding it possible to take any food. As a result of continuous X-ray treatment, I am somewhat better and much less uncomfortable.

May 7, 1947

TO Shirley Fisher, Honesdale, Pa.

I am glad to hear from a little Lady of eleven. As for the discussion on whether the Jewish people are a race or religion, I have only to say that a people cannot be a religion. A people can have a religion, but not be one. The Jewish people have a religion. It is the Jewish religion. The Jewish people are not a race; they are a part of the Semitic division of the white race. We were a people. We are a people. We remain a people. Most Jews, though alas, not all, have a religion. That religion is the religion of Israel.

Someone will explain to you the big words which I am now going to use: Our religion is an ethical monotheism—faith in God, plus the will to live by God's law of the right.

June 13, 1947

TO Miss M ...... J ......, Mt. Vernon, N.Y.

I thank you for your sweet note. It is good to think that I could be of a little help to you in your great sorrow over the passing of dear brother, Edward. Let me remain in your prayers as you are in mine.

The enclosure I cannot accept. If I did, it would go into a special fund which is entirely devoted to the care of the neediest of cases and the worthiest of causes. But in this case, with you and Edward old friends and children of the Synagogue, I really cannot. So please forgive me if I return it and send it to you with deepest sympathy and much affection.

October 30, 1947

TO Roland Gittelsohn, Rockville Center, Long Island

I want to congratulate you with all my heart upon your report ["To Secure These Rights," of the Committee on Civil Rights, appointed in 1946] to the President [Harry Truman]. It is a very real achievement and I have "underground" information to the effect that you have been very helpful in drafting it.

. . . It is a very great document. It will leave its mark in American history. It makes all anti-democratic things seem trivial and absurd and it may now set the nation on the right way. . . .

November 26, 1947

TO Chaim Weizmann

Even though I thought I could come to you last night and sit with you [on the platform of the Convocation], I have been so ill as a result of an attack of acute indigestion on Sunday that I was not able to come in for more than the last part of the evening's exercises [at the Jewish Institute of Religion]. I did hear your fine word.

I must add that, in view of my illness and the excitement of the days, I did not feel equal to seeing you. It would have been too much. My happiness over your birthday and over the great tribute would have overflowed in tears, and I did not wish even for a moment to mar the occasion. As I sat listening to you last night and thought of the imminent decision [on the U. N. Partition Plan for Palestine], I could only remember the words of your English poet [Samuel Taylor Coleridge in "The Good Great Man"]:

> It sounds like stories from the land of spirits
> If any man obtains that which he merits,
> Or any merit that which he obtains.

As a great American said upon another occasion: "Both conditions were fulfilled" last night, and it may be they will, under God, be fulfilled today. [The U.N. General Assembly voted the partition of Palestine three days later, November 29.]

December 5, 1947

TO Fanny Mayer Korn

I know you will be sorry to hear that on coming home I found Louise [Waterman Wise] in a state of complete breakdown. She is very, very ill. The doctor sees her every day. . . . She has a nurse; she probably will have nurses. It is so sad and most depressing. The night I came home [from a speaking engagement in a distant city] I heard her calling at five in the morning. She had fallen in her room and could not rise; and lifting her and putting her back to bed gave me a day of awful pain, but that is somewhat better. . . .

December 8, 1947

TO Fanny Mayer Korn

. . . I am most unhappy to tell you that Louise is critically ill. The doctor says this morning that it is now become very grave. We have an oxygen tank for her to help her pneumonia, which, as you know, is very serious. There is still hope, but not too much, alas; and she is so uncomfortable, but lucid, and happy to have Jim, whose birthday was yesterday, and Justine and me around her. One hopes and prays for the best, but one is very doubtful. . . .

February 9, 1948

TO Mrs. Abram L. Elkus

What great, good news—triplets born to James and his wife! What a wonderful experience; what a heavenly blessing for the heads of Planned Parenthood. We shall have to change the line of the poet—"They builded better than they knew"—to: "They builded better than they planned."

March 16, 1948

TO Michael Stephen Lelyveld (19 days old)

I want you to know that I have been thinking about you, and hope that when I see you, you will be as extraordinarily handsome a boy as you were when [as godfather] I had part in the savage and bloody [circumcision] rites of about a week ago. But

I am writing not only to hope that you are quite yourself again after the reverse of decapitation, but to say to you—don't let anyone give you a cup from which to drink. One [inscribed: "To Mike From Steve"] is coming to you with my love and my love for your parents and your brothers. It will take a few weeks to get it ready, but I think you can comfortably wait and drink in some other way, without the help of a cup.

April 26, 1948

TO Gross Alexander, Redlands, California

. . . But I am in the midst of such pressing burdens that I cannot do more than make my modest personal contribution toward the sum that you need. Finally, after forty-two years of waiting, we are building the [Free] Synagogue. I have the budget of the Jewish Institute of Religion, running well over a hundred thousand dollars, to secure. I have had to "pawn" my insurance in order to lend the American Jewish Congress money. So you can see how pressed I am. But I send you this trifling sum [$25] with every good wish in the world.

May 3, 1948

TO Frank L. Sveska, Omaha, Nebraska

As for your query, I must answer frankly, as I am sure you wish me to do. I do not consider the lack of adequate playgrounds and recreational facilities a substantial factor in contributing to juvenile delinquency. Juvenile delinquency results, as you cannot help knowing, from broken homes, from inadequacy of family incomes, from wretched housing conditions, from social causes, which are very much more substantial as factors in contributing to juvenile delinquency than lack of adequate playgrounds and recreational facilities. These, too, are needed, and a democracy worth its salt must provide these. But before it provides recreational facilities, it must make possible the building of decent housing; and the whole scale of living of the nation must be improved.

May 4, 1948

TO Roy Wilkins

Your invitation to have part in the 39th annual conference [of the National Association for the Advancement of Colored People] at Kansas City, June 22–27, is before me. I wish I could accept, and it may become possible for me to do so. At present the following is the situation: the World Jewish Congress is scheduled to hold its session in Geneva, June 27. In confidence I may say to you that this date may change. I ought to know within a few weeks. If you can wait two or three weeks, until the end of May, I shall be able to let you know. I want to go to you if I can. I will speak for you if my schedule makes it at all possible.

It is good that you know that I was one of the founders of the Association and have never ceased to be interested in its magnificent service.

Three cheers for the decision—though this has nothing to do with your invitation—of the Supreme Court on the restrictive covenants, for which, I must tell you, the American Jewish Congress, under Shad Polier and Leo Pfeffer, has long been fighting.

May 17, 1948

TO Lorna Wingate, Aberdeen

I know we share each other's happiness in the great and blessed consummation [of the establishment of Israel]. I write to thank you for all that you have done and, above all, that Orde did for our cause. I spoke of him last night at a Madison Square Garden rally, as one among the great friends and furtherers of our cause. I have the feeling that Haganah [the Jewish self-defense movement in Palestine] has done so wondrously because of the help he gave it and us. . . .

May 17, 1948

TO Harry Friedenwald, Baltimore

You are the one fellow-Zionist in our country to whom I offer my congratulations. We have stood together so long, and I am sure that both of us have over and over said, "Shehecheyanu" [traditional Jewish thanksgiving benediction]. Therefore I wish you to have this word of heartfelt congratulations to an old and cherished comrade. God has indeed helped us. May the Republic of Israel and, we hope, the Golah [the Dispersion] be worthy of His continued help.

May 28, 1948

TO David Petegorsky

Do you as a Britisher [a Canadian citizen] realize how very serious is the defeat of [Jan Christiaan] Smuts? I am not thinking of him or concerned about him, but I am concerned about the rise and growth of fascism in South Africa. [Daniel F.] Malan was considered a lunatic a few years ago. Today he is evidently to succeed Smuts. Fascism is making the gravest inroads upon the life of the people. . . .

June 10, 1948

TO David Niles, Boston

I cannot let the day go by without telling you that I know how deeply you must be grieved, as I am, over the passing of Josh [Joshua Loth Liebman, rabbi of Temple Israel, Boston]. As I have just written to Sol Goldman [rabbi of Anshe Emet Synagogue, Chicago], his other closest friend, we shall have to find solace, but where shall we find someone to take his place? Josh was a lovable person, to begin with, not a little of the most uncommon genius. How greatly he would have served in the years to come, but the Eternal Wisdom has willed otherwise.

July 29, 1948

TO Chaim Weizmann, Montreux

It is good to hear from you, especially because of my disappointment in failing to see you at the Glion. I was very ill for two days at Montreux and was ordered home by the surgeon who helped me.

Now I am back in New York. Alas, the doctors, including [Dr. Albert] Berg, the surgeon, will not let me go to the Adirondacks with the children, and I must spend the summer practically in or near New York. The hard thing is that I am denied the privilege, I had long cherished, of going to Palestine and attending a meeting of the Actions Committee, perhaps the last. . . .

Keep well and strong, and may the time not be distant when England will have the good sense to welcome you back as President of the Government of the State of Israel.

October 8, 1948

TO Meyer W. Weisgal

I do not know where you are and I am not sure that you know; but, wherever you are, I send you heartfelt thanks for your New Year's message, which I deeply appreciate.

I have been reading [Chaim Weizmann's autobiography] *Trial and Error*. C. W. [Weizmann] has done a wonderful job and I learn that Maurice [Samuel] has been helpful. I am happy to think it is to be serialized in the [N.Y.] *Herald Tribune*. I sent a blurb to Harper's [Harper and Brothers, publisher].

I think it is Maurice rather than Weizmann, who, in a rather less appreciative moment, must have written of me. After all I was not merely helpful in the Wilson Administration and brought Weizmann to Wilson in Paris, but it was I—not L. D. B. [Brandeis] alone—who changed the wording of the [Balfour] Declaration as it came to us from London.

I find the reference to me a little queer. It sounds like Maurice after he had lost a game with heavy stakes at "gin rummy." But it should not matter, for after all he treated you rather well, though,

of course, not well enough; and to [Louis] Lipsky, C. W. and
M. S. are most kind.

October 20, 1948

TO Fanny Mayer Korn

. . . I have been thinking very carefully about the . . . question
which you put to me—namely, whether Jews ought not to help
the so-called Arab refugees at this time. There are a number of
reasons why I think this should not be done. Let me state them
as I see them—Of the two hundred and fifty million dollars asked
for by the U.J.A. [United Jewish Appeal], not more than one
hundred and fifty million is in sight; and not much more than
one hundred million has been forwarded. It is going to be hard
sledding to get the rest of the funds so desperately needed, and I
tremble to think how great will be the difficulty of securing even
comparable sums in 1949, in view of the possible beginnings of
a very real recession.

As for helping the Arabs, I wonder whether you noted that
the moment some Arabs deserted their Palestinian homes—they
were never driven out—the British government, through dear
Mr. Bevin, made a generous offer of one hundred thousand
pounds for their help and relief, though Britain had never given
one penny for the Jews, however terrible their need. Far from
giving relief, throughout the war, and especially after the White
Paper, they denied Jews the right to enter into Palestine and
save themselves from Nazism.

Two things should be remembered, which people who have
not carefully studied the Palestine situation do not quite understand. The Palestine Arabs have not warred against the Jews,
are not warring against them now. Under the cruelest coercion,
some of them have been compelled to take up arms against us,
lest they perish at the hands of their fellow-Arabs—I mean the
extra-Palestinian Arabs from the so-called Christian Lebanon
and from the Arab states, Iraq, Syria, Transjordan, Saudi Arabia,
Egypt. If today the Arabs were free, they would effect a lasting
truce, indeed peace, with the Jews of Palestine or the Jewish

state, to which they are more deeply indebted than anyone can know who has not seen, as I have seen on three different widely separated visits to Palestine, the transformation in economic and social standards which Jews have achieved for the Arabs, and only incidentally for themselves. The fullest assurance was given to the Arabs of Palestine, after the Arabs of neighboring lands began to war against the State of Israel, that they were safe, that their rights and status would be respected. But the coercion of the Arabs states compelled them to flee, against their own will and judgment. If and when the Arabs return to their former homes in Palestine, they will find that no wrong has been done to them, and they will enjoy every right within the Jewish state which is the lot of the Jews who dwell therein.

I feel this way about any organized gift to the Arabs. It seems an acknowledgment of wrong, for one thing. It is we who have been wronged. I feel so strongly about this. The Arabs states took part in the discussion for weeks and weeks preceding the Partition decision of November 29. Immediately thereafter, they began to war upon Israel. If we now set out to help the Arabs, who have chosen to flee—I repeat, under the coercion of fellow-Arabs—there will be involved an acknowledgment of wrong on our part, which we have not committed.

And there is yet another aspect, which is distasteful to me. I think we Jews have no occasion to set out to do things which will make non-Jews feel that we are helpful and unvindictive. We have done that throughout two thousand years of Christian life. It is non-Jews who practice less than justice to the Jew. It is Jews who practice more than charity to Christians. I think it would be an act of needless self-chastisement for Jews to send help to the Arab refugees, and thus appeal to the friendly judgment of the Christian world.

The Christian world has permitted six million, two hundred thousand Jews to be slain, with the very minimum of protest. Christendom does nothing for the Jew, or next to nothing. If Arabs are in difficulty at this time, let the Christian world help a handful of Arabs, as it has neglected and wronged and even permitted to be slain, millions of Jews.

I hope, dear Fanny, you will not think me vindictive. I am

speaking out of the deeps of my heart and out of the strongest convictions of which I am capable. . . .

January 12, 1949

TO A. Leon Kubowitzki, Tel Aviv

After having written to you in mild protest against your failure to have written me, comes your very delightful and full letter of the 29th of December. It is the most informing and significant letter which I have had from Israel in a long time.

Thanks for your generous reference to my place in the life of Israel! There are just two things I want to do before the end of my days: one is to finish my book, *Challenging Years: An Autobiography;* the other is to visit Israel in order that I may get a glimpse of the glory of the State of Israel.

It is fine to read your word about "the calmness and the discipline" of the people and you put it very aptly: it simply means that the Yishub has in fact been, quoting your very word, "a self-governing nation for almost a generation."

I am more deeply interested than you can imagine by what you write of two fields in which American Jews could bring a real contribution to Israel—in American economic democracy, and in the religious life of the country. What I am afraid of is that in trying to bring order into the old-fashioned synagogue, we may achieve something as pallid and unvital as is the American Reform temple. I have, therefore, been inclined to give not the slightest interest or support to the attempt to reform or liberalize the synagogue of Israel. The Yishub must work out its own problem in its own way. I think we have not done well enough in American life to be helpful to the Yishub herein.

As for what you write regarding American economic democracy, all of us feel very deeply about the right of the Yishub to build up its own economic and political life without interference on our part such as the Z.O.A. [Zionist Organization of America] and kindred bodies might be tempted to offer. . . .

January 13, 1949

TO Wilfrid Gibson, Isle of Wight

I am afraid I omitted to send you a little gift for Christmas. I am sending one now, which comes a little late, but I hope you and Geraldine and dear little Roland will enjoy some of the contents.

I have been far from well and I sometimes wonder whether I am ever going to be really well again.

Recently we had a beautiful service in memory of Louise, at which noble addresses were made by my associate, Rabbi [Edward E.] Klein, and the famous Unitarian minister, Dr. [John Haynes] Holmes. When they are published in *Opinion,* I will try to remember to send you a copy of them. In the meantime I send you a little pamphlet which contains what was said about dear Louise when she passed.

With affectionate greetings and wishing you might be good enough to tell me which of the items is particularly useful so that I may send you a [CARE] package which would fit your needs. [The package arrived April 20, 1949, the day following Wise's death.]

January 13, 1949

TO James W. Parkes, Herts, England

. . . Excepting for one or two rather stiff snowstorms, it has been a beautiful and very mild winter from the American point of view, with temperatures running to fifty and over fifty day after day. There are spots in America in which we have equalled the perennial British miracle of crocuses appearing in January.

I am sorry to say that I have been far from well; and while far from well, I have tried to work on an autobiography under the title *Challenging Years.* Thanks to [Ernest] Bevin, 1949 is to be the most challenging of all years. How tragic that the Balfour Declaration, which made everything else possible, should have come from the country whose Minister for Foreign Affairs seems bent upon the destruction of the State of Israel. I know that we, too, have sinned; but it is not our Minister for Foreign Affairs who has sinned, but poor wretched creatures [the assassins of United Nations Palestine mediator Count Folke Bernadotte, slain in Jerusalem on September 17, 1948], crazed with anger because of the injustice of the onetime Mandatory Power, now, alas, become the enemy of Israel.

. . . As you know, I am no longer president of the Jewish Institute of Religion. A brilliant younger man has taken my place; and he is, at one and the same time, president of the Hebrew Union College and Jewish Institute of Religion, which are now joined within the Union of American Hebrew Congregations. I shall send you a copy of *Opinion*, the January number of which contains the addresses of President [Nelson] Glueck and myself upon his installation as president.

February 8, 1949

TO John Gunther

I think we have met casually, but I believe you will understand if I write to you about your inexpressibly beautiful tribute to your son under the [John] Donne title, *Death Be Not Proud*. I not only read it, but could not put it down, and finished it in one sitting of three or four hours.

It is a beautiful tale solely of a beautiful life. I wish I might have known the boy. What extraordinary gifts, what broken promise! Perhaps I should not say this to you, but I wish I had known you and Frances better, for I happen to be an intimate friend of Professor Einstein, and I might have brought him to see Johnny. Perhaps it is tactless on my part to say this, but, knowing Einstein as I do, I feel that he would have been deeply interested in the gallant and brilliant effort of Johnny, and bringing something to him with regard to the Relativity and Quantum Theory.

I write chiefly to thank you personally for a service that you have rendered many. Perhaps I ought to be ashamed to tell you that, old as I am—on the verge of seventy-five and suffering from a fine collection of diseases of older people—your story of Johnny has reinforced my own patience and helped somewhat to renew my courage. If that dear boy of fifteen and sixteen could endure what he did, what right has a person, who has lived and labored as I have, to complain of anything that he may be called upon to endure? Some day I hope to see you and talk further to you about a high service which you rendered many, many parents and even older folk like the writer by telling the story of a most heroic battle on the part of a mere boy, doomed to go down with his flag flying.

P.S. I must add by way of postscript that, when months ago I saw Frances, I had not known about your boy's going. She seemed surprised, but I had had a hard year. My beloved wife has passed, and so I did not quite know the things that were happening about me, as I should have known.

February 9, 1949

TO Samuel Caplan

. . . Did you and Dave [Petegorsky] notice that the first article in this issue [of *Commentary*] is by [Arnold] Toynbee—"Can Western Civilization Save Itself?" Why the devil should he find a place in a Jewish magazine? He is not so much an enemy of Israel as completely incapable of decently evaluating the significance of Hebraism, the contribution of Israel to world civilization. If I were writing my column [in the *Congress Weekly*] now, as I will, beginning in April or May, I would have something to say about Toynbee's welcome by the Philistines [i.e., the American Jewish Committee, which sponsors *Commentary*].

I think the whole number is poor. I have gone through it pretty carefully.

February 11, 1949

TO Bernard Ehrenreich, Brunswick, Ga.

. . . My people are making a great fuss over my seventy-fifth birthday. I suppose it is the best possible substitute for funeral excitement.

Yes, indeed, Bernard, I have the clearest recollection of the beginnings of the Federation of American Zionists [in 1897–98], when we elected [Richard] Gottheil president, though he was abroad. And I, who had done the work, modestly made myself honorary secretary. You are right, [Chaim] Weizmann's *Trial and Error* is a great book, but I wish he had been a little more generous to [Theodor] Herzl and [David] Ben-Gurion and Hadassah. He seems incapable of generosity even to the dead. . . .

March 1, 1949

TO Edward E. Klein

My first reaction upon reading the resignation at midnight of [John Haynes] Holmes was naturally that of pain. We have gone along together so long—forty-two years it will be in April—that it is like parting with an arm or a leg to have him withdraw from the ministry. But I am afraid he is right and that he must do this and that he has no choice.

He is a free man, but I am not. You know that I would have withdrawn a year or two ago if it had not been for your feeling and that of the Executive Council, which I came to share, that I was needed for the completion of the Building Fund Campaign. The moment we dedicate the building, if I live to see it, I will resign as Holmes has done; and you will become Rabbi without encumbrance as far as I am concerned, and I hope that my going will give you the opportunity to lay down conditions about your leadership as Rabbi. . . . You will understand what I mean, for we have talked it over. I would not lightly share this thought with anyone else, neither Fred [Guggenheimer] nor members of the Council, until you and I are ready to act. I hope I can have some part in the dedication, even if such dedication be of a building not quite completed. And then, of course, I withdraw. How strange it will be—Holmes and I started together, and we will virtually go together, both of us in the year 1949. In the meantime I just want you to know that I have perfect faith in your devotion to the work and your capacity to carry on, and in the future of the Synagogue under your leadership. . . .

March 9, 1949

TO David Ben-Gurion, Tel Aviv

I am writing this letter at the direction of the Executive Committee of the American Jewish Congress which referred to me the happy task of sending you its congratulations upon your becoming Prime Minister of the State of Israel.

May I be permitted to add that these congratulations are more than formal? All of us rejoice in the high wisdom and extraordinary statesmanship with which you have guided the new state through its infancy up to this day. I know how safe in your hands lies the destiny of Israel. I know something of what you did throughout a generation to bring it about and that your conduct of its affairs will always be marked by wisdom and nobility growing out of your understanding of your people, your faith in them and your hopes for a better future for Klal Yisroel [the entire Jewish People] and all mankind.

This note is, therefore, to convey to you not only the congratulations and best wishes of the Executive Committee of the American Jewish Congress, but my own sense, as a Zionist veteran, of my deep indebtedness to you for all that you have greatly wrought and will continue to achieve on behalf of Israel.

April 1949

TO His Children

I am not tearful or maudlin as I write this, but I am so wretched that I would be insensitive and stupid not to write as I do. When something happens to me, Ed [Edward Klein, associate rabbi] knows about the things I prefer for the Service.

Ed, of course, is to have charge of the service, whether at the Synagogue House or in Carnegie Hall, where I preached for thirty years and with which I became associated during the stronger years of my life—or, best of all, in the new building.

In view of the large part which the [American Jewish] Congress and Zionism have had in my life, I think that, just as in the case of Mummie, I would like Dave [Petegorsky] to speak the word of farewell if he were equal to it. Dave [executive director of the Congress] has grown very dear to me. He knows what it is that I most deeply care for: the State of Israel and freedom and justice for Jews everywhere. If an address is to be made, it shall be made by Dave. He has become very dear to me and he is a loyal and faithful comrade.

I would like a prayer or the reading of a poem by my beloved friend Holmes.

You won't see this while I am alive. When you do see it, I beg you to understand that my release, whenever it comes, is a great mercy. I am far from well and comfortable. As you know, I hate to leave you both and Shad [Polier, Justine's husband] and Helen [James' wife] and my precious grandchildren, but I feel the time is drawing very near for me to go Home. If God will, it will mean the reunion of my spirit with that of Mummie's, and you know that I want my dust to be placed in the niche wherein she lies.

All love forever to you who have taken such wonderful care of me and will do so, I know, to my end, whenever it is to be. You will love and care for each other always.

Into the Hand of God I commend my spirit. May He continue to vouchsafe me His grace and mercy.

Stephen Wise's directions were carried out in every detail; and the memorial service, held in Carnegie Hall on April 22, 1949, was attended by three thousand people, fifteen thousand more listening to the loudspeakers on West 57th Street. He was laid to rest in the Free Synagogue Cemetery by the side of Louise Waterman Wise.

Several days later a letter arrived from Princeton, New Jersey.

April 25, 1949

TO *James Waterman Wise and Justine Wise Polier*

He has been taken not only from you, but from all of us. He left a gap among us which cannot be filled. He always knew how to help and how to arouse people's consciences wherever it was necessary. In times of great adversity, he helped the Jewish people to maintain dignity and to win their independence, and to every individual he was an understanding friend. No effort was ever too much for him when he felt the obligation to go into action. He knew neither fear nor did he ever hesitate to act, nor did he ever make unprincipled compromises.

I consider it a blessing to have been close to him personally. For it is due to the few of his stature that one does not completely despair of man. His deep, moral influence will continue although he is no longer among us. This knowledge will be a real comfort in your sorrow.

With affectionate sympathy,

Yours,
Albert Einstein

GLOSSARY OF ABBREVIATIONS

A.C.L.U.—American Civil Liberties Union

A.F.L. (also A.F. of L.) —American Federation of Labor

A.J.C.—American Jewish Committee (although sometimes used to refer to American Jewish Congress)

A.J.R.C.—American Jewish Relief Committee

A.Z.E.C. (also A.Z.C.) —American Zionist Emergency Council (also American Provisional Committee for Zionist Affairs)

B.G.—David Ben-Gurion

C.C.A.R.—Central Conference of American Rabbis

C.C.N.Y.—College of the City of New York

C.W.—Chaim Weizmann

F. F.—Felix Frankfurter

G.A.C.— (also A.C. and G.A.U.) Larger Actions Committee of the World Zionist Organization

H.U.C.—Hebrew Union College

I.C.A.—The Jewish Colonization Association

I.T.O.—The Jewish Territorial Organization

J.D.C.—[American Jewish] Joint Distribution Committee

J.I.R.—Jewish Institute of Religion

J.T.S.—Jewish Theological Seminary

J. W. M.—Julian W. Mack

L. D. B.—Louis Dembitz Brandeis

N.A.A.C.P.—National Association for the Advancement of Colored People

U.A.H.C.—Union of American Hebrew Congregations

U.J.A.—United Jewish Appeal

U.N.R.R.A.—United Nations Relief and Rehabilitation Agency

U.P.A.—United Palestine Appeal

W.Z.O.—World Zionist Organization

Z.O.A.—Zionist Organization of America

BIOGRAPHICAL REGISTER

ABRAHAMS, ISRAEL, 1858–1925; scholar; author; teacher; reader, rabbinics and talmudic lit., Cambridge Univ., 1902–25.

ACHESON, DEAN GOLDERHAM, 1893–19 ; lawyer; undersec'y. of treas., 1933; asst. sec'y. of state, 1941–45, undersec'y., 1945–47, sec'y., 1949–53.

ADDAMS, JANE, 1860–1935; founder, social settlement (Hull House), Chicago; peace advocate.

ADLER, CYRUS, 1863–1940; sec'y., Smithsonian Inst.; founder, Am. Jewish Hist. Soc.; ed., Am.-Jewish Yearbook, 1899–1940; pres., Dropsie Coll., Phila., Pa., 1908–40; pres., J.T.S., 1924–40.

ADLER, FELIX, 1851–1933; lecturer; teacher; writer; son of Rabbi Samuel Adler; founder, Ethical Culture Soc.

ADLER, SAMUEL, 1809–1891; rabbi in Germany: Worms, 1836–42, Alzey, 1842–57; rabbi, Temple Emanu-El, N.Y.C., 1857–74; father of Felix Adler.

ALTHEIMER, BENJAMIN, 1850–1938; banker; philanthropist; civic leader.

ANDERSON, CHARLES PALMERSTON, 1864–1930; clergyman; bishop, Epis. diocese, Chicago, 1900–1930.

BAERWALD, PAUL, 1871–1961; banker; communal leader; chrmn., J.D.C., 1932–45; co-chrmn., U.J.A.

BAKER, NEWTON DIEHL, 1871–1937; lawyer; city solicitor, Cleveland, O., 1902–12, mayor, 1912–16; sec'y. of war, 1916–21.

BAKSTANSKY, LAVEY; staff member, Jewish Agency for Palestine, London.

BALFOUR, ARTHUR JAMES, 1848–1930; 1st lord of treas. 1891–92, 1895–1902; prime min., 1902–5; foreign min., 1916–19; repr., Gt. Brit., Disarmnt. Conf., 1921–22.

BAMBERGER, LOUIS, 1855–1944; merchant; civic leader; philanthropist.

BARUCH, BERNARD MANNES, 1870–1965; economist; financier; chrmn., War Industries Brd., 1918–19; U.S. repr., U.N. Atomic Energy Comm., 1946.

BATTLE, GEORGE GORDON, 1868–1949; N.Y. lawyer; active in Dem. party.

BECK, JAMES MONTGOMERY, 1861–1936; lawyer; congressman, 1927–36.

BEILIS, MENDEL; found not guilty of "blood ritual" charges in trial by jury; emigrated from Russia to Palestine, 1913, then to U.S., 1921; died in Saratoga Springs, N.Y., 1934.

BEN-GURION, DAVID, 1886–19 ; genl. sec'y., Genl. Fedtn. Labor, Palestine, 1921–35; chrmn., brd., Jewish Agency, 1935–48; head of provisl. govt., Israel, 1948, prime min. and min. defense, 1949–53, 1955–63.

BERKOWITZ, HENRY, 1857–1924; educator; rabbi, Kansas City, Mo., 1888–92, Phila., Pa., 1892–1921.

BERLE, ADOLF AUGUSTUS, SR., 1865–1960; clergyman; author, *The World Significance of a Jewish State* (1916).

BERMAN, MORTON MAYER, 1899–19 ; asso. rabbi, dir. of educ., Free Syn., 1927–29; dir., field activities, J.I.R., 1929–37; rabbi, Chicago, 1937–57; exec., Keren Hayesod, Jerusalem, 1957– .

BERNAYS, ELI; merchant; brother-in-law of Leonard Lewisohn.

BERNSTEIN, SIMON GERSON, 1882–1962; Zionist exec., Leningrad, later in Berlin and in Copenhagen, 1908–19; ed., *Dos Yiddische Folk*, 1922–53.

BEVERIDGE, WILLIAM, 1879–1963; economist; dir., London Sch. Econ., 1919–37; Oxford, 1937; author, plan for social sec., Gt. Brit.

BILLIKOPF, JACOB, 1883–1950; social worker; community leader Cin., O., Milwaukee, Wis., Kansas City, Mo., Phila., Pa., and N.Y.C.

BISGYER, MAURICE, 1897–19 ; social worker; exec. sec'y., B'nai B'rith, 1937–56, exec. v-pres., 1956–65.

BLOCH, CHARLES EDWARD, 1861–1940; publisher; sec'y., pres., trustee, Free Syn.; trustee, J.I.R., 1922–40.

BLUM, LEON, 1872–1950; writer; premier, France, 1935–37, 1938, 1946–47.

BLUMENTHAL, BENJAMIN; pres., Congrtn. Rodeph Sholom, N.Y.C.

BORAH, WILLIAM EDGAR, 1865–1940; U.S. sen., Idaho; chrmn., Senate Comm. For. Affairs, 1925–33; Ind. Republican.

BRADY, JOHN GREEN, 1848–1918; Protestant missionary at Sitka, Alaska; gov. of Alaska, 1897–1909.

BRANDEIS, LOUIS DEMBITZ, 1851–1941; author; Zionist leader; lawyer; asso. justice, U.S. Supreme Court, 1916–38.

BREWER, DAVID JOSIAH, 1837–1910; jurist; lecturer; member, state, fed. judiciary, 1861–89, U.S. Supreme Court, 1889–1910.

BRICKNER, BARNETT ROBERT, 1892–1958; welfare leader, N.Y.C., Cincinnati; rabbi, Toronto, 1920–25, Cleveland, 1925–58.

BROOKS, JOHN GRAHAM, 1846–1938; economist; author, *The Social Unrest* (1903), *Labor's Challenge to the Social Order* (1920), etc.

BROWN, DAVID, 1875–1958; Detroit industrialist; publisher; active in J.D.C., U.A.H.C., Palestine Fdtn. Fund, Crimean project.

BRÜNING, HEINRICH, 1885–19   ; educator; author; statesman; Roman Cath. layman; chancellor, German Reich, 1930–32.

BRYAN, WILLIAM JENNINGS, 1860–1925; congressman, 1891–95; Dem. party candidate for pres., 1896, 1900, 1908; sec'y. of state, 1913–15.

BÜCHLER, ADOLF, 1867–1939; historian; theologian; talmudist; principal, Jews' Coll., London, 1907–39.

BURCH, CHARLES SUMNER, 1855–1920; bishop, Epis. Diocese, N.Y.C., 1919–20.

BURLINGHAM, CHARLES C., 1858–1959; lawyer; Protestant layman.

CAPLAN, SAMUEL, staff member, Am. Jewish Congress; ed., *Congress Weekly.*

CARDOZO, BENJAMIN NATHAN, 1870–1938; lawyer; elected, N.Y. Supreme Court, 1913, Court of Appeals, 1914, chief justice, Court of Appeals, 1926; apptd. asso. justice, U.S. Supreme Court, 1932–38.

CAVERT, SAMUEL MCCREA, 1888–19   ; clergyman; genl. sec'y., Natl. Council of Churches of Christ in Am. (formerly Federal Council), 1921–57; exec. sec'y., World Council of Churches, 1954–57.

CECIL, ROBERT, 1864–1958; British statesman; co-author, covenant of League of Nations; recipient, 1937 Nobel Peace Prize.

CHURCHILL, WINSTON LEONARD SPENCER, 1874–1965; British soldier and statesman; cabinet officer, 1910–15, 1917–21, 1924–29; prime min., 1940–45, 1951–55.

CLINCHY, EVERETT ROSS, 1896–19   ; clergyman; pres., Natl. Conf. of Christians and Jews, 1928–58; pres., Council World Tensions, 1958–   .

COFFIN, HENRY SLOANE, 1877–1954; min., Madison Ave. Pres. Ch., 1905–26; pres., Union Theol. Sem., N.Y.C., 1926–45.

COHEN, J. X., 1889–1955; rabbi, Free Syn., N.Y.C., 1927–55.

COHEN, MORRIS RAPHAEL, 1880–1947; philosopher; prof., C.C.N.Y., 1912–38, Univ. of Chicago, 1938–42.

COLBY, BAINBRIDGE, 1869–1950; U.S. sec'y. of state, 1920–21.

COLEMAN, GEORGE WILLIAM, 1867–1950; publicist; labor arbitrator; Baptist layman; founder, Sun. eve. Ford Hall Forum, 1908.

COLLIER, JOHN, 1884–1967; social worker; author; exec. sec'y., Am. Indian Defense Asso., 1923–33; commsr., Ind. Affrs., 1933–53.

CRAVATH, PAUL, 1861–1940; lawyer; staff member, U.S. delegation, Paris Peace Conf., 1918–19; pres., Metropolitan Opera Asso.

CROSSMAN, RICHARD HOWARD STAFFORD, 1907–19   ; journalist; author; House of Commons, 1945–   ; member, Anglo-Am. Comm. Inquiry on Palestine, 1946.

CRUM, BARTLEY CAVANAUGH, 1900–1959; lawyer; publisher; author; member, Anglo-Am. Comm. Inquiry on Palestine, 1946.

CUTLER, HARRY, 1875–1920; legislator, Rhode Island, 1908–11; active in work of Natl. Jewish Welfare Brd., Z.O.A., A.J.C., U.A.H.C., etc.

DANIELS, JOSEPHUS, 1862–1948; ed., Raleigh (N.C.) *News and Observer;* sec'y. of navy, 1913–21; amb. to Mexico, 1933–42.

DAVIDSON, THOMAS, 1840–1900; philosopher; scholar; founder, head, Breadwinner's Coll., Croton-on-Hudson, N.Y.

DAVIS, JOHN WILLIAM, 1873–1955; W. Va. state legis., 1899; U.S. House of Repr., 1911–13; U.S. sol. genl., 1913–18; U.S. amb. to Gt. Brit., 1918–21; Dem. party candidate for pres., 1924.

DAVIS, NORMAN HEZEKIAH, 1878–1944; staff member, Peace Conf., 1918–19; asst. sec'y. of treas., 1919–20; undersec'y. of state, 1920–21; chief, delegation, Disarmnt. Conf., Geneva, 1932–33; amb.-at-large, 1933; chrmn., Am. Red Cross, 1938–44.

DEEDES, WYNDHAM, 1883–1956; military attaché, Constantinople, 1918–19; chief sec'y., Palestine adm., 1920; knighted, 1921.

DEVINE, EDWARD THOMAS, 1867–1948; social worker; author; dir., N.Y. Sch. of Philanthropy, 1904–7, 1912–17; ed., *Survey,* 1897–1912.

DITTENHOEFER, ABRAHAM JESSE, 1836–1917; authority on jurisprudence; son of Isaac Dittenhoefer, a founder of Temple Emanu-El, N.Y.C.

DUBNOW, SIMON, 1860–1941; Jewish historian; resident, Berlin, 1922–33.

EHRENREICH, BERNARD, 1876–1955; rabbi and educator, Ala., Wis.; a founder, Fedtn. of Am. Zionists.

EHRICH, LOUIS R., 1849–1911; patron of the arts; author.

EINHORN, DAVID, 1809–79; rabbi, Baltimore, 1852–61, Philadelphia, 1861–66, and N.Y.C., 1866–79.

EINSTEIN, ALBERT, 1879–1955; physicist; mathematician; prof., Prague, Zürich, Berlin, 1920–33, Princeton, N.J., 1933–45.

ELBOGEN, ISMAR, 1874–1943; educator; scholar; lecturer, Hochschule fuer die Wissenschaft des Judentums, Berlin, 1902–4; dir., 1904–38; research prof., J.I.R., H.U.C., J.T.S., and Dropsie Coll., 1938–43.

ELKUS, ABRAM I., 1867–1947; lawyer; amb. to Turkey, 1916–19; jurist; diplomat.

EPSTEIN, ABRAHAM, 1892–1942; founder-exec. sec'y., Am. Asso. for Old Age Sec.; author; teacher.

FECHHEIMER, SAMUEL MARCUS, 1864–1933; Cincinnati businessman; member, Natl. Advisory Brd., U.A.H.C.

FELS, MARY F., 1863–1953; active Zionist during World War I and early 1920s; associated with husband, Joseph (1854–1914), in Single Tax advocacy, prison reform, social welfare.

FELSENTHAL, BERNHARD, 1822–1908; rabbi, Madison, Ind., 1854–57, Chicago, 1858–87.

FINLEY, JOHN HOUSTON, 1863–1940; pres., Knox Coll., 1892–99, C.C.N.Y., 1903–13, Univ. State of N.Y., 1913–21; asso. ed., N.Y. *Times,* 1921–37, ed., 1937–38.

FISHMAN, JACOB, 1876–1946; Zionist leader; founder-managing ed., *Jewish Morning Journal.*

FLEISCHER, CHARLES, 1871–1942; rabbi, Boston, 1893–1911; organizer, Sunday Commons, Boston, 1911–22; lecturer; writer.

FLEXNER, ABRAHAM, 1866–1959; exec., Carnegie Fdtn. for Adv. Teaching, 1908–29; author, *Medical Education in the U.S. and Canada,* 1910; dir., Inst. for Adv. Study, Princeton, 1930–39.

FOHS, FERDINAND JULIUS, 1844–1965; oil geologist; lecturer; conducted surveys of water, mineral, and petroleum resources in Palestine; active, Palestine Econ. Corp.

FOSDICK, HARRY EMERSON, 1878–19 ; author; min., Montclair, N.J., 1904–15, N.Y.C., 1921–23, 1928–46; prof., Union Theol. Sem., 1908–46.

FRANKEL, LEE KAUFER, 1867–1931; insurance exec.; pioneer, social ins.; v-pres., Metropolitan Life Ins. Co.; trustee, J.I.R.

FRANKFURTER, FELIX, 1882–1964; author; prof., Harvard Law Sch., 1914–39; asso. justice, U.S. Supreme Court, 1939–63.

FRIEDENWALD, HARRY, 1864–1950; ophthalmologist; a founder, Fedtn. of Am. Zionists, pres., 1904–18.

FRIEDMAN, ELISHA MICHAEL, 1889–1951; consulting economist; author.

GASTER, MOSES, 1856–1939; scholar; author; lecturer, Univ. of Bucharest, 1881–85, Oxford, 1886–91; chief rabbi, Sephardic communities, Gt. Brit., 1887–1919; Zionist leader.

GEORGE, HENRY, 1839–97; economist; author, *Progress and Poverty,* 1879; founder of Single Tax movement.

GERMAIN-LEVI, LOUIS; rabbi, Union Liberale Israélite, Paris; leader among anti-Zionists.

GIBSON, WILFRED WILSON, 1878–1962; English poet; author, *Daily Bread* (1910), *Livelihood* (1917), *Fuel* (1934), etc.

GITTELSOHN, ROLAND, 1910– ; author; rabbi, Lawrence, L.I., Boston, since 1952.

GLADDEN, WASHINGTON, 1836–1918; clergyman; author; hymn writer; leader, Social Gospel movement.

GOLDMAN, FRANK, 1890–1965; Lowell, Mass. lawyer; pres., B'nai B'rith, 1947–53.

GOLDMAN, SOLOMON, 1893–1953; rabbi, Brooklyn, N.Y., 1917–18, Cleveland, O., 1919–29, Chicago, Ill., 1929–53; pres., Z.O.A., 1938–40; author.

GOLDMANN, NAHUM, 1894–19 ; ed., Berlin, 1920–35; repr., Jewish Agency for Palestine, Geneva, 1935–40, U.S., 1940–46, chrmn., Am. sect., 1949–51, exec. comm., 1951– ; pres., W.Z.O. 1956–68; chrmn., adm. comm., World Jewish Congress, 1945–53, pres. since 1953; pres., Conf. Jewish Mat'l. Claims Ag. Germany.

GOLDSCHMIDT, SIGMUND; court steno.; recorded Stephen Wise's sermons, Carnegie Hall.

GOLDSTEIN, ISRAEL, 1896–19 ; rabbi, N.Y.C., 1918–60; pres., Z.O.A.,

1943–45, Am. Jewish Congress, 1951–58, and World Confedtn., Genl. Zionists, 1947–56; Keren Hayesod, Jerusalem, 1960– .

GOLDSTEIN, SIDNEY EMANUEL, 1879–1955; rabbi, founder-dir., social serv. dept., Free Syn., 1907–55; prof., J.I.R., 1922–55.

GOMPERS, SAMUEL, 1850–1924; labor leader; pres., A.F.L., 1886–94, 1896–1924; chrmn., War Comm. on Labor, World War I.

GOTTHEIL, GUSTAV, 1827–1903; rabbi, Manchester, Eng., 1860–73, Temple Emanu-El, N.Y.C., 1873–99.

GOTTHEIL, RICHARD JAMES HORATIO, 1862–1936; head of Oriental Dept., N.Y. Publ. Lib., 1896–1936; prof., Columbia Univ., 1887–1930; pres., Fedtn. of Am. Zionists, 1898–1904.

GRANT, PERCY STICKNEY, 1860–1927; rector, Ch. of the Ascension, N.Y.C., 1893–1924.

GRAYSON, CARY TRAVERS, 1878–1938; naval officer; surgeon; personal physician to Theodore Roosevelt, William Howard Taft, and Woodrow Wilson.

GREEN, WILLIAM A., 1873–1952; labor leader; sec'y.-treas., A.F.L., 1912–24, pres., 1924–52.

GREER, DAVID HUMMELL, 1844–1919; bishop, Epis. Diocese, N.Y.C. 1908–19.

GREY OF FALLODON, EDWARD GREY, 1862–1933; British statesman; foreign sec'y., 1905–16; amb. to U.S., 1919–20.

GRIES, MOSES J., 1868–1918; rabbi, Chattanooga, Tenn., 1889–92; Cleveland, O., 1892–1917.

GUEDALLA, PHILIP, 1889–1944; historian; English Zionist.

GUGGENHEIM, DANIEL, 1856–1930; industrialist; philanthropist.

GUGGENHEIMER, FREDERICK, L., 1882–1956; exec. sec'y., Free Syn., 1916–26, pres., 1926–52, hon. pres., 1952–56; exec. sec'y., City Affairs Comm.

GUNTHER, JOHN, 1901– ; foreign correspondent; author, *Inside Europe, Inside Asia,* etc.

HAAS, JACOB DE, 1872–1937; exec. sec'y., Fedtn. Am. Zionists; ed., *The Maccabaean,* 1902–20.

HALIFAX, EDW. FREDK. LINDLEY WOOD, 1881–1959; gov. genl., India, 1926–31; foreign sec'y., 1938; amb. to U.S., 1941–46.

HARLOW, S. RALPH, 1884–19 ; clergyman; author; teacher; prof., relig. and sociology, Smith College, 1924–50.

HARRIS, MAURICE H., 1859–1930; rabbi, Temple Israel, N.Y.C., 1888–1930.

HARVEY, GEORGE BRINTON MCCLELLAN, 1864–1928; journalist; diplomat; ed., *N. Am. Rev.,* later *Harper's Weekly;* founder, publisher, *Harvey's Weekly.*

HAUSER, GERTRUDE; cousin of Louise Waterman Wise.

HAYDEN, JOEL B.; min., Fairmount Pres. Ch., Cleveland Heights, O.

HAYES, PATRICK JOSEPH, 1867–1938; archbishop, N.Y.C., 1919–38; elevated, cardinal, 1924.

HAYS, DANIEL, 1854–1923; lawyer; pres., Temple Israel, N.Y.C.; chrmn., exec. comm., U.A.H.C.

HEARST, WILLIAM RANDOLPH, 1863–1951; journalist; publisher; congressman, 1903–7; owner, N.Y. *Journal-American,* San Fran. *Examiner,* etc.

HECHT, BEN, 1894–1964; author; playwright; chrmn., Emergency Comm. to Save the Jews of Europe; sympathetic to Irgun Zvai Leumi.

HEINRICHS, WALDO, 1892–1959; Y.M.C.A. sec'y., Calcutta and Lahore, later Jerusalem; prof., Middlebury Coll., 1934–56.

HELD, ADOLPH, 1885–19 ; banker; chrmn., Jewish Labor Comm.; city ed., later, bus. mgr., *Jewish Daily Forward.*

HELLER, MAXIMILIAN, 1860–1929; rabbi, Houston, Texas, 1886, Temple Sinai, New Orleans, 1886–1927; prof., Hebrew lit., Tulane Univ., 1912–28; pres., C.C.A.R., 1909–11.

HENEY, FRANCIS JOSEPH, 1859–1937; lawyer; atty. genl. Ariz., 1893–94; judge, Superior Court, Calif., 1931–37.

HENRIQUES, BASIL L. Q., 1890–1961; rabbi; social worker; pioneer, youth club work, Gt. Brit.; for 19 yrs., chrmn., E. London Juvenile Court.

HERZL, THEODOR, 1860–1904; journalist; critic; dramatist; author, *Der Judenstaat (The Jewish State)*; convened First Zionist Congress, Basle, 1897.

HEWITT, ABRAM STEVENS, 1822–1903; industrialist; lawyer; congressman, 1874–86; mayor, N.Y.C., 1886–90.

HILBORN, WALTER S., 1879–19 ; lawyer, N.Y.C., later, Calif.; for many years, pres., Free Syn., N.Y.C.

HILLMAN, SIDNEY, 1887–1946; labor leader; pres., Amalgamated Clothing Workers, 1915–46.

HINDENBURG, PAUL VON, 1847–1934; field-marshal; pres., Germany, 1925–34.

HIRSCH, EMIL GUSTAV, 1851–1923; rabbi, Chicago, Ill., 1880–1923; social reformer; prof., rabbinic lit. and philos., Univ. of Chicago, 1892–1923.

HIRSCH, SOLOMON, 1839–1902; merchant; member, Ore. state legis., later, state senate; U.S. min. to Turkey, 1889–92; pres., Temple Beth Israel, Portland, 1899–1902.

HOCKING, WILLIAM ERNEST, 1873–1966; author; philosopher; prof., Harvard Univ., 1914–41.

HOLMES, JOHN HAYNES, 1879–1964; min., Community Ch., N.Y.C., 1907–49; with Stephen Wise, a founder of N.A.A.C.P., 1909, and A.C.L.U., 1920; chrmn., A.C.L.U., 1940–50.

HOOVER, HERBERT CLARK, 1874–1964; chrmn. Comm. for Relief in Belgium, 1915–19, Am. Relief Adm. and European Relief Council, 1920; sec'y. of commerce, 1921–29; pres., U.S., 1929–33.

HORTHY DE NAGYBANYA, NICHOLAS, 1868–1957; admiral, Austro-Hungarian fleet, World War I; regent, Hungary, 1920–44.

HOUSE, EDWARD MANDELL, 1858–1938; bore Texas title of "Colonel"; Woodrow Wilson's confidant and trouble-shooter, esp. at Peace Conf., World War I.

HOUSTON, DAVID FRANKLIN, 1866–1940; scholar; educator; sec'y. of agric., 1913–20; sec'y. of treas., 1920–21.

HOWE, LOUIS MCHENRY, 1871–1936; confidant and exec. asst. to Franklin Delano Roosevelt, 1915–36.

HUGHES, CHARLES EVANS, 1862–1948; gov., N.Y., 1906–10; asso. justice, U.S. Supreme Court, 1910–16; sec'y. of state, 1921–25; chief justice, U.S., 1930–41.

HYLAN, JOHN FRANCIS, 1868–1936; lawyer; city magistrate, 1906–14; judge, county court, 1914–18; mayor, N.Y.C., 1918–25.

JACKSON, FREDERICK JOHN FOAKES-, 1855–1941; church historian; author; fellow, Jesus Coll., Cambridge Univ., 1886–95, dean, 1895–1916; prof., Union Theol. Sem., N.Y.C., 1916–34; lecturer, J.I.R. 1924.

JEROME, WILLIAM TRAVERS, 1859–1934; lawyer; justice, Court of Special Sessions, 1895–1900; distr. atty., N.Y. county, 1901–9.

JOHNSON, JAMES WELDON, 1871–1938; author; lawyer; govt. offcl.; prof., Fisk Univ., 1930–38; sec'y., N.A.A.C.P., 1916–30.

JOHNSON, JOHN ROSAMOND, 1873–19 ; musician; composer; anthologist; brother of James Weldon Johnson.

JONES, JENKIN LLOYD, 1843–1918; clergyman; ed.; founder, All Souls Ch., 1885, Abraham Lincoln Ctr., 1905, Chicago, Ill.; ed. *Unity*, 1880–1918.

KALLEN, HORACE M., 1882–19 ; member faculty, Harvard, Clark Univ., Wis., New Sch. for Soc. Research, N.Y.C., 1919–52; author.

KAPLAN, ELIEZER, 1891–1952; treas., Jewish Agency for Palestine, 1933–48; fin. min., State of Israel, 1948–52.

KAPLAN, MORDECAI, 1886–19 ; educator; theologian; author; prof., J.T.S.; founder, Soc. for Advmnt. of Judaism.

KAPLAN, NATHAN D.; leader, "Knights of Zion," Chicago; migrated to Palestine as early settler.

KAUFMANN, EDMUND I., 1886–1950; merchant; pres., Z.O.A., 1940–42.

KENNEDY, JOSEPH PATRICK, 1888–19 ; banker; ship-builder; financier; chrmn., Sec. and Exch. Comm., 1934–35; chrmn., U.S. Maritime Comm., 1937; U.S. amb. to Gt. Brit., 1937–40.

KESSELMAN, ROBERT; a Palestinian pioneer, emigrated from U.S.A., early 1920s.

KLEIN, EDWARD E., 1913–19 ; exec. dir., Hillel Fdtn., Berkeley, Calif., 1942–43; rabbi, Free Syn., 1940–42, 1943–19 .

KOHLER, KAUFMANN, 1843–1926; rabbi, Detroit, 1869–71, Chicago, 1871–79, N.Y.C., 1879–1903; pres., H.U.C., Cin. O., 1903–21.

KOHUT, ALEXANDER, 1842–1894; rabbi, N.Y.C., 1885–94; prof., J.T.S. N.Y.C.

KOHUT, GEORGE ALEXANDER, 1874–1933; son of Alexander Kohut; rabbi, Dallas, Texas, 1899–1900, Mt. Vernon, N.Y., 1906–7; principal, religious sch., Temple Emanu-El, N.Y.C., 1902–12; founder, Kohut Sch. for Boys, Columbia Grammar Sch., 1920–33.

KOHUT, REBEKAH, 1864–1951; educator; wife of Alexander Kohut; established Kohut Sch. for Girls, 1899.

KORN, FANNY MAYER; friend of Stephen and Louise Wise; supporter (with husband, William Korn) of Am. Jewish Congress and liberal causes.

KOUSSEVITZKY, SERGE, 1874–1951; conductor, Boston Symphony Orch., 1924–49, Berkshire Symphonic Festivals, 1936–51.

KRASS, NATHAN, 1880–1949; rabbi, Muncie, Ind., Owensboro, Ky., Lafayette, Ind., Rochester, N.Y., Brooklyn, N.Y., Central Synagogue, N.Y.C., 1918–23, Temple Emanu-El, N.Y.C., 1923–45; prof. in homiletics, J.I.R.

KRAUS, ADOLF, 1850–1928; lawyer; philanthropist; owner-ed., Chicago *Times;* internatl. pres., B'nai B'rith, 1905–25; organized Anti-Defamation League.

KRENSKY, MILTON AND ROSEMARY; relatives and personal friends of Stephen and Louise Wise; communal leaders, Chicago.

LA FOLLETTE, ROBERT, 1855–1925; lawyer; political reformer; pacifist; Progressive party candidate for pres., 1924.

LA GUARDIA, FIORELLO HENRY, 1882–1947; public official; Congressman, 1916–17, 1923–33; mayor, N.Y.C., 1933–45.

LAKE, KIRSOPP, 1872–1946; scholar; prof., Univ. of Leiden, 1904–13, Harvard, 1919–37.

LANDMAN, ISAAC, 1880–1946; rabbi, Philadelphia, 1906–16, Far Rockaway, N.Y., 1917–28, Brooklyn, 1931–46; ed., *The American Hebrew,* 1918–37; ed., *The Universal Jewish Encyclopedia.*

LANDON, ALFRED MOSSMAN, 1887–19 ; banker; oil operator; gov., Kansas, 1933–37; Rep. party candidate for pres., 1936.

LANE, HARRY, 1855–1917; practiced medicine, San Fran., later Portland; mayor, Portland, Ore., 1905–9; U.S. sen., 1913–17.

LANSING, ROBERT, 1864–1928; internatl. lawyer; govt. official; sec'y. of state, 1915–20.

LASKER, ALBERT DAVIS, 1880–1952; founder, Lord and Thomas advtng. agency; chrmn., U.S. Shipping Brd., 1921–23.

LASKI, HAROLD, 1893–1950; economist; political scientist; author; prof., London Sch. Econ., 1920–50, Univ. of London, 1926–50; chrmn., British Labour party, 1945–46.

LEHMAN, HERBERT H., 1878–1963; banker; statesman; lt. gov., N.Y. state, 1928–32; gov., 1932–52; dir. genl., U.N.R.R.A., 1943–46; U.S. sen., 1949–56.

LEHMAN, IRVING, 1876–1945; brother of Herbert; lawyer; justice, N.Y.

Supreme Court, 1908–23; asso. justice, N.Y. Court of Appeals, 1923–39, chief justice, 1939–45; pres., Temple Emanu-El, N.Y.C., 1929–38; pres., Natl. Jewish Welfare Brd., 1921–40.

LEIPER, HENRY SMITH, 1891–19 ; clergyman; missionary, 1913–14, 1918–22; exec. denmtl. ecumenical orgs., 1922–59.

LEON, MAURICE, 1880–1952; lawyer; brother-in-law of Richard Gottheil.

LEVEN, NARCISSE, 1833–1915; statesman; philanthropist; founder-pres., Alliance Israelite Universelle.

LEVIN, SCHMARYAHU (Shemaryahu Halevi), 1867–1935; rabbi; ed.; publisher; Zionist leader.

LEVINE, JOSEPH, 1883–1963; lawyer; jurist; a founder, Free Syn. and pres., 1933–45; chrmn., brd. of trustees, J.I.R., 1940–49; v- chrmn., H.U.C.–J.I.R.

LEVY, REUBEN, 1891–1966; prof., librarian, J.I.R., 1924–27; prof., Cambridge Univ., 1927–57.

LEWISOHN, ADOLPH, 1849–1938; mining entrepreneur; philanthropist; art collector.

LEWISOHN, LEONARD, 1847–1902; brother of Adolph; merchant; philanthropist; helped reorganize J.T.S. as an incorporator and founder of endowment fund.

LEWISOHN, LUDWIG, 1882–1955; author; teacher; drama critic, *The Nation,* 1919, asso. ed., 1920–24; ed., *The New Palestine,* 1943–48; prof., Brandeis Univ., 1948–55.

LEWISOHN, SAM ADOLPH, 1884–1951; banker; philanthropist; communal leader.

LIBMAN, EMANUEL; pathologist; staff, Beth Israel Hosp., later, Mt. Sinai Hosp., N.Y.C.

LICHTWITZ, LEOPOLD; staff, Montefiore Hosp.; prof., Columbia Univ.

LIEBMAN, JOSHUA LOTH, 1907–1948; author, *Peace of Mind,* as Charles W. Eliot lecturer, J.I.R., 1945; rabbi, Temple Israel, Boston, 1940–48.

LINDHEIM, IRMA, 1886–19 ; student at J.I.R. in 1920s; settled at Mishmar Haemek in Palestine with husband and children, 1933; pres., Hadassah, 1926–28.

LINDSAY, SAMUEL MCCUNE, 1869–1959; sociologist; economist; prof., Univ. of Penna., 1896–1907; prof., Columbia Univ., 1907–39.

LINDSEY, BENJAMIN BARR, 1869–1943; judge, juvenile court, Denver, Colo.; author (with Wainwright Evans), *The Companionate Marriage,* 1927.

LIPSKY, LOUIS, 1876–1963; journalist; author; Zionist leader; prominent in work of W.Z.O., Am. Jewish Congress, U.P.A., U.J.A., etc.

LIVINGSTON, JULIUS; Zionist leader in Southwest; petroleum entrepreneur, Tulsa.

LODGE, HENRY CABOT, 1859–1924; ed.; author; U.S. sen. from Mass., 1893–1924.

LONG, JOHN D.; chrmn. speakers comm., Christian Socialist Fellowship.

McAdoo, William Gibbs, 1863–1941; lawyer; political leader; sec'y. of treas. 1913–21; U.S. sen. from Calif., 1933–39.

McConnell, Francis John, 1871–1953; clergyman; educator; author; Methodist pastorates, 1894–1909; pres., De Pauw Univ., 1909–12; bishop, Methodist Ch., Denver, 1912–19, Pittsburgh, 1919–30, N.Y. East Conf., 1930–44.

MacDonald, James Ramsay, 1866–1937; prime min., Gt. Brit., 1922, 1929–31, Labour govt., and 1931–35, Natl. govt.

McGiffert, Arthur Cushman, Sr., 1861–1933; theologian; church historian; pres., Union Theol. Sem. N.Y.C., 1917–26.

Mack, Julian, W., 1866–1943; prof., Northwestern Univ., 1895–1902, Univ. of Chicago, 1902–11; judge, U.S. Commerce Court, 1911–13, U.S. Circuit Court of Appeals, 1911–41; pres., Am. Jewish Congress, 1917–18 and Z.O.A., 1918–21; chrmn., brd. of trustees, J.I.R., 1922–41.

Mackay, Clarence, 1874–1938; financier; chrmn., Postal Telegraph Cable Co.

MacLeish, Archibald, 1892–19 ; poet; librarian, Lib. of Congress, 1939–44; asst. sec'y. of state, 1944–45.

MacMahon, Thomas; pres., United Textile Workers, 1920s.

Magnes, Judah Leon, 1877–1948; rabbi, Brooklyn, N.Y., 1904–6, Temple Emanu-El, N.Y.C., 1906–10, Congrtn. B'nai Jeshurun, N.Y.C., 1911–12, Soc. for the Advancement of Judaism, 1919–20; chancellor, Hebrew Univ., Jerusalem, 1925–35, pres., 1935–48.

Manning, William T., 1866–1949; rector, Trinity Parish, N.Y.C., 1908–21; Epis. bishop, N.Y.C., 1921–46.

Markham, Edwin, 1852–1940; poet, author, "The Man with the Hoe," etc.

Marshall, Louis, 1856–1926; lawyer; chrmn. brd. and exec. comm., J.T.S.; pres., Am. Jewish Comm.; pres., Temple Emanu-El N.Y.C. Temple Emanu-El, N.Y.C.

Mattuck, Israel Isidor, 1883–1954; rabbi, Lincoln, Neb., Far Rockaway, N.Y. 1905–12; Liberal Jewish Syn. of London, 1912–54; a founder, World Union for Progressive Judaism.

Melish, John Howard, 1874–19 ; clergyman; rector, Cincinnati, O., 1895–1905; Brooklyn, N.Y. 1905–48.

Mendes, Henry Pereira, 1852–1937; rabbi, Congrtn. Shearith Israel, N.Y.C.; a founder, Fedtn. of Am. Zionists.

Menuhin, Moshe; father of Yehudi.

Meyer, Martin, 1879–1923; rabbi, Albany, N.Y., 1902–6, Brooklyn, 1906–10, San Francisco, 1910–23; active in civic, rabbinical, and Zionist affairs.

Monsky, Henry, 1890–1947; lawyer; pres., B'nai B'rith, 1938–47; co-chrmn., Am. Jewish Conf., 1943–47.

Montagu, Samuel (Baron Swaythling), 1832–1911; banker; philanthropist; member Parliament, 1885–1907; communal leader.

MONTAGU, EDWIN SAMUEL, 1879–1924; Liberal party member Parliament; occupied various govt. posts, 1906–22.

MONTAGUE, RICHARD WARD, 1862–1935; lawyer; reform leader in northwest; Unitarian layman.

MONTEFIORE, CLAUDE GOLDSMID, 1858–1938; scholar; philanthropist; founder-ed., *Jewish Quarterly Review;* founder-pres., World Union for Progressive Judaism, 1926–38.

MONTEFIORE, SIR FRANCIS ABRAHAM, 1860–1935; for many years head of Zionist movement, Gt. Brit.

MORGENSTERN, JULIAN, 1881–19 ; rabbi, Lafayette, Ind., 1904–7; professor, H.U.C., Cin., O., 1907–21, acting pres., 1921, pres., 1921–46; scholar; author.

MORGENTHAU, HENRY, SR., 1856–1946; banker; philanthropist; fin. chrmn., Dem. Natl. Comm., 1912–16; U.S. amb. to Turkey, 1913–16; a founder, Free Syn. 1907, pres., 1907–17.

MORRISON, CHARLES CLAYTON, 1874–1966; clergyman; author; ed. *The Christian Century,* 1908–47.

MORROW, DWIGHT WHITNEY, 1873–1931; banker; amb. to Mexico, 1927–30; sen. from N.J., 1930–31.

MOSKOWITZ, BELLE, 1877–1933; active in admin. of N.Y. state agencies, advisor, Gov. Alfred E. Smith.

MOSKOWITZ, HENRY, 1879–1936; social reformer; journalist; pres., N.Y.C. Civil Serv. Comm.

MOTON, ROBERT RUSSA, 1867–1940; successor to Booker T. Washington as principal, Tuskegee Inst., 1915; later, pres. until 1935.

MURRAY, GEORGE GILBERT AIMÉ, 1866–1957; classical scholar; regius prof. Greek, Oxford Univ., 1908–36.

NASH, ARTHUR, 1870–1927; Ohio clothing manufacturer; dev. "Nash Plan" of co-ownership of industry by workers.

NATHAN, OTTO, 1893–19 ; economist; econ. advisor, Weimar Republic, 1922–33; later, taught at Princeton, N.Y.U., Columbia, and Howard Univ.

NEARING, SCOTT, 1883–19 ; author; prof., Univ. of Penna., Temple Univ., etc.

NEUMANN, EMANUEL, 1896–19 ; pres., Z.O.A. 1946–48; active in J.N.F., Jewish Agency for Palestine, etc.

NEWMAN, LOUIS ISRAEL, 1893–19 ; rabbi, Free Syn., N.Y.C., 1917; Bronx Free Syn., 1917–21, Temple Israel, N.Y.C., 1921–24, Temple Emanu-El, San Francisco, Calif., 1924–30, Congr. Rodeph Sholom, N.Y.C., 1930– .

NIEBUHR, REINHOLD, 1892–19 ; author; ed.; min., Detroit, 1915–28; prof., dean, v-pres., Union Theol. Sem., 1928–60.

NILES, DAVID K., 1890–1952; dir. Ford Hall Forum; exec. asst., pres. F. D. Roosevelt and H. Truman.

OBERMANN, JULIAN JOEL, 1889–1956; instructor, Univ. of Hamburg, 1915–24; prof., J.I.R., 1924–31; prof., Yale Univ., 1932–53.

OSBORNE, THOMAS MOTT, 1859–1926; prison reformer; warden, Sing Sing Prison, 1914–15, U.S. Naval Prison, Portsmouth, N.H., 1917–20; author, *Prisons and Common Sense,* etc.

OTTINGER, ALBERT, 1878–1938; lawyer; N.Y. state sen. 1917–21; asst. U.S. atty. genl., 1921–24; atty. genl., N.Y. state, 1925–26.

PARET, BERTHA; sec'y. of Women's Trade Union League, until marriage to Prof. Thomas I. Emerson.

PARKES, JAMES WILLIAM, 1896–19   ; scholar; author, many books on Jewish-Christian relations.

PARKHURST, CHARLES HENRY, 1842–1933; min., Lenox, Mass., 1874–80, N.Y.C., 1880–1918; author, *Our Fight with Tammany* (1895), *My Forty Years in New York* (1923).

PEABODY, GEORGE FOSTER, 1853–1938; financier; philanthropist, trustee, many colls., univs.; treas., Dem. Natl. Comm., 1904–5; advisor, Woodrow Wilson, Alfred E. Smith, Franklin Delano Roosevelt, etc.

PERKINS, MILO RANDOLPH, 1900–19   ; U.S. agric. dept. posts, 1935–41; exec. dir., Brd. of Econ. Warfare, 1941–42.

PERLES, FELIX, 1874–1933; scholar; linguist; rabbi, Königsberg, 1899–1933; hon. prof., Univ. Königsberg, 1924–33.

PETEGORSKY, DAVID, 1915–56; author; exec. dir., Am. Jewish Congress, 1946–56.

PETERS, MADISON CLINTON, 1859–1918; lecturer; clergyman; author, *Justice to the Jews* (1899), *The Wit and Wisdom of the Talmud* (1900), *The Jews as Patriots* (1902), etc.

PHILIPSON, DAVID, 1862–1949; rabbi, Baltimore, 1884–88; Cincinnati, 1888–1938; prof., H.U.C., 1891–1949; pres., C.C.A.R., 1907–9.

PHILLIPS, WILLIAM, 1878–1968; asst. sec'y. state, 1917–20; undersec'y. state, 1922–24, 1933–36; min. to Netherlands and Luxembourg, 1920–22, Canada, 1927–29; amb. to Belgium, 1924–27, Italy, 1936–41, India, 1942–43.

PINCHOT, AMOS, 1873–1944; lawyer; publicist; brother of Gifford (1865–1946).

PINCHOT, GIFFORD, 1865–1946; conservationist; gov., Pa., 1923–27, 1931–35; prof., Yale Sch. Forestry, 1903–36.

POLACHEK, JOHN; member, Free Syn.; friend of Stephen Wise.

POLIER, JUSTINE WISE, 1903–   ; daughter of Stephen and Louise Wise; judge, N.Y. state family court; pres., Wom. Div., Am. Jewish Congress, 1947–57; chrmn., Louise Wise Serv., 1947–   .

POLIER, SHAD, 1906–   ; lawyer; positions, govt. legal serv., 1937–45; chrmn., governing council, Am. Jewish Congress; sec'y. Meml. Fdtn. Jewish Culture; member, exec. comm., World Jewish Congr., Conf. Jewish Mat'l. Claims Ag. Germany, and N.A.A.C.P. Educ. and Defense Fund.

POLLAK, JACOB B.; rabbi; N.Y. educator; staff member, U.A.H.C.

POTTER, HENRY CODMAN, 1834–1908; bishop, Epis. Diocese, N.Y.C., 1883–1908.

PROSKAUER, JOSEPH M., 1877–19 ; lawyer; justice, Supreme Court of N.Y., 1923–30; pres., Am. Jewish Comm.

RASKOB, JOHN JAKOB, 1879–1950; resigned as chrmn. fin. comm., Genl. Motors Corp., 1928, to become chrmn., Dem. Natl. Comm.; later, treas. and v-pres., E. I. du Pont de Nemours Co.

RAUH, JOSEPH L., JR., 1911– ; lawyer; law sec'y., Justices Cardozo and Frankfurter, 1936–39.

RAUSCHENBUSCH, WALTER, 1861–1918; prof. church history, Rochester Theol. Sem., 1902–18; author, *Christianity and the Social Crisis, Christianizing the Social Order,* etc.

READING, LADY EVA; daughter of the first Baron Melchett; wife of Gerald Rufus Isaacs, second Marquess of Reading; communal leader in Gt. Brit.; active in World Jewish Congress.

REINACH, THEODORE, 1860–1928; historian; musician; composer; philologist; numismatist; author.

RICHARDS, BERNARD G., 1877–19 ; journalist; communal worker; exec. sec'y., Am. Jewish Congress, 1915–32; exec. dir., Jewish Info. Bureau, 1932– .

RIEGNER, GERHARD; dir., Geneva off., World Jewish Congress.

RIIS, JACOB AUGUST, 1849–1914; journalist; philanthropist; social worker; author, *How the Other Half Lives.*

ROCKEFELLER, JOHN DAVISON, JR., 1874–1960; philanthropist; donor, Riverside Ch., N.Y.C., Univ. of Chicago chapel, etc; built Rockefeller Center.

ROOSEVELT, ANNA ELEANOR, 1884–1961; wife of Franklin Delano Roosevelt; member U.S. delegation, United Nations, 1945–52; chrmn., U.N. Comm. on Human Rights.

ROOSEVELT, FRANKLIN DELANO, 1882–1945; N.Y. state sen., 1910–13; asst. sec'y. of navy, 1913–20; gov., N.Y. state, 1928–32; pres., U.S., 1933–45.

ROOSEVELT, THEODORE, 1858–1919; author; historian; statesman; v-pres., U.S., 1901, pres., 1901–9.

ROSENAU, WILLIAM, 1865–1943; rabbi, Baltimore, 1892–1943.

ROSENBERG, JAMES, 1874–19 ; lawyer; artist; communal leader; active, J.D.C., Dominican Republic Settlement Asso.

ROSENWALD, JULIUS, 1862–1932; merchant and philanthropist.

ROTHENBERG, MORRIS, 1885–1950; pres., Z.O.A., 1932–36; magistrate, N.Y.C. courts, 1937–50; active in U.P.A., Jewish Agency for Palestine, W.Z.O.

ROTHSCHILD, ALFRED CHARLES DE, 1842–1918; a dir., Bank of England, Natl. Gallery, and other art museums.

ROTHSCHILD, EDMUND JAMES DE, 1845–1934; philanthropist; art collector; donor art collections to Louvre, assistance to agric. colonies in Palestine.

ROTHSCHILD, LIONEL WALTER, 1868–1937; naturalist; recipient, letter containing Balfour Declaration.

RUTENBERG, PINCHAS, 1879–1942; engineer; industrialist; founder-dir., Palestine Electric Corp.

SACKETT, FREDERICK MOSELEY, JR., 1868–1941; lawyer; U.S. sen., Kentucky, 1925–31; U.S. amb. to Germany, 1930–33.

SAMUEL, HERBERT, 1870–1963; philosopher; author; British statesman; first High Commissioner for Palestine, 1920–25.

SAMUEL, MAURICE, 1895–19   ; translator; lecturer; author, *You Gentiles, The World of Sholem Aleichem, Harvest in the Desert, The Professor and the Fossil,* etc.

SASSOON; family of Sephardic Jews in Gt. Brit.; famed for its scholars, merchants, and philanthropists.

SCHACHT, HJALMAR HORACE GREELEY, 1877–19   ; German financier; pres., Reichsbank, 1923–30, 1934–39.

SCHECHTER, SOLOMON, 1847–1915; scholar and rabbi; reader in rabbinics, Cambridge Univ., England, 1892–1902; pres., J.T.S., N.Y.C., 1902–15.

SCHIFF, JACOB HENRY, 1847–1920; financier; philanthropist; co-founder, Henry Street Settlement; endowed Temple Emanu-El, J.T.S., Montefiore Home, etc.

SCHIFF, MORTIMER L., 1877–1931; son of Jacob Henry Schiff; financier; philanthropist; active in Boy Scouts of Am. (pres.), J.T.S., etc.

SEABURY, SAMUEL, 1873–1958; lawyer; justice, N.Y. Supreme Court, 1906–14; N.Y. Court of Appeals, 1914–16; apptd. by Gov. F. D. Roosevelt to head investigation of N.Y.C. politics, magistrate courts, 1930–31.

SELIGMAN, EDWIN R. A., 1861–1939; economist; prof., Columbia Univ., 1885–1931.

SENIOR, MAX, 1862–1939; Cin. businessman; communal leader; philanthropist.

SHULMAN, HERMAN, 1897–1945; lawyer; Zionist leader.

SILVER, ABBA HILLEL, 1890–1963; rabbi, Wheeling, W. Va., 1915–17, Cleveland, O., 1917–63; pres., Z.O.A., 1943–45; co-chrmn. (with Stephen Wise), A.Z.E.C., 1943–48; pres., C.C.A.R., 1945–47; chrmn., Am. sect., Jewish Agency for Palestine, 1943–49.

SILVERMAN, SAMUEL SIDNEY, 1895–1968; Labour party member, House of Commons, 1935–68; pres., British division, World Jewish Congress, 1940–50.

SIMKHOVITCH, MARY KINGSBURY; social worker; founder, dir., Greenwich House, N.Y.C., 1902–46.

SLOMOWITZ, PHILIP; publisher and ed., Detroit *Jewish News.*

SMUTS, JAN CHRISTIAAN, 1870–1950; statesman; philosopher; soldier; prime min., Union of S. Africa, 1919–24, 1939–48; author, *Holism and Evolution.*

SOKOLOW, NAHUM, 1860–1936; journalist; classicist; author; sec'y., W.Z.O., 1904–20, chrmn., Zionist Exec., 1920–31, pres., 1931–35.

SPEYER, JAMES, 1861–1941; banker; philanthropist.

SPRECKLES, ADOLPH BERNARD, 1857–1924; manufacturer; owner, Spreckles Sugar Co., Oceanic Steamship Co., etc.; park commissioner, San Francisco.

STETTINIUS, EDWARD REILLY, JR., 1900–49; industrialist; statesman; Genl. Motors Corp., 1926–34; chrmn. brd., U.S. Steel Corp.: undersec'y. of state, 1933–44, sec'y. of state, 1944–45; U.S. repr., U.N., 1945–46.

STONE, ELIHU, 1888–1952; atty.; Zionist leader.

STORRS, RONALD, 1881–1955; military gov. of Jerusalem, 1917–20; civil gov. of Jerusalem, Jaffa, and Judaea, 1920–26.

STRAUS, ISIDOR, 1845–1912; merchant, philanthropist; congressman; died, with wife, on S.S. *Titanic.*

STRAUS, NATHAN, 1848–1931; merchant and philantropist; supported colonies, health projects in Palestine.

STRAUS, NATHAN, JR., 1889–1961; journalist; bus. exec.; legislator; admr., U.S. Housing Authority, 1937–42; author; radio exec.

STRAUS, OSCAR SOLOMON, 1850–1926; jurist; merchant; author; philanthropist; diplomat; min. to Turkey, 1887–89, 1898–1900; amb. to Turkey, 1909–10.

STRAUSS, LEWIS LICHTENSTEIN, 1896–19 ; corp. exec.; member, Kuhn, Loeb & Co.; member, U.S. Atomic Energy Comm., 1946–50, chrmn., 1953–58; sec'y. of commerce, 1958–59; admiral, U.S. navy.

STROOCK, SOLOMON MARCUSE, 1873–1941; lawyer; sec'y., Congrtn. B'nai Jeshurun, 1896–1906; chrmn., brd. dir., J.T.S. 1930–41; chrmn., exec. comm., Am. Jewish Comm., 1934–40, pres., 1941.

SULZBERGER, MAYER, 1843–1923; lawyer; judge; Hebraist; a founder Jewish Pub. Soc. of Am., chrmn. publications comm., 1888–1923; first pres., Am. Jewish Comm.

SULZBERGER, RACHEL HAYS, wife of Cyrus Leonard Sulzberger (1858–1932, merchant and communal leader); mother of Arthur Hays Sulzberger (1891–1968, pub.), N.Y. *Times).*

SVESKA, FRANK L.; dir., Youth and Recreation, Omaha, Neb., 1948.

SZOLD, HENRIETTA, 1860–1945; scholar; teacher; humanitarian; sec'y., Jewish Pub. Soc. of Am., 1892–1916; founder-pres., Hadassah, women's Zionist org., 1912–26; resident, Palestine, 1920–45.

SZOLD ROBERT, 1889–19 , lawyer; active in Palestine Econ. Corp., Z.O.A., Jewish Agency for Palestine, etc.

TAFT, WILLIAM HOWARD, 1857–1930; lawyer; statesman; jurist; pres., U.S., 1909–13; chief justice, U.S., 1921–30.

TAYLOR, MYRON CHARLES, 1874–1959; lawyer, industrialist; diplomat; v-chrmn., Inter-govtl. Comm. Polit. Refugees, 1938–44.

TCHERNOWITZ, CHAIM, 1871–1949; talmudist; author; rabbi; prof., J.I.R., 1923–47.

THOMAS, NORMAN MATTOON, 1884–1968; author; clergyman; pacifist; socialist; Socialist party candidate, gov. of N.Y. (1924, 1938), mayor, N.Y.C. (1925, 1929), pres., U.S. (1928, 1932, 1936, 1940, 1944).

TORCZYNER (TUR-SINAI), NAPHTALI HIRSCH, 1886–19 ; orientalist; biblical scholar; prof., Hochschule, Berlin, 1919–32; prof., Hebrew Univ., Jerusalem, 1933–56.

TUMULTY, JOSEPH; private sec'y. to Pres. Woodrow Wilson.

UPHAUS, WILLARD; clergyman; exec. dir., Natl. Religion and Labor Fdtn.

VILLARD, OSWALD GARRISON, 1872–1949; journalist; author; pub., N.Y. *Evening Post,* 1900–18; ed., pub., *Nation,* 1918–32, contributor, 1932–40.

VOGELSTEIN, LUDWIG, 1871–1934; industrialist; philanthropist; chrmn., exec. comm. U.A.H.C., 1925–34.

WAGNER, ROBERT FERDINAND, 1877–1949; N.Y. state assembly, 1904–10; N.Y. state sen., 1910–18; justice, N.Y. Supreme Court, 1919–26; U.S. Sen., 1927–49.

WALD, LILLIAN, 1867–1940; social worker, founder, Henry Street settlement, N.Y.C., 1893; co-founder, U.S. Children's Bureau, 1912.

WALDMAN, MORRIS, 1879–19 ; social worker; exec. dir., Am. Jewish Comm.; author, *Nor by Power.*

WALKER, JAMES JOHN, 1881–1946; lawyer; song writer; N.Y. state sen., 1914–25; mayor, N.Y.C., 1925–32; arbiter, garment industry, 1940–46.

WALLACE, HENRY AGARD, 1888–1965; ed., pub., *Wallace's Farmer,* 1910–33; sec'y. of agriculture, 1933–41; U.S. v-pres. 1941–45; sec'y. of commerce, 1945–46; ed., *New Republic,* 1946–48.

WALSH, DAVID IGNATIUS, 1872–1947; gov., Mass., 1914–15; U.S. sen., Mass., 1919–47.

WALSH, FRANK, 1864–1939; lawyer; pub., ed., Kansas City *Post;* chrmn., War Labor Conf. Brd., 1918; chrmn., Power Authority, N.Y. state, 1931–39.

WARBURG, FELIX M., 1871–1937; banker; philanthropist; communal leader.

WARBURG, PAUL MORITZ, 1868–1932; banker; philanthropist; communal leader.

WATERMAN, EDMUND; food exporter, co-chrmn., N.Y. Joint Defense Appeal, 1946.

WATERMAN, JENNY AND LEO; sister and brother of Louise Waterman Wise.

WAUCHOPE, ARTHUR GRENFELL, 1874–1947; soldier; diplomat; high commissioner and commander-in-chief, Palestine and Transjordania, 1931–38.

WEBB, SIDNEY, 1859–1947; Fabian socialist; civil servant; appointed

Colonial Sec'y., 1929; his wife, Beatrice Potter Webb (1858–1943), refused to share title, "Baron Passfield," with him.

WEISGAL, MEYER, 1894–19 ; active in Zionist org. and publishing from 1916; exec. v-pres., Weizmann Institute, Rehovoth, 1947–67, pres., 1967– ; author.

WEIZMANN, CHAIM, 1874–1952; lecturer in chemistry, Univ. of Geneva, 1900–1903; later, Univ. of Manchester; dir., British admiralty labs., 1916–19; pres., World Zionist movement, 1920–31, 1935–46, 1948; founder, Hebrew Univ., Jerusalem, 1918, chrmn., brd. of govs., 1919–48; first pres., Israel, 1948–52.

WELLES, SUMNER, 1892–1961; diplomat; amb. to Cuba, 1933; asst. sec'y. of state, 1933–37; undersec'y. of state, 1937–43.

WELLIVER, JUDSON CHURCHILL, 1871–1943; journalist; described by *Review of Reviews* as "having a confidential relationship with the White House," during terms of Warren G. Harding and Calvin Coolidge; later, ed., Pittsburgh *Post-Gazette*.

WERTHEIM, MAURICE, 1886–1950; banker; active in affairs of For. Pol. Asso., New Sch. Soc. Research, Am. Jewish Comm., etc.

WICKERSHAM, GEORGE WOODWARD, 1858–1936; lawyer; govt. official, state and natl. level; chrmn., Natl. Comm. on Law Observance and Law Enforcement, 1929–31.

WILLIAMS, CHARLES, 1860–1923; clergyman; bishop, Epis. diocese, Michigan.

WILSON, EDITH BOLLING, married to Pres. Woodrow Wilson, Dec. 18, 1915.

WILSON, THOMAS WOODROW, 1856–1924; pres., Princeton Univ., 1902–10; gov., N.J., 1911–13; pres., U.S., 1913–20.

WISE (WEISZ), AARON, 1844–96; father of Stephen Wise; rabbi, Congrtn. Rodeph Sholom, N.Y.C., 1875–96; a founder, J.T.S.

WISE, HELEN BROOKS; wife of James Waterman Wise.

WISE, ISAAC MAYER, 1819–1900; rabbi, Albany, N.Y., 1846–54, Cincinnati, O., 1854–1900; founder, pres., H.U.C., 1875–1900; founder, U.A.H.C., 1873; founder, pres., C.C.A.R., 1889–1900; founder, ed., *American Israelite* (Eng. lang.) and *Deborah* (German).

WISE, JAMES WATERMAN, 1901– ; son of Stephen and Louise Wise; writer, lecturer, art critic; founder and ed., *Opinion,* 1931.

WISE, JONAH B., 1881–1959; rabbi, Chattanooga, Tenn., 1904–6, Portland, Oregon, 1906–1925, N.Y.C., 1925–59; son of Isaac Mayer Wise.

WISE, LOUISE WATERMAN, died 1947; wife of Stephen S. Wise; artist; founded Free Nurses Asso., Portland, Ore.; founder, pres., Free Syn. Child Adoption Comm.; founder, pres., Wom. Div., Am. Jewish Congress; founder, pres., Congress House for Refugees in N.Y.C.

WISE, OTTO IRVING, 1872–1918; lawyer; brother of Stephen S. Wise.

WOLF, GERTRUDE; private sec'y. to Stephen Wise, 1907–23.

WOLF, SIMON, 1836–1923; lawyer; pres., B'nai B'rith, 1904–5; active in U.A.H.C. and Am. Jewish Comm.

WOLFFSOHN, DAVID, 1856–1914; merchant, Cologne, Germany; Zionist leader; collaborator and successor of Theodor Herzl.

WOLFSON, HARRY, 1887–19　; scholar; prof., J.I.R., 1922–25, Harvard Univ., 1925–　; author, *Philo, The Church Fathers,* etc.

WORRELL, WILLIAM HOYT, 1879–1953; orientalist and author; dir., Am. Sch. of Oriental Research, Jerusalem, 1919–20; Gustav Gottheil lecturer, Semitic languages, Columbia Univ., 1921–24; prof., Univ. of Michigan, 1924–53.

ZANGWILL, ISRAEL, 1864–1926; author; dramatist; journalist; founder head, ITO to settle Jews in any available territory.

ZEELAND, PAUL VAN; diplomat; chrmn., Intergovtl. Comm. Polit. Refugees.

ABOUT THE EDITOR

CARL HERMANN VOSS, clergyman, teacher, and author, was born and educated in Pittsburgh, Pennsylvania, receiving the degrees of Bachelor of Arts and Doctor of Philosophy from the University of Pittsburgh. He pursued graduate studies in Chicago, at Yale and abroad, earning the Bachelor of Divinity degree at the Union Theological Seminary in New York City. Ordained a Congregational minister in 1935, he is also a member of the Unitarian Universalist Ministerial Association. His other books include THE UNIVERSAL GOD: *The Eternal Quest in Which All Men Are Brothers;* IN SEARCH OF MEANING: *Living Religions of the World;* THE PALESTINE PROBLEM TODAY: *Israel and Its Neighbors; and* RABBI AND MINISTER: *The Friendship of Stephen S. Wise and John Haynes Holmes.* He is editor of Excalibur Books.

INDEX

Abraham Lincoln Center (Chicago), 34
Abrahams, Israel, 71–72, 77, 103–105, 115, 120, 122, 131, 301
Abrahams, Phyllis, 131
Achad Ha'am, 80
Acheson, Dean, 250–251, 301
Addams, Jane, xviii, 48, 49, 66, 301
Adler, Cyrus, 89, 180, 222–223, 301
Adler Felix, 38–39, 41, 301
Adler, Samuel, 37, 301
Agudah (Union of Orthodox Rabbis), 132–134, 257
Alexander, Gross, 284
Allen, Henry W., 173–174
Allied Supreme Council, 99
Altheimer, Ben, 109, 301
Amalgamated Clothing Workers of America, 143
"America First" Movement, xx
American Association for Social Security, 147, 164, 262
American Civil Liberties Union, xix, 139–140
American Colony (Jerusalem), 160–161
American Council for Judaism, 266
American Federation of Labor, 87–88, 147–148, 257
American Hebrew, The, 9
American Indian Defense Association, 202–203
American Israelite, 37
American Jewish Committee, 64, 69, 90, 173, 181, 209–210, 215, 226, 231–232, 253–255, 257–259, 293
American Jewish Conference, xx
American Jewish Congress, xix, xx, 68–72, 75, 80–91, 182–188, 215, 226–228, 231–232, 237, 253–259, 265, 273, 277–280, 284–286, 295–296
American Jewish Joint Distribution Committee, 156, 242
American School of Oriental Research, 36, 38
American Union Against Militarism, xix
American Zionist Emergency Council, xx, 256, 267
Anna Clare, (Sister), 265
Anderson, Charles P., 57, 301
Anglo-American Commission of Inquiry on Palestine, xxi, 269, 271, 273–274
Anglo-Jewish Association, 85
Arab Refugees, 288–290
Arabs, 229, 247–248
Armaments Conference, 108
Armenia, 85, 100
Attlee, Clement, 271–274

Baeck, Leo, 116, 301
Baerwald, Paul, 227, 239, 301
Baker, Newton Diehl, xix, 125, 127–128, 196, 209–210, 301
Bakers Union, 44
Bakstansky, Lavey, 227, 251–252, 301
Baldwin, Stanley, 184

321]